IMAGES
of America

MIDDLETOWN

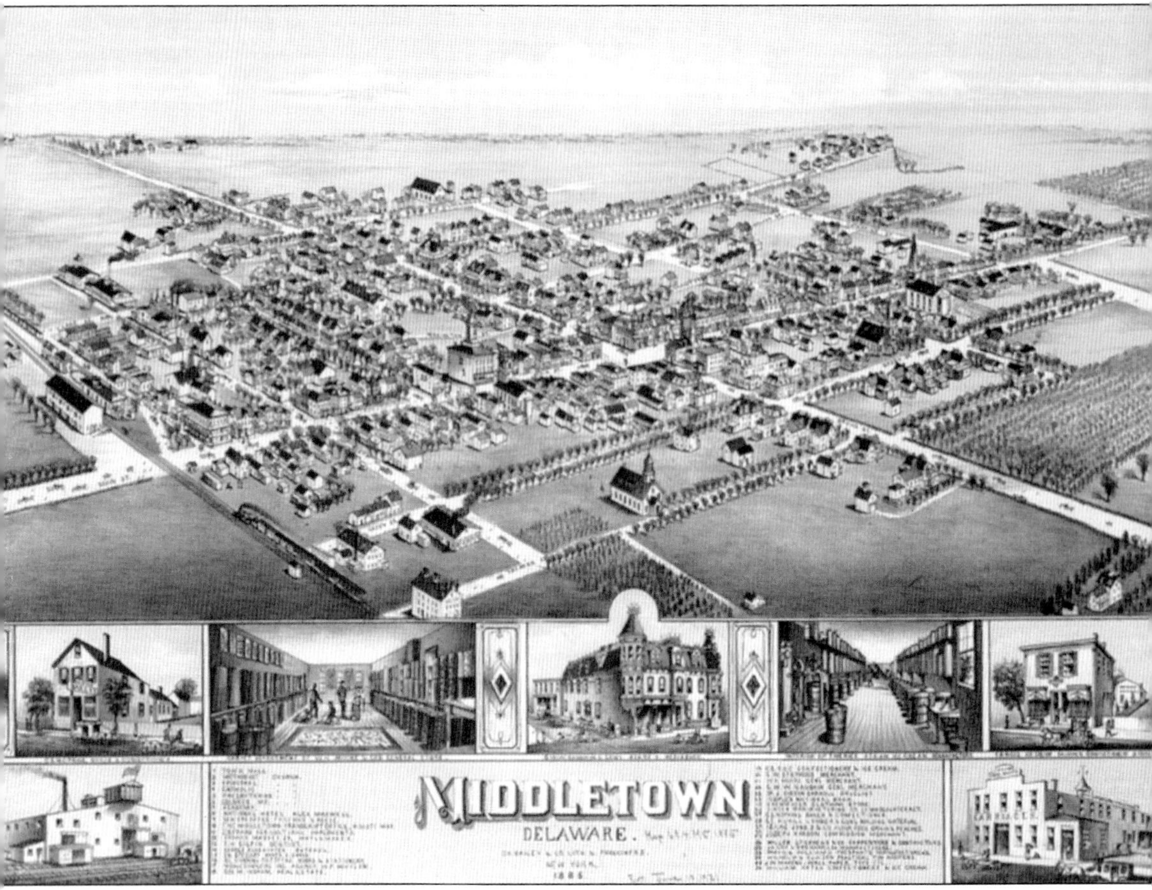

This 1885 map shows a three-dimensional sketch of the original village of Middletown during its early prosperity. West Main Street is visible at left as the map extends east to Catherine Street and north to Lockwood Street, surrounded by large swaths of land that have since been developed. The population around that time was fewer than 1,500 people. (Courtesy of Middletown Historical Society.)

On the Cover: This August 17, 1950, photograph shows one of several post office locations in Middletown. The building at 23 and 25 West Main Street was constructed in the early 20th century. The post office was previously located in a three-story building that also housed the Middletown Town Hall, an auditorium, and a Masonic lodge. A newer building at 30 West Main Street was the town's mail headquarters until an even newer structure was built along East Main Street in the early 21st century. (Courtesy of Delaware Public Archives.)

IMAGES
of America

MIDDLETOWN

Shauna McVey with the
Middletown Historical Society

ARCADIA
PUBLISHING

ISBN 978-1-4671-2078-4

Published by Arcadia Publishing
Charleston, South Carolina

Printed in the United States of America

Library of Congress Control Number: 2013942637

For all general information, please contact Arcadia Publishing:
Telephone 843-853-2070
Fax 843-853-0044
E-mail sales@arcadiapublishing.com
For customer service and orders:
Toll-Free 1-888-313-2665

Visit us on the Internet at www.arcadiapublishing.com

Dedicated to my hometown.

Contents

Acknowledgments 6

Introduction 7

1. Street Scenes and Landscapes 9
2. Historic Structures 25
3. Commerce 39
4. Agriculture 63
5. Residents and Community 73
6. Education 91
7. Athletics 113
8. Modern Times 125

Bibliography 127

Acknowledgments

Many hands helped in the creation of this book, and I am forever grateful to those who took time to assist me with locating photographs and information.

Historian George Contant deserves endless thanks for his invaluable organization of the Middletown Historical Society's accessions and the hours he dedicated as my on-call historian. Dave and Alison Matsen, the heart and soul of the Middletown Historical Society, have a praiseworthy passion for preserving Middletown's past.

My editor, Julia Simpson, was an endless source of encouragement and guidance.

Much appreciation goes to the Delaware Public Archives staff, including Katie Hall, Sarah Denison, Cynthia Caldwell, Michele Peterson, Dawn Mitchell, Lori Hatch, Margaret Dunham, David Littleton, Rich Hays, Bruce Hasse, Randy Goss, and director Stephen Marz.

It was a pleasure to meet with longtime area residents who graciously invited me into their homes and stores. I greatly enjoyed catching up with my Middletown High School English teacher George Atkinson and his wife, Julie. It was good to finally meet fellow former *Middletown Transcript* editor Scott Lawrence. I knew I could pick the brains of W.D. Hatton and Charlie Biggs in their shops. Richard and Marlene Green's collection of photographs was a treasure to view. My visits with Betty Todd and Corbit Collins were rewarding. Vice mayor Jimmy Reynolds Jr., as always, was just a phone call and a short drive away. The exhaustive efforts of Louisa Price Zeh, Dorothy Taylor, Mike Handlin, Richard Taylor, Buddy Jefferson, and Vontiva Williams are commendable. Credit also goes to the recipients of many phone calls to friends and familiar families in search of material.

My parents, Mike and Debbie McVey, deserve recognition for their decision to raise my sisters and me in Middletown. My interest in the town and its history—and the creation of this book—would never have happened without them.

To Shane Martin, thank you for your patience with and support of me as I completed my first book, and Romeo, who was right by my side.

Those who donated photographs to the Middletown Historical Society or Delaware Public Archives will never know the depth of my gratitude for helping to preserve the history of the town we all cherish.

INTRODUCTION

Beneath Middletown's abundant and relatively new suburban neighborhoods, big-box stores, and strip malls lie the bones of what was formerly just a resting point for travelers halfway between two ports of trade and became the fastest-growing municipality in Delaware, the First State.

Middletown started as a tavern stop nearly 350 years ago and grew into a small, close-knit community that has recently transformed into the home of some of the most sought-after real estate in the region. Numerous new residents have relocated to below the Chesapeake & Delaware Canal from northern New Castle County and surrounding states; many of these new residents may not be aware of the rich history of the town they now call home. I hope the images of Middletown's past contained within these pages will further all readers' appreciation for this central hub of activity in southern New Castle County.

The Lenni-Lenape tribe was the first to live among this land of rich soil. In the late 1600s, European settlers made their way to the area, which is conveniently situated along a trail between the Appoquinimink River in present-day Odessa and the Bohemia River in Maryland.

Two of the earliest Middletown establishments were David Witherspoon's hotel and tavern in the center of town and Thomas Noxon's mill to the southeast of the town's limits; both were important to Middletown's development because of the services they provided to visitors and inhabitants alike. As agricultural and milling industries began to flourish, "Middletown" came to be known for its central location.

The bodies of water that flank Delaware provided easy access to the Middletown area, and Swedish, Scottish, Irish, and Dutch families were the earliest to build homes on the land. Nearby Odessa deserves much credit for its hub of trade and settlement that enabled interested minds to travel a few miles west. The Lenni-Lenape tribe, upon the continuous arrival of European settlers and the devastation the tribe incurred due to the diseases and strife that these new settlers introduced, abandoned the land and moved farther west.

With religion an integral part of early settlers' lives, Episcopal and Presbyterian places of worship arose among beautiful landscapes to serve the population. At the start of the 19th century, 120 people called Middletown home and, soon after, the Middletown Academy was established as a private educational institution. A tannery, a wheelwright, dry goods stores, and several other early businesses led to the steady growth of what had become a village. By the middle of the 19th century, Middletown boasted nearly 400 inhabitants.

Residents initially built homes spanning east of Broad Street toward Odessa. The people of Odessa later denied the establishment of a railroad there, which resulted in the construction of the Delaware Railroad on the west end of Middletown. After its completion in 1855, the railroad brought prosperity to the town and spurred the construction of homes and businesses west of Broad Street. Train transportation made it easier for residents and visitors to travel north and south of the village, bringing convenience to Middletown. The accessibility of the railroad put Middletown on the map for what was grown on its invaluable land; wheat and corn made for prosperous trade, as did peaches and other crops. The farmers of Middletown earned a reputation for the crops they produced, and the stage was set for incorporation.

Middletown was granted its charter on February 12, 1861. Workers laid streets among the town's official boundaries, which extended a half-mile in each direction and formed a diamond. Improved infrastructure followed the installation of water and electricity. After several devastating fires, volunteers founded the desperately-needed Volunteer Hose Company of Middletown to protect businesses and homes.

The population grew to about 1,500 at the start of the 20th century as modernization made its way into Middletown. Locals could find entertainment at the Everett Theatre, and a number of other options for recreation became available. Residents formed baseball and football leagues, along with multiple organizations like the Middletown-Odessa Rotary Club, the Middletown Lions Club, the Masonic Union Lodge No. 5 AF & AM, and the Middletown-Odessa Garden Club, plus children's groups like the M.O.T. Little League and M.O.T. Youth Football and Cheerleading League, formerly M.O.T. Pop Warner.

Middletown residents developed an unwavering passion for youth and high school sports. After the dominating Middletown High School football teams of the 1960s, Friday night games on South Broad Street became a weekly highlight for countless residents. Area schools were desegregated in the mid-1960s, and for several decades, the only schools in town were Middletown High School, Louis L. Redding Middle School, and Silver Lake Elementary School.

Farmers continued to set the town's scenic country backdrop with corn, wheat, and soybean crops. For much of its existence, familiar faces could be found in Middletown and the surrounding area. Everyone knew just about everyone else, and country life prevailed. The close-knit community atmosphere endured through the 1980s, as the town still contained fewer than 3,000 residents.

In the late 20th century, developers took notice of Middletown's extensive farmland and began to purchase parcels on which to build suburban neighborhoods, and commercial businesses followed suit. The town's population surpassed 5,000 in the 1990s, then nearly quadrupled—to around 19,000—from 2000 to 2010. Development quickly came to the areas surrounding the official town limits, making Middletown the center of civilization in southern New Castle County. The Appoquinimink School District did its best to keep pace and built 11 new schools in 15 years to accommodate the influx of families. Private, charter, and vocational schools also appeared in the area and, along with what became a reputable public school district, added to the residential attraction of Middletown. Youth and adult sports are still abundant, as are town celebrations such as the Victorian Stroll, the Olde-Tyme Peach Festival, and Memorial Day and Fourth of July parades.

Today's Middletown represents a transformation from its early years. Major national chain stores seek to set up shop among its boundaries, and proposed large-scale residential developments promise to usher in an even busier way of life. More than 50,000 people now call the land "below the canal" home—a population number easily estimated when thousands gather around the popular Silver Lake Park for fireworks each July.

Middletown has grown from a stopping point to a destination. Amid modern construction, historic buildings stand proudly as a testament to those who once lived here. The small-town charm has managed to permeate into the large-town atmosphere that now exists. Friendly and familiar faces are still abundant, and minor traffic delays give way to the remaining beautiful countryside that borders town limits. With its historic roots, community appeal, and modern conveniences, Middletown is truly a charming place.

One

Street Scenes and Landscapes

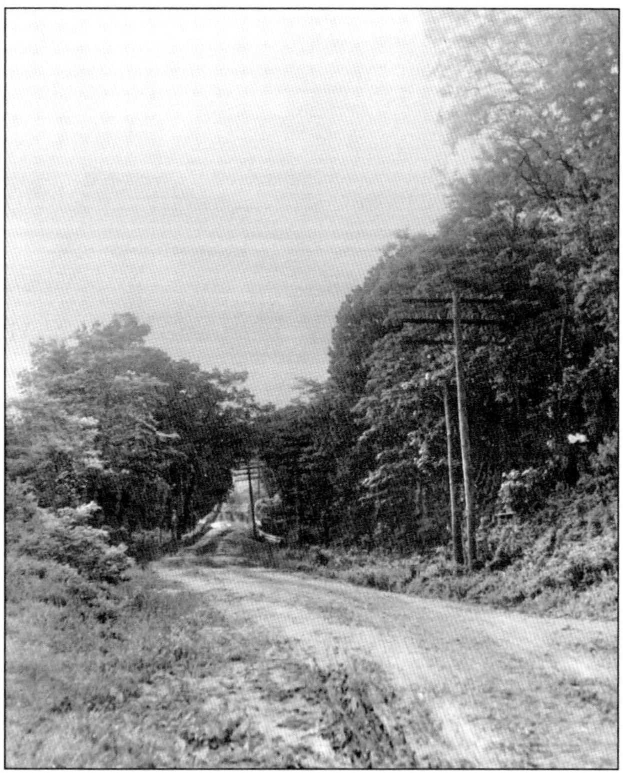

This familiar roadway is nearly unrecognizable to modern residents of and visitors to Middletown. It was taken near Old St. Anne's Church and shows what is now South Broad Street (also known as Delaware Route 71 and Summit Bridge Road) heading into downtown Middletown. Currently, drivers along this road experience a much smoother ride than those who traveled on this dirt causeway. (Courtesy of the author.)

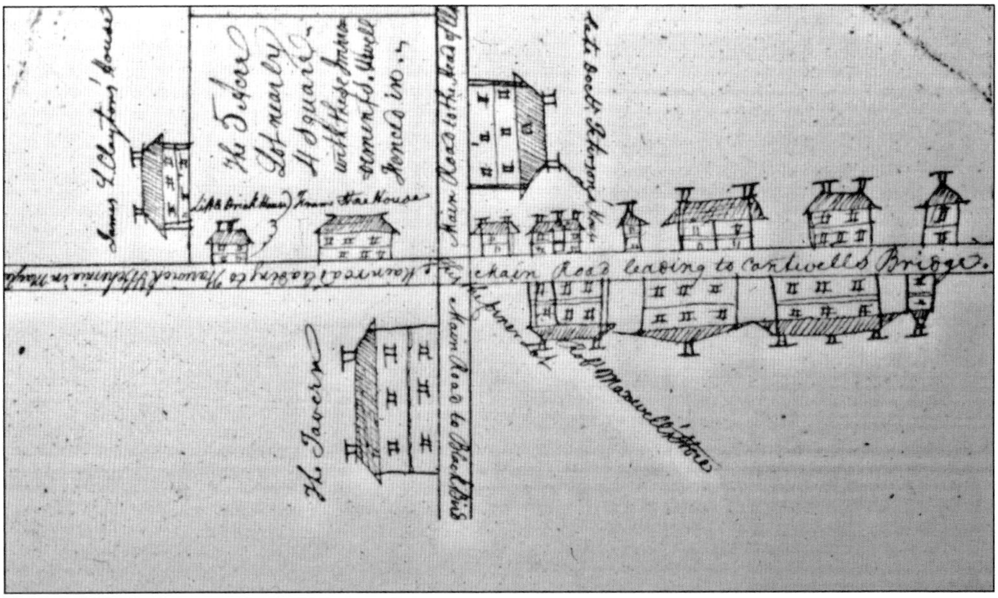

This 1799 sketch of Middletown was drawn for use in a court case. It shows the homes of several residents of the time, including James L. Clayton and the prominent Peterson farming family. The Witherspoon Inn is featured as "The Tavern," as is a roadway labeled as "leading to Cantwell's Bridge"—a former name for Odessa. (Courtesy of Middletown Historical Society.)

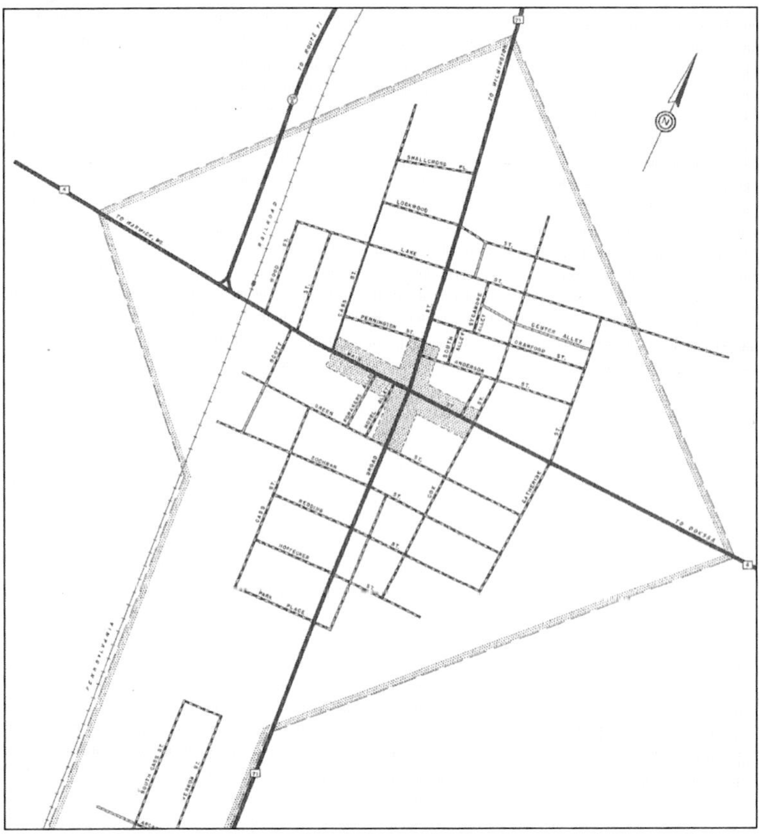

Middletown was incorporated on February 12, 1861, and the town limits extended a half-mile in each direction from the intersection of Main and Broad Streets. The boundary lines resulted in a diamond. This 1955 map shows that diamond with one of the first annexations as indicated here by a rectangular outline. (Courtesy of Middletown Historical Society and Delaware Public Archives.)

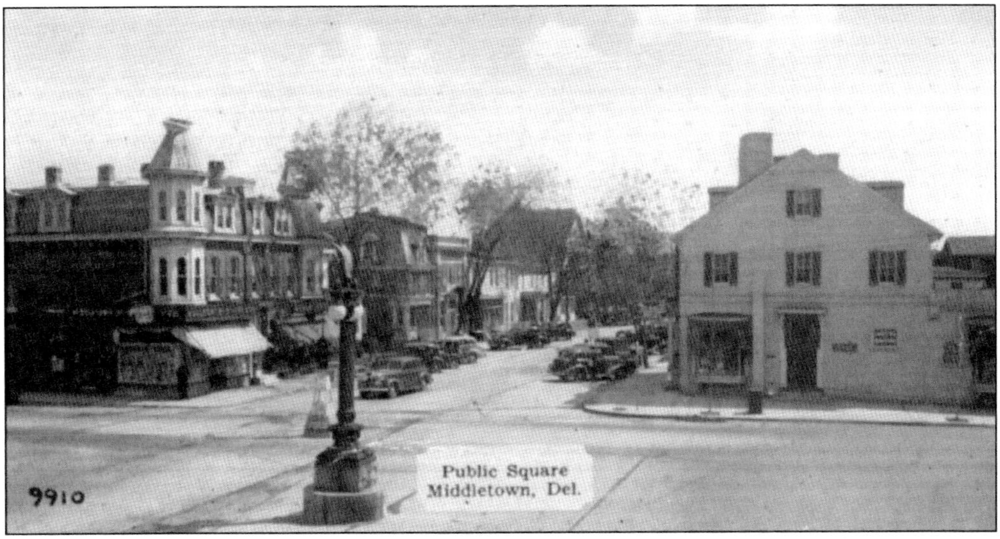

Cochran Square is the center and crossroads of Middletown on which two of the town's most popular landmarks are situated—the Witherspoon Inn and an eagle-topped memorial dedicated to the local men who died in World War I. Robert A. Cochran purchased the inn in 1844 and also owned the stores on the south side of the square. He gave his own name to the entire square of the southeast corner of the intersection at Main and Broad Streets. The photograph below, taken sometime after 1944, shows Cochran Square when ample parking was available to patrons of its businesses and those across the street. (Above, courtesy of Delaware Public Archives; below, courtesy of the author.)

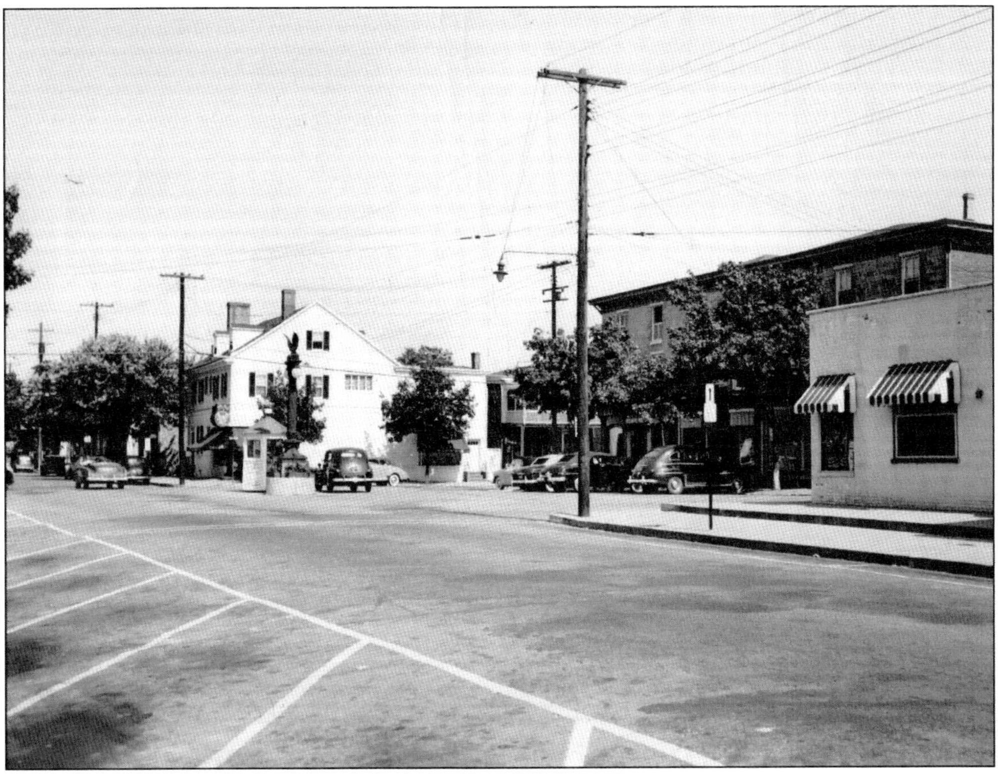

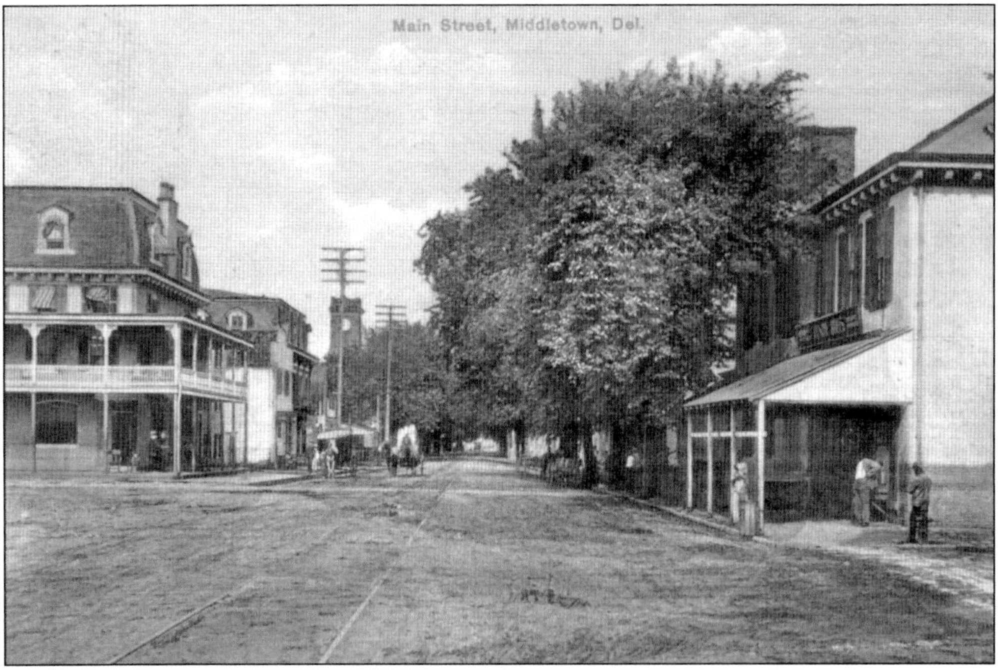

While the hub of historic Main Street business buildings is located west of the town center, Middletown grew mostly east in its earliest days. The arrival of the railroad spurred commerce along West Main Street toward the train depot. These two views of West Main Street, taken near the intersection of Main and Broad Streets, show how the town evolved with the times. Above is a 1909 image with the Lundy Brothers grocery store on the right and trolley rails still visible in the street. Below, automobiles and traffic lights indicate a busier street and quicker pace of life. (Both, courtesy of Middletown Historical Society.)

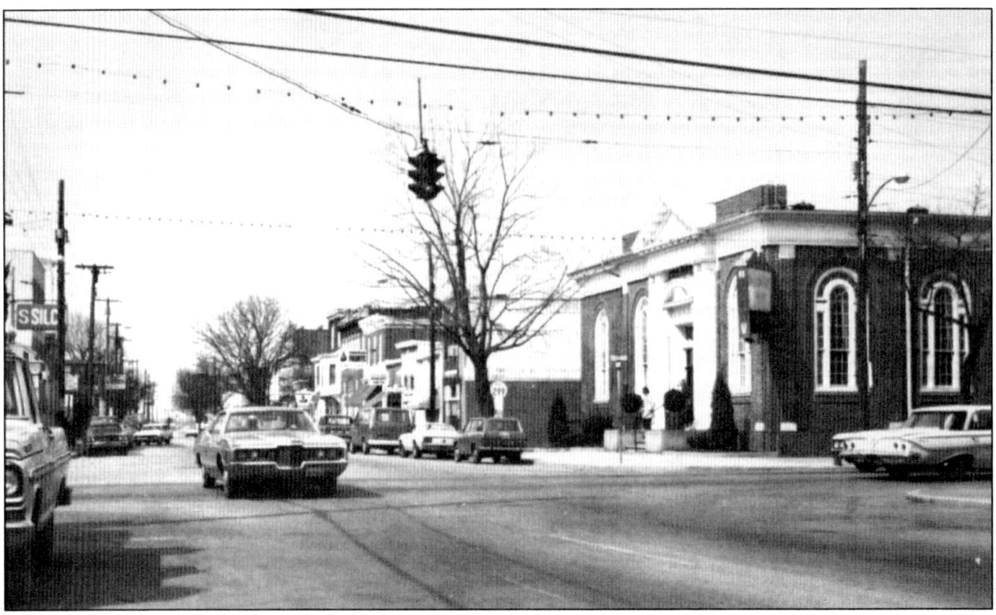

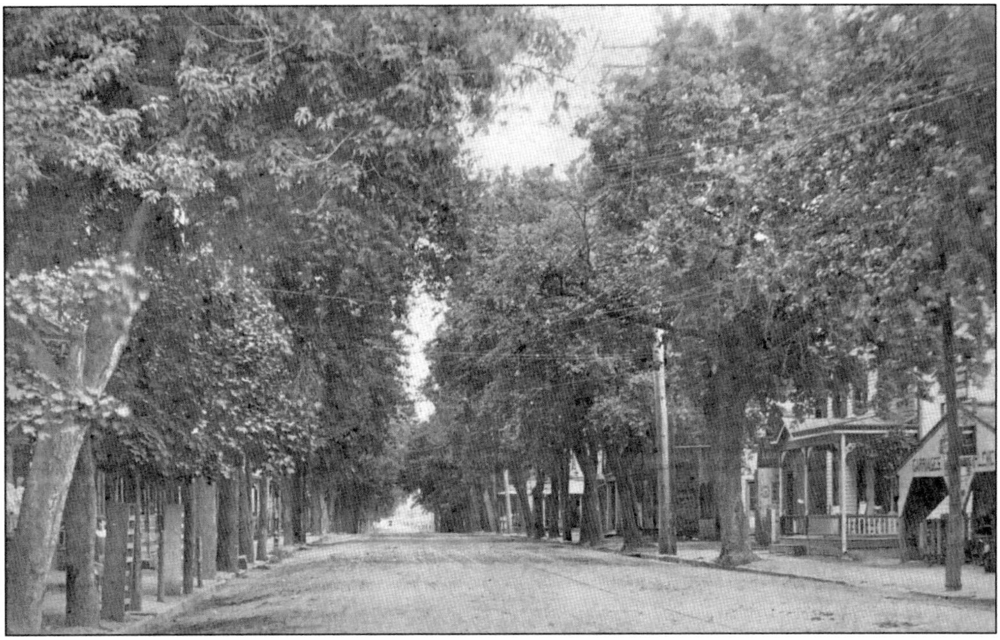

Many of Middletown's original streets were named for prominent men of the town, and the earliest houses were built along Main Street. East Main Street (above) is lined with residences that were once owned by those with family names that can be found on original town streets, including former governor John P. Cochran, C.E. Anderson, the Crawford family, and Jesse Lake. Other homeowners on this side of the street included Dr. J.R. Niles, M.E. Walker, M.L. Walker, a Mrs. Grears, and John Whitlock. When the town was incorporated, there were no houses on Lockwood, Crawford, or Green Streets. Lake Street had a few structures between Broad and Cass Streets. Previous residents of North Broad Street (below) included a Mrs. Roberts, P. Denney, E.G. Gibbs, Nimrod French, a Mrs. McIntyre, and E.T. Evans. Middletown Academy is also located on North Broad Street. (Above, courtesy of Charlie Biggs; below, courtesy of Scott Lawrence.)

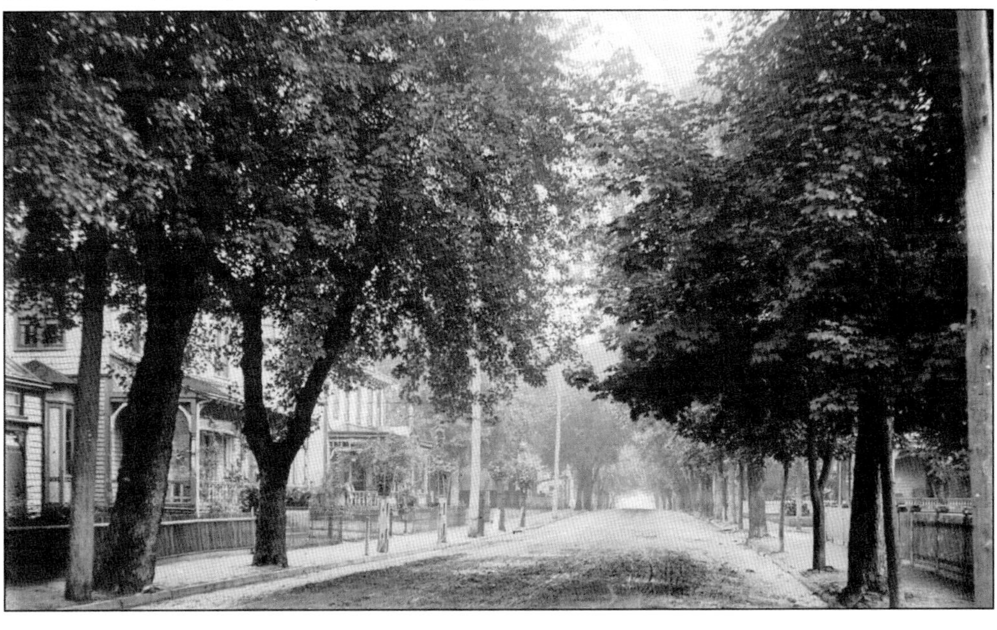

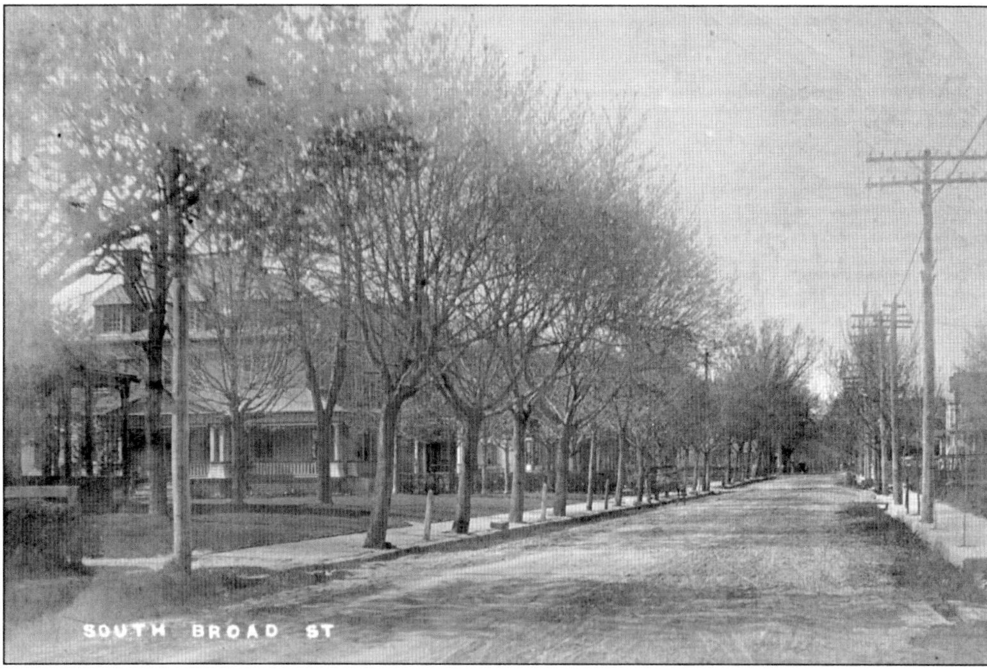

Broad Street's massive historic homes have remained a time capsule of Middletown's past. Various businesses that served as a backbone of commerce in the town are no longer visible, including the carriage factory of J.M. Cox, site of a disastrous 1882 fire that destroyed an entire block; the machine shop of J.T. Budd, who made power corn-shellers; and Pennington's improved reapers, iron veranda, and porch railings, which are still visible on some West Main Street buildings. Business owner Albert Pennington, a machinist and inventor, built several of the houses in Middletown. (Above, courtesy of Richard and Marlene Green; below, courtesy of Delaware Public Archives.)

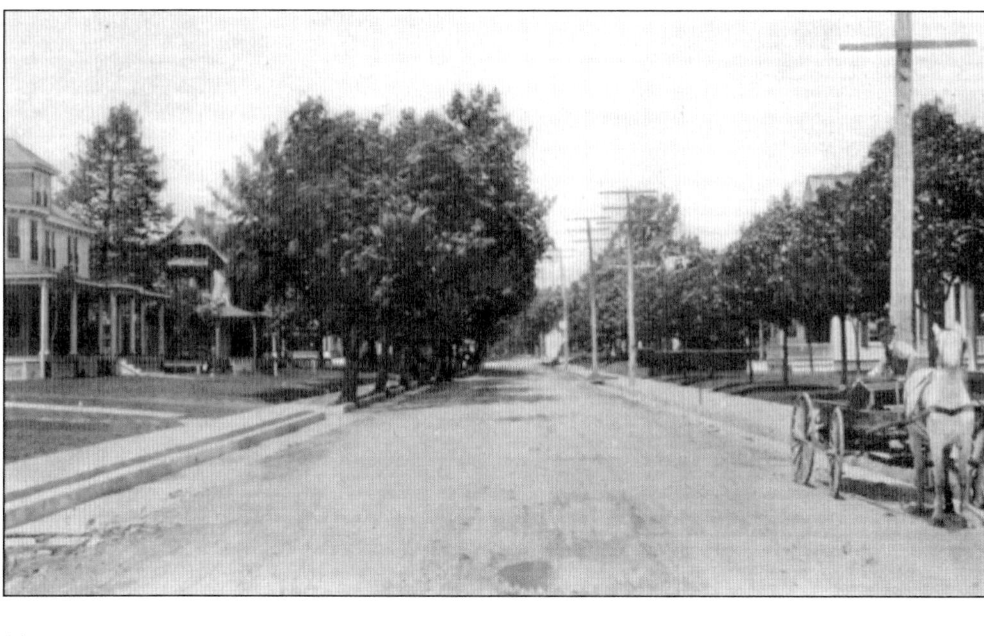

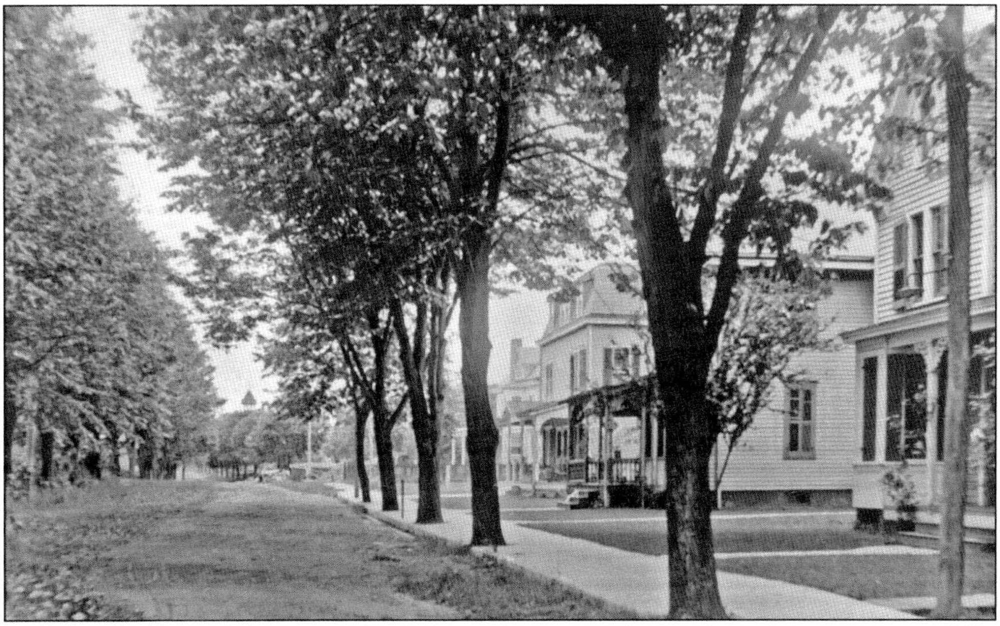

Cochran Street may have been named after Robert A. Cochran, who, at one point, owned the Witherspoon Inn, named Cochran Square after himself, and held claim to about 70 acres of land that contained much of the original town. In 1861, Cochran was elected as a Democrat to the Delaware General Assembly, and he was said to be a respectable man who was instrumental in the incorporation of Middletown. (Courtesy of Middletown Historical Society.)

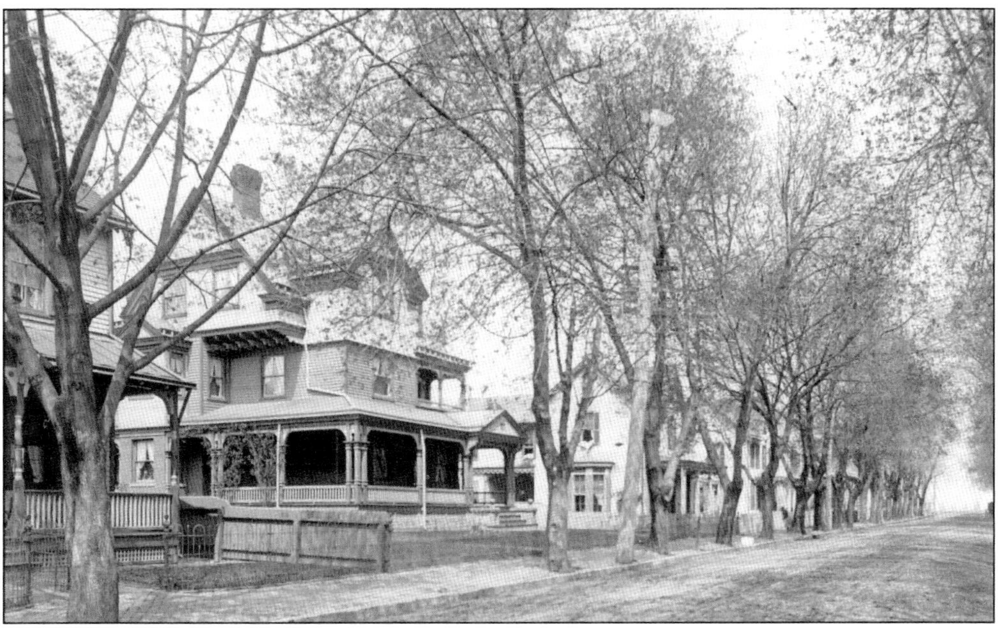

North Cass Street is home to some of the most beautiful residences in Middletown. The locally famous Biggs Mansion, once occupied by Delaware's 48th governor, Benjamin T. Biggs, sits at 210 Cass Street. Dr. Louis Levinson, a Middletown mayor and veterinarian, lived at 206 Cass Street and worked to pass a bill in Delaware that required the testing of cows for tuberculosis, resulting in a reduction of the disease in humans. (Courtesy of Middletown Historical Society.)

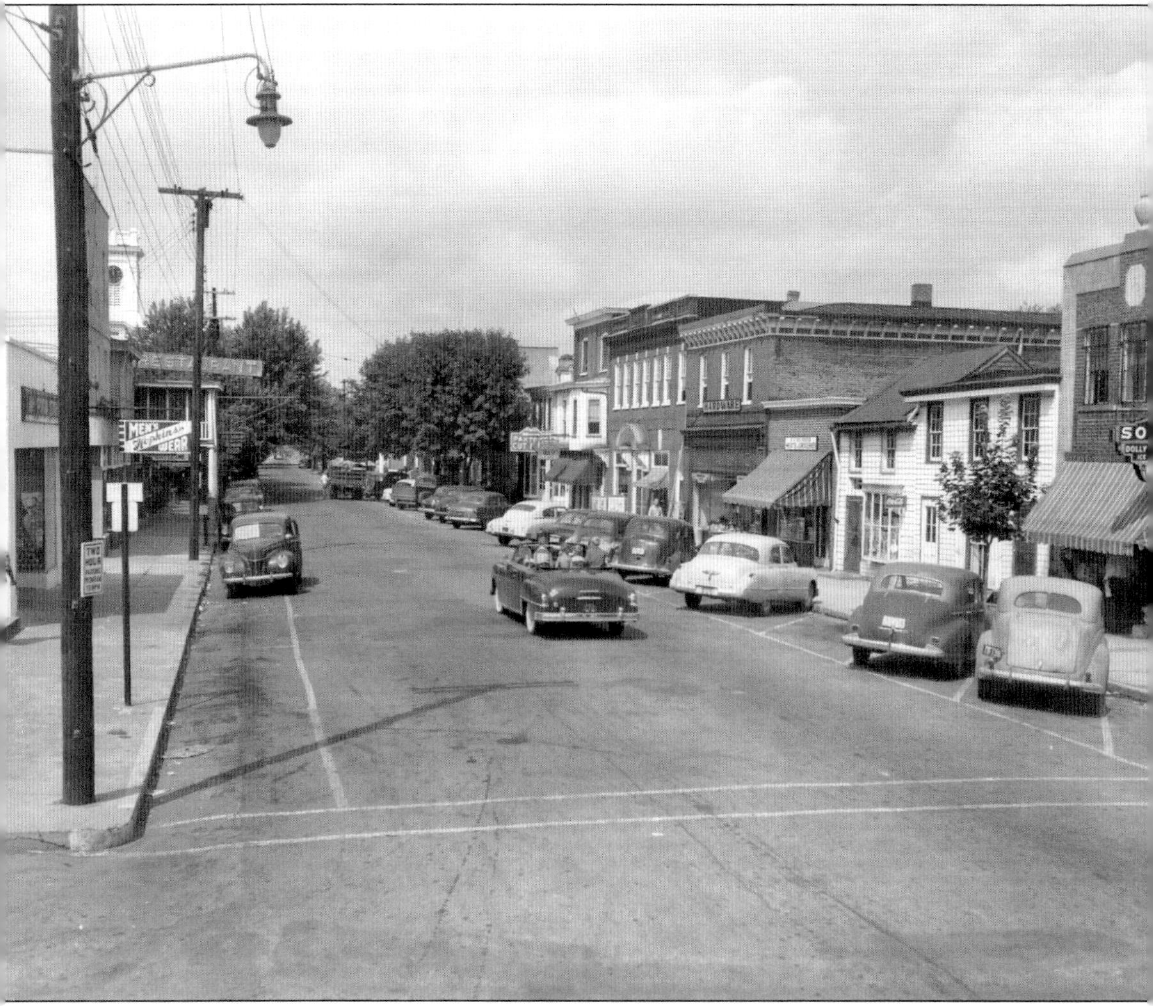

Downtown streetlights have long been a common backdrop in town, but they were once a much-celebrated luxury. Middletown became one of the first towns in Delaware to have electricity when the Light and Water Commission was founded in 1893. Streets, such as West Main Street (pictured), had previously been lit by oil lamps that were installed in 1866. Gas lights replaced the lamps in 1880, and in 1886, ten-candlepowered electric lights were installed. As the town's lighting evolved, town planners also worked to fulfill water needed to help fight fires. A water standpipe was built in 1871, but water was not abundant enough, and a viable water supply system was not available until 1887, when a waterworks system was constructed with a 37,000-gallon water standpipe and 20 driven wells set at 50-foot intervals. (Courtesy of Delaware Public Archives.)

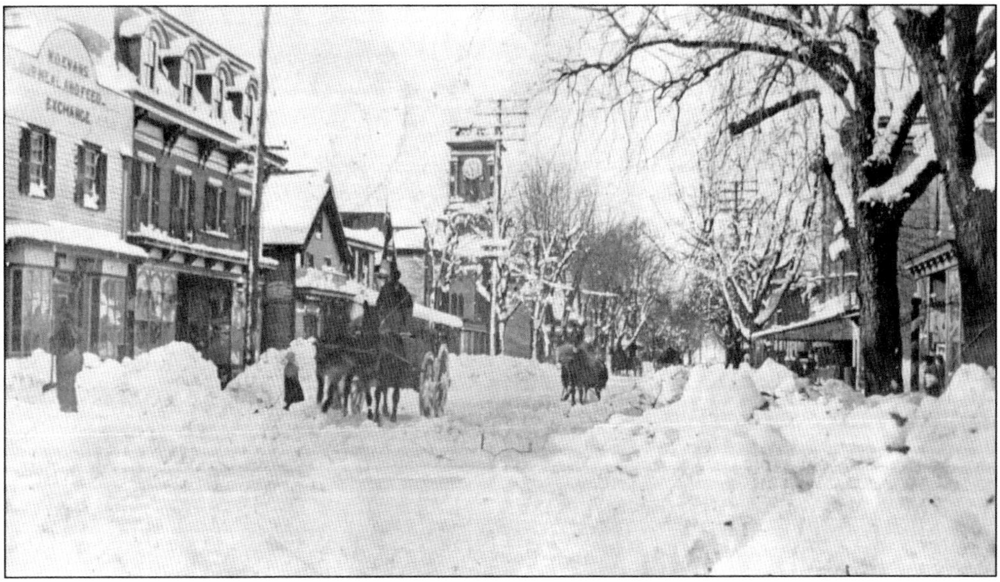

White Christmases are rarer now in the Mid-Atlantic, but in 1909, several states were hammered by more than two feet of snow that started to fall on Christmas Day. Delaware received the brunt of the storm, with 23 inches reported in Wilmington and 25 in Milford. With downed wires and stalled trade, Middletown residents gathered outdoors to enjoy the snow and work to get back to normal. These photographs from December 26, 1909, show horses pulling carriages down West Main Street (above) and Cochran Square alive with activity (below). (Above, courtesy of the author; below, courtesy of Middletown Historical Society.)

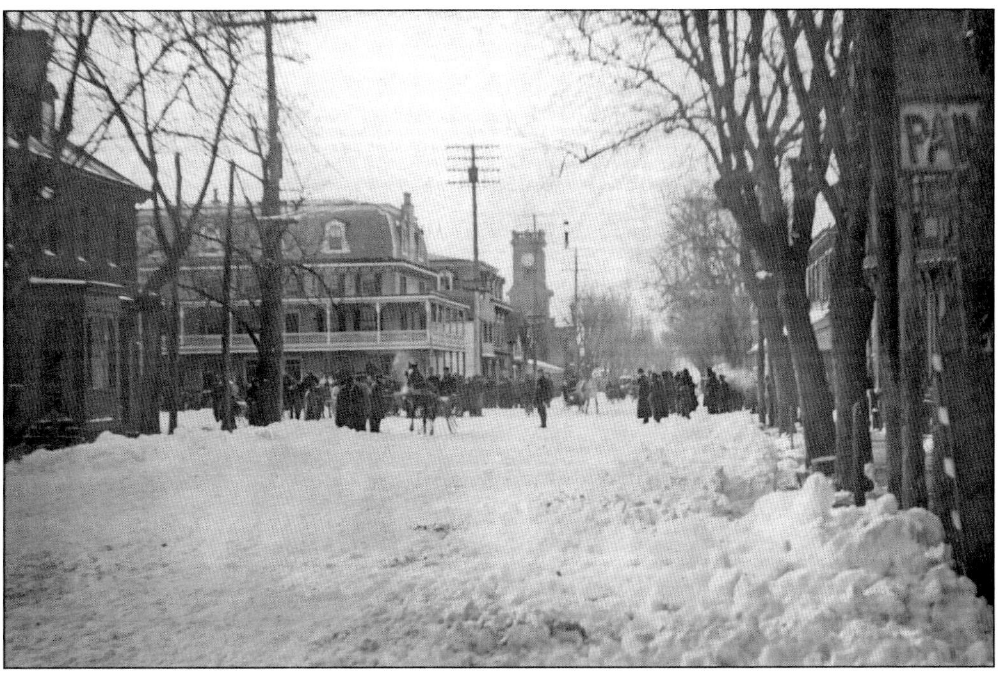

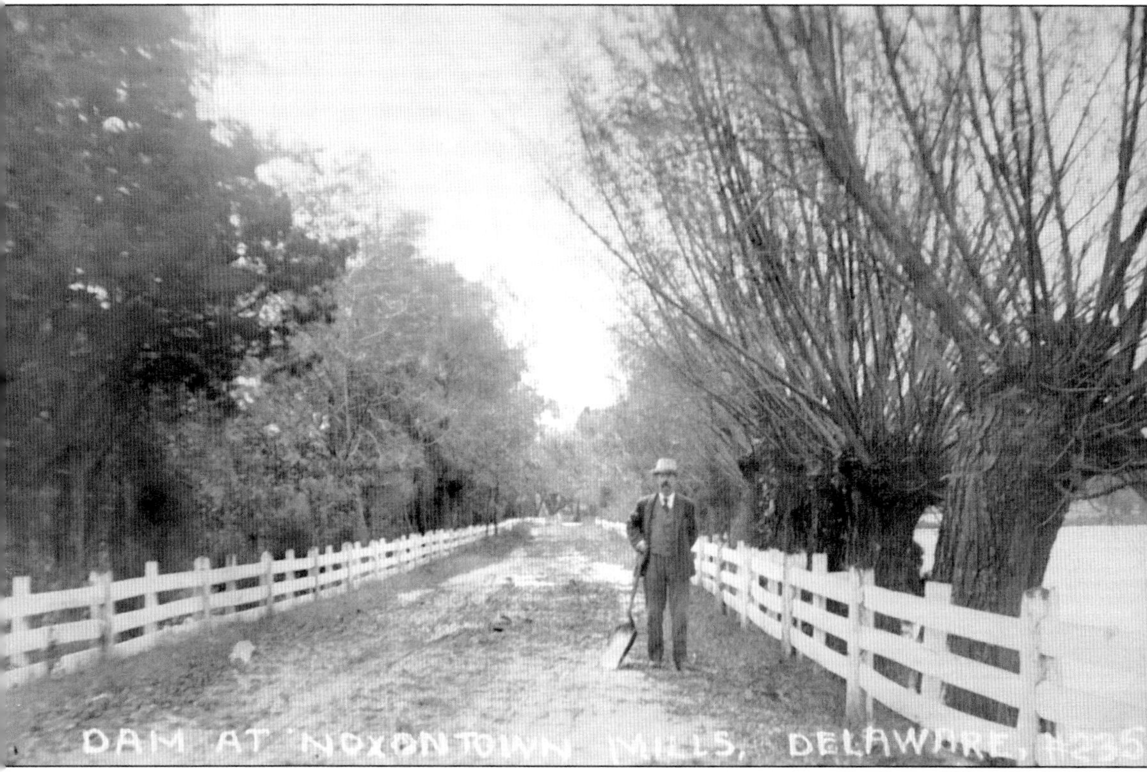

Thomas Noxon, who began to acquire property in Delaware in 1726 and owned several mills on branches of the Appoquinimink River, can be credited with the beautiful landscape that surrounds St. Andrew's School a few miles south of Middletown. Noxon built a dam for a millpond about two miles southeast of Middletown on the Appoquinimink River, then constructed a gristmill beside the dam. Noxon lived in a large brick house by the mill, and a small community called Noxontown was chartered in the area surrounding his home in 1742. Noxon died the following year, leaving his estate to his son, Benjamin. In August 1777, Caesar Rodney set up camp with the Kent County Militia at the Noxon Mill to protect against foraging by the British, who invaded northern Delaware via the Elk River. The mill still stands on present-day Noxontown Road. (Courtesy of Delaware Public Archives.)

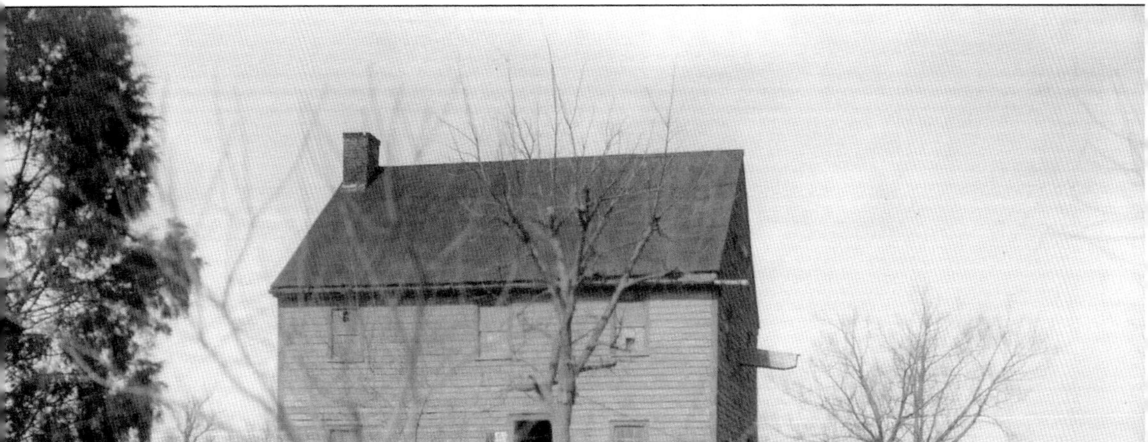

The Noxon Mill, situated on a hill along a sharp curve of Noxontown Road, may go unnoticed by passersby unaware that the surrounding historic structures owe their existence to it. The operations of the Noxon Mill spurred a community to rise around the structure, including a bakehouse, a brewhouse, a malthouse, and a hotel that served residents and visitors who flocked to the famous 18th-century Noxontown Fair. The mill operated as a merchant mill until 1855, when it transitioned to custom work. In the 1890s, W.D. Evans purchased the property and continued production at the mill with an emphasis on feed and agricultural uses. The majority of the homes directly adjacent to the mill are now owned and used by St. Andrew's School, which was founded on the Noxontown Pond in 1929. (Courtesy of Delaware Public Archives.)

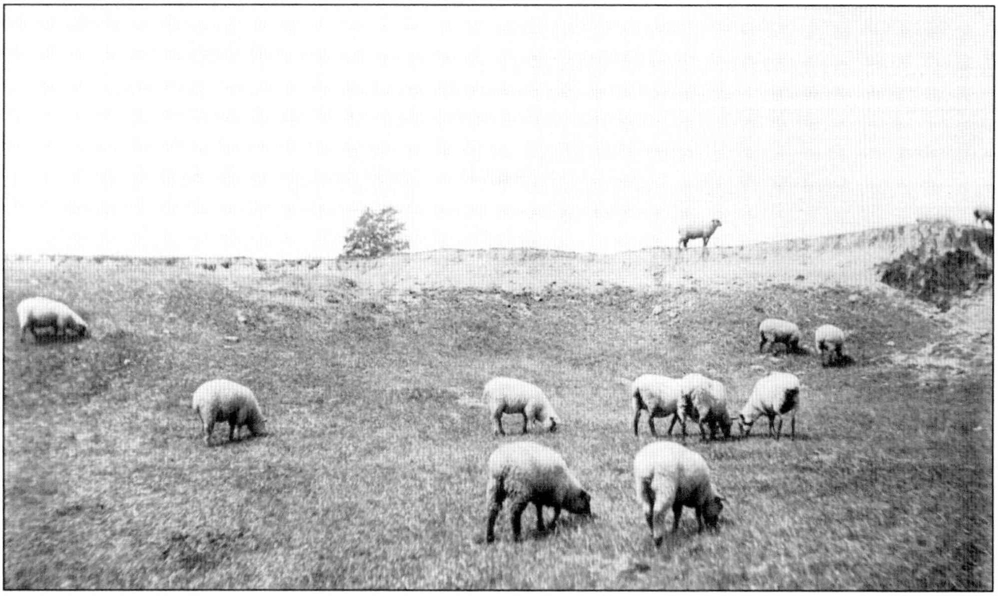

William Green operated a gravel pit on the south end of his farm and allowed contractors to remove gravel—for use in constructing roads and sidewalks—from a giant hole in the ground. This photograph shows sheep grazing at the gravel pit. The entrance to what became known at "the pit" was located off South Broad Street, and the area is now home to the Lakeside neighborhood. (Courtesy of Scott Lawrence.)

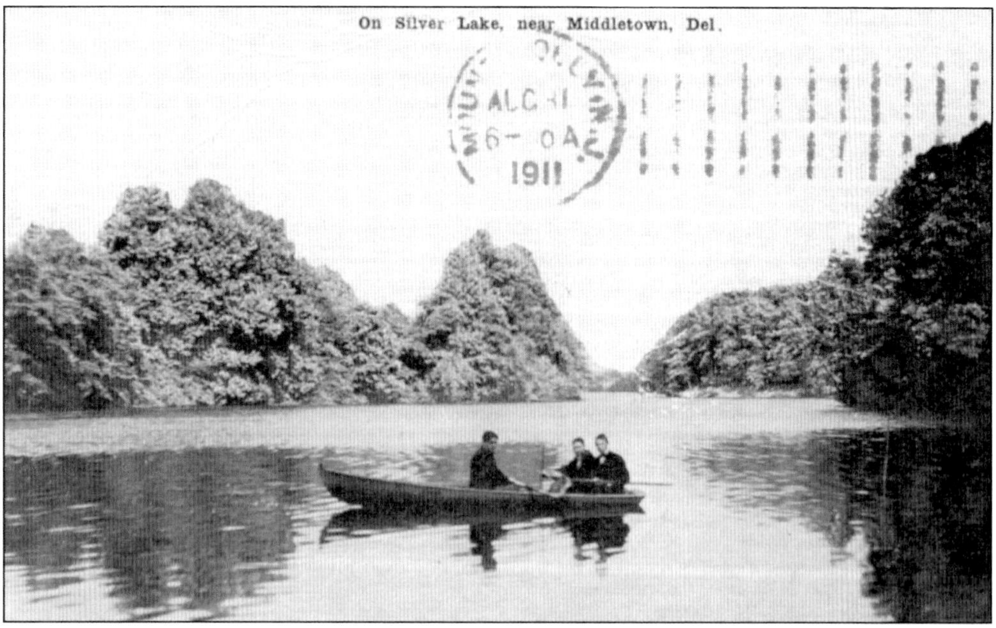

Silver Lake, utilized by Thomas Noxon in the 18th century, was a popular recreational area in both the summer and winter months. Clarence Weber founded the Black Duck Club and taught swimming at the lake. When the lake froze in winter, residents used it for ice-skating. A March 1, 1924, article in the *Middletown Transcript* tells of when Lloyd M. Bragdon drowned after ice under his feet gave way. The lake is now under private ownership. (Courtesy of Delaware Public Archives.)

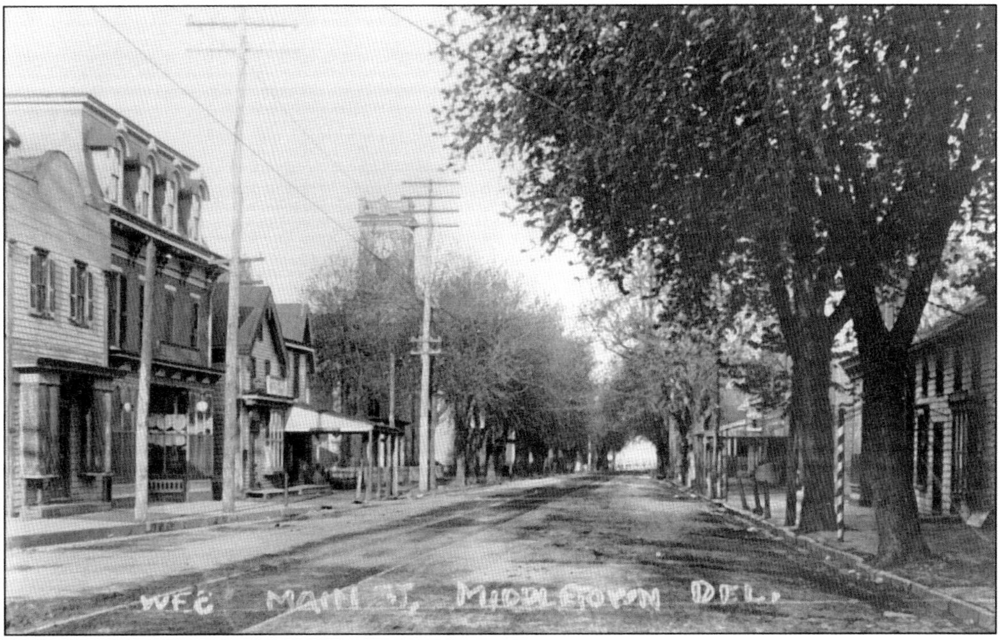

Opposite views of the same section of West Main Street show just two of the often-changed facades of businesses that came and went. The sleepy street scene above, in a view looking west, shows trolley lines, several shops, and the Forest Presbyterian Church tower and clock. In the 1960s photograph below, with a view looking east, one can see gas-powered lawnmowers, money-wiring services, a restaurant, and one of the former locations of the US post office. W.D. Hatton's clock-repair business and Charlie "Chopper Charlie" Biggs's barbershop have weathered many decades and still stand on the north side of this section. (Both, courtesy of Delaware Public Archives.)

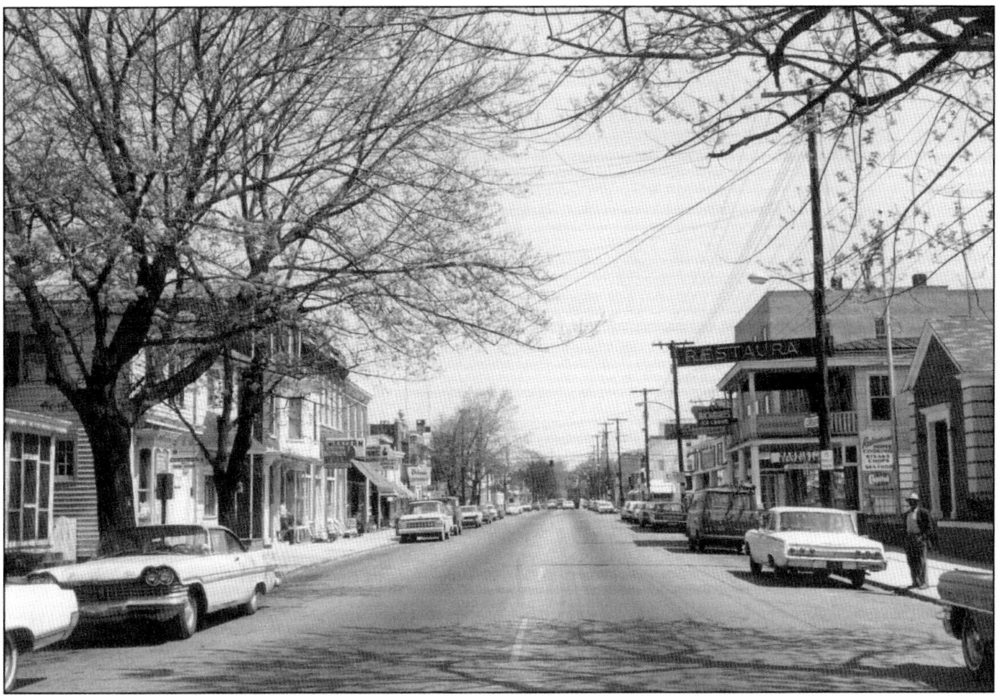

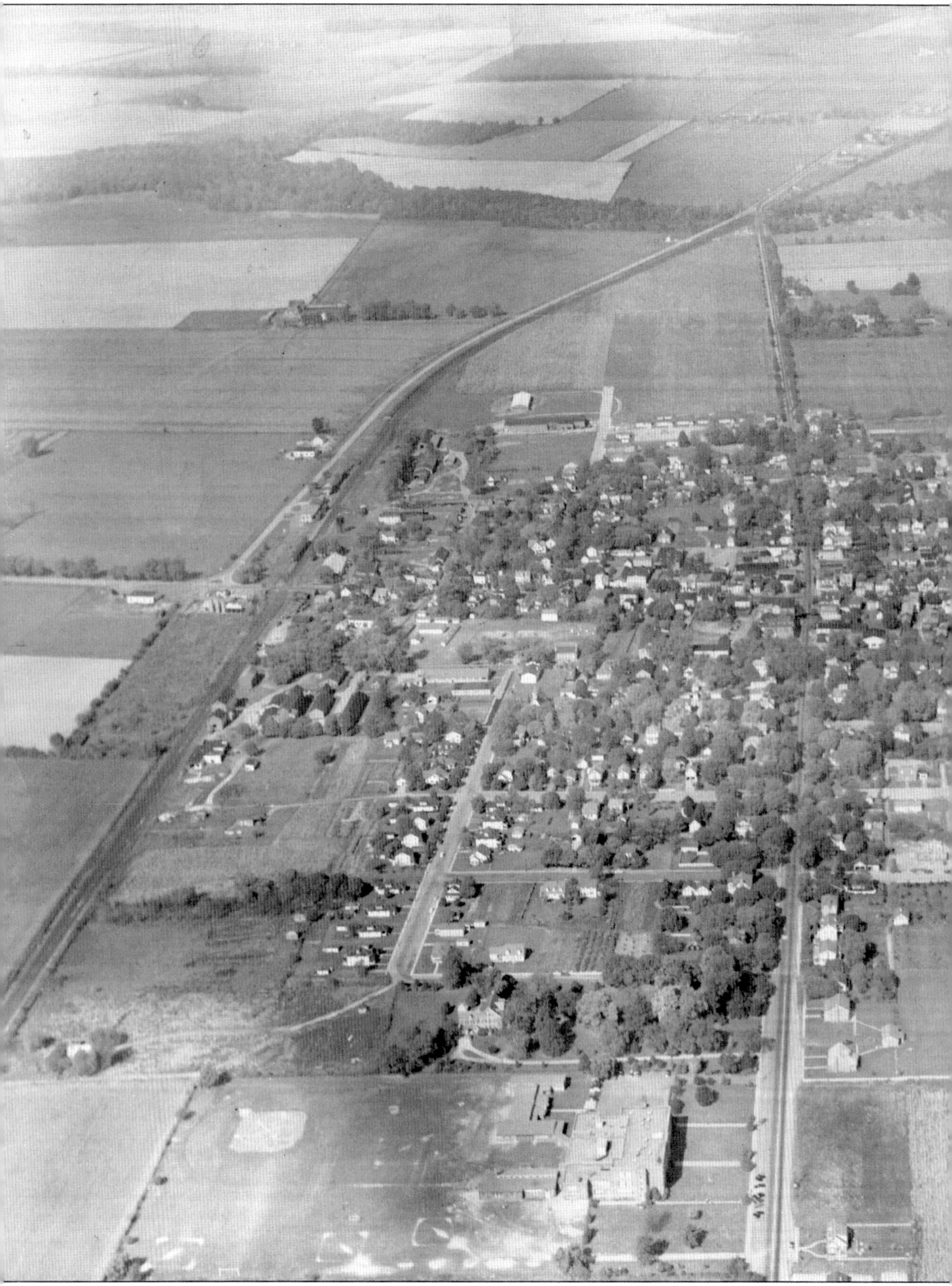

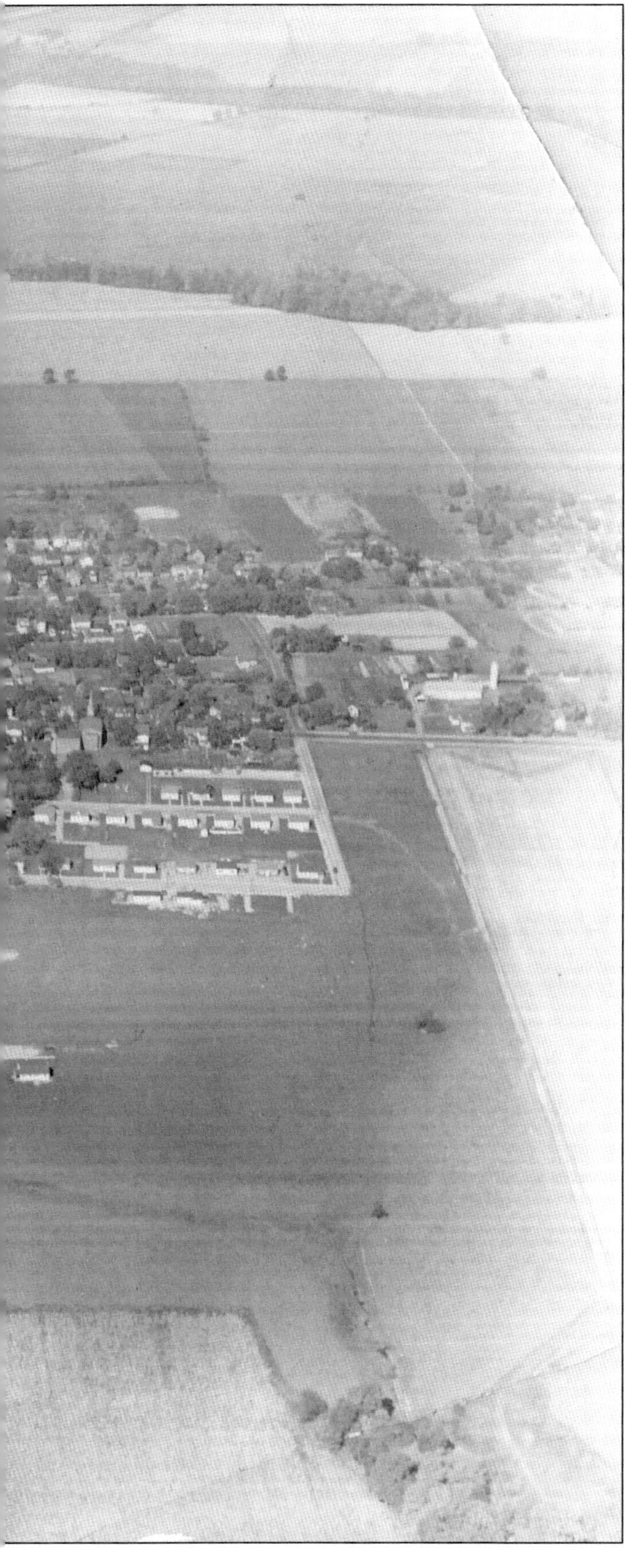

This 1950s-era bird's-eye view of Middletown shows the original structure of the town limits, with the former Middletown High School building at the bottom of the image and the intersection of Routes 71 and 301 toward the top of it. Route 301, which extends into Maryland, stopped at Route 299, or East Main Street, at that time. Residential and commercial structures now cover the majority of the open space shown here. The area at lower right is now home to the Laurel Creek neighborhood and Silver Lake Elementary School, which is situated among Silver Lake Park, one of Middletown's most popular recreational areas. (Courtesy of the author.)

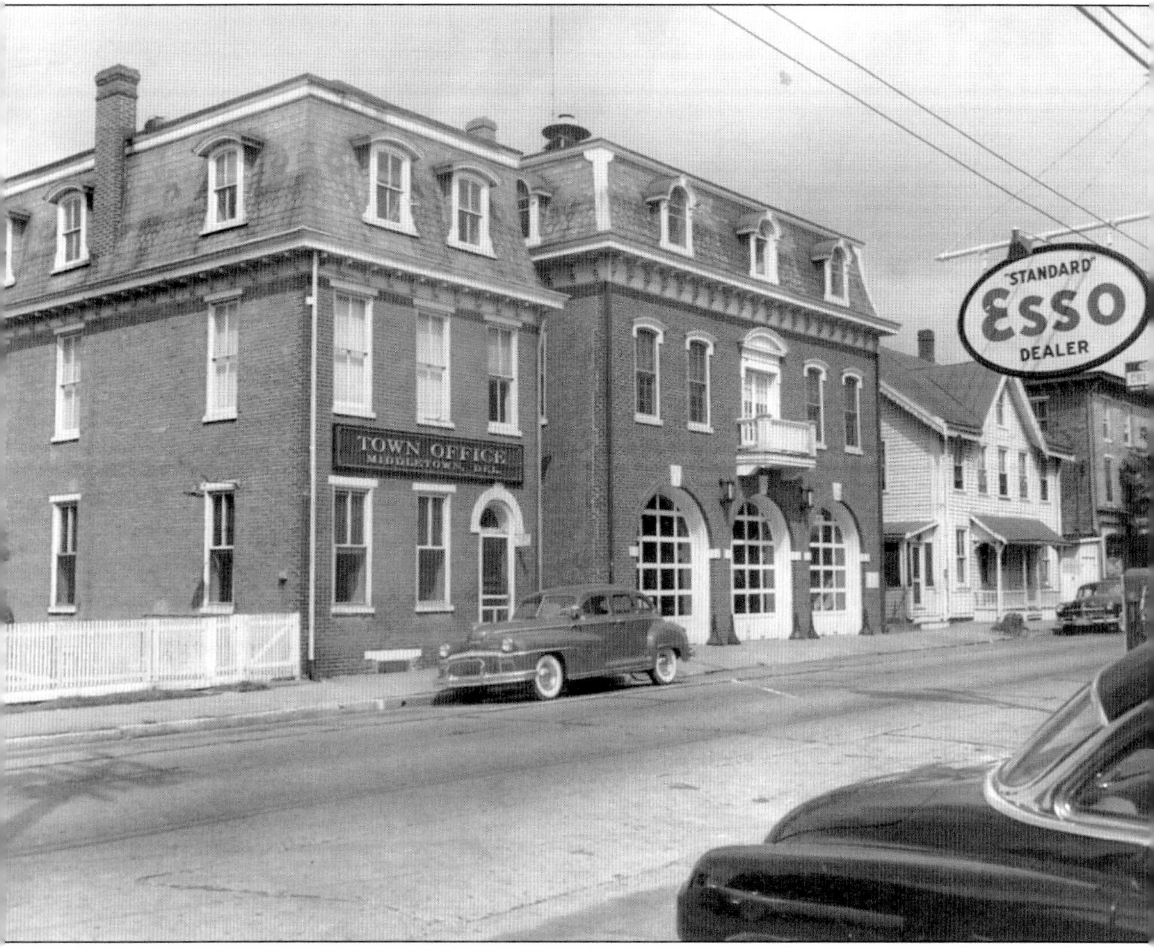

In 1919, the Masonic Lodge No. 5 had this building constructed at 18 South Broad Street after the Middletown Opera House and Town Hall, where the lodge previously conducted business, was destroyed by fire in December 1918. While the lodge members seemingly lost all their possessions in that fire, the organization's Duncan Beard–made silver Masonic square-and-compass "jewel" survived by chance. Mason Walter S. Letherbury accidentally left a lodge meeting while still wearing the jewel, later placing it in the safe of his hardware store. Fire struck the opera house and town hall that night, and Letherbury's mistake made the jewel the lodge's only remaining (and hence very prized) possession. The first floor of the building was then rented to the Town of Middletown for use as a town office until the Volunteer Hose Company of Middletown purchased it and the building next door, which was owned by the forerunner of the Delaware Trust Co. (Courtesy of Delaware Public Archives.)

Two

HISTORIC STRUCTURES

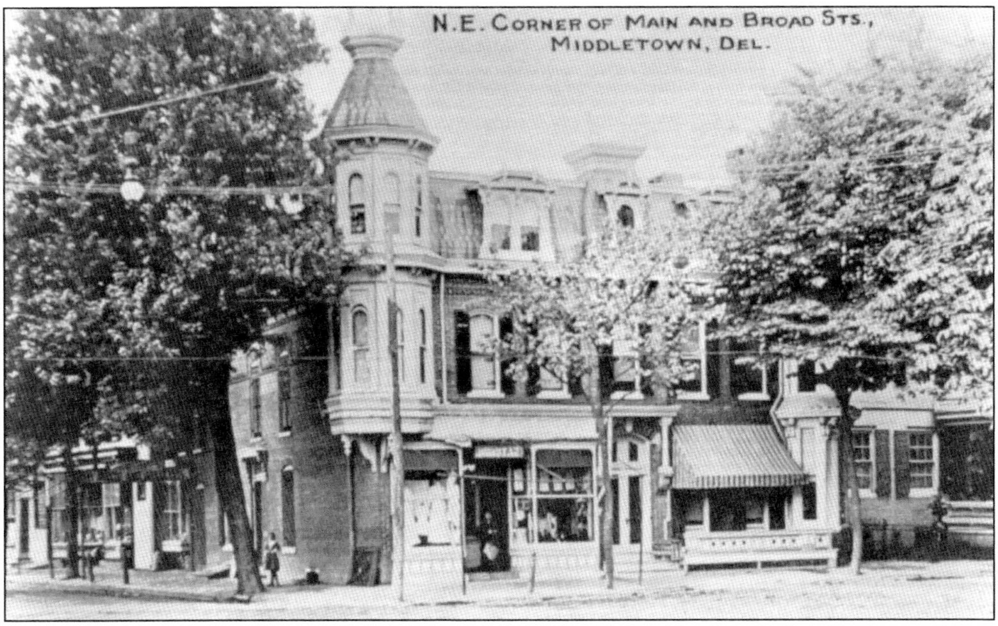

One of Middletown's most prominent structures literally towers over the northeast corner of Main and Broad Streets. This late-1800s building at 1–5 East Main Street is a commercial and residential structure covered in intricate details. It once housed the popular and memorable Naudain's dry goods store and businesses such as the Citizens' Bank of the State of Delaware and Middle-of-the-Town Antiques. (Courtesy of Delaware Public Archives.)

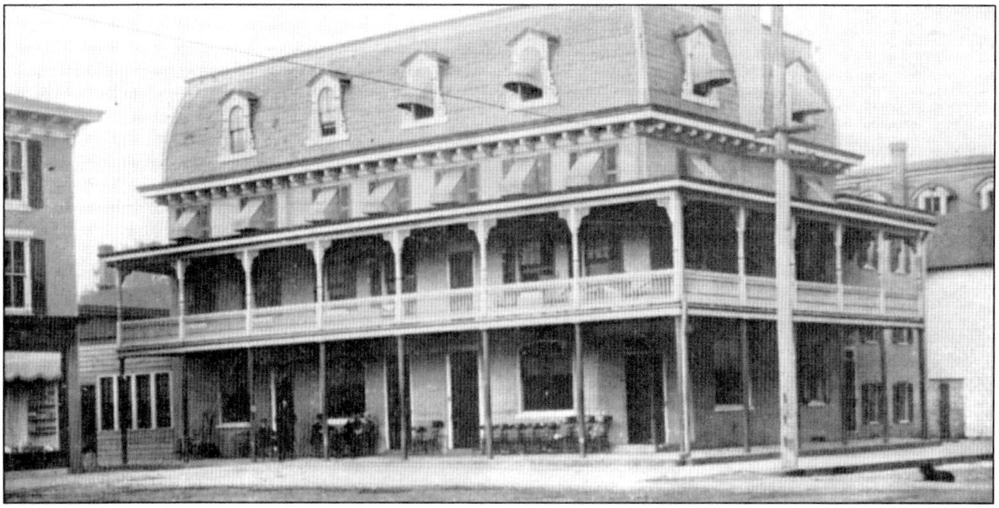

The Witherspoon Inn, shown above around the 1920s, has varied in appearance and use since it was constructed in 1761. Its biggest face-lift came after it was gutted by the infamous fire of February 14, 1946 (below), which broke out in the nearby hardware store. High winds kept flames alive for nearly two hours as hundreds of residents grabbed fire hoses and struggled to help the fire department save the landmark. At one point, five firemen were trapped on the inn's second floor when it collapsed, forcing them to crawl out into the street. The inn was rebuilt within its surviving walls and reopened two years to the day after the fire. It was remodeled in the early 2000s and is now a two-story building that currently houses Sully's Irish Pub, with a small and separate restaurant space currently occupied by Middletown Seafood at the south end. (Above, courtesy of Middletown Historical Society; below, courtesy of Delaware Public Archives.)

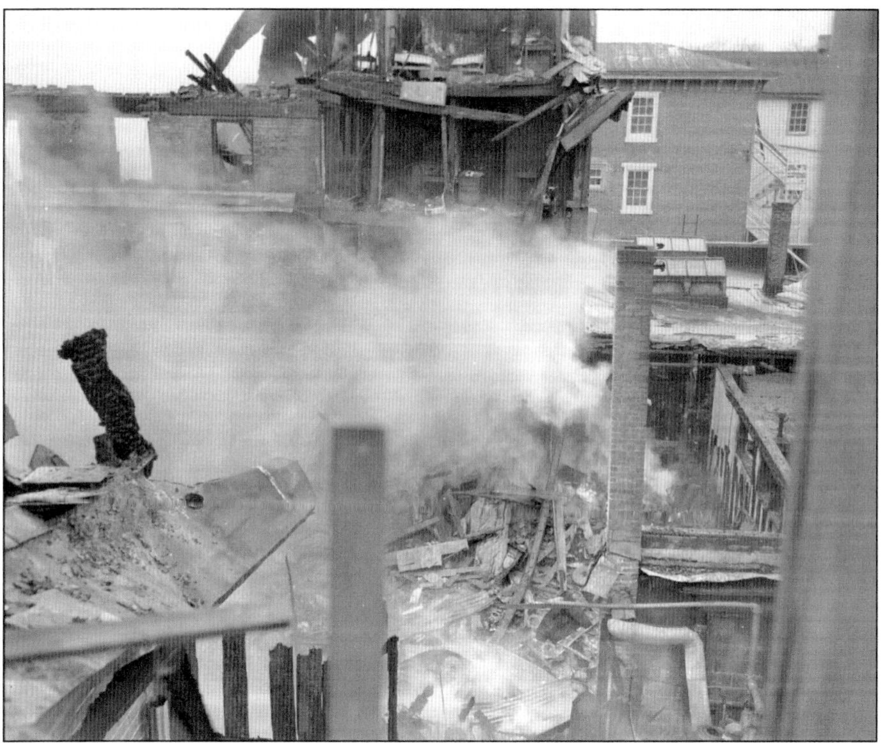

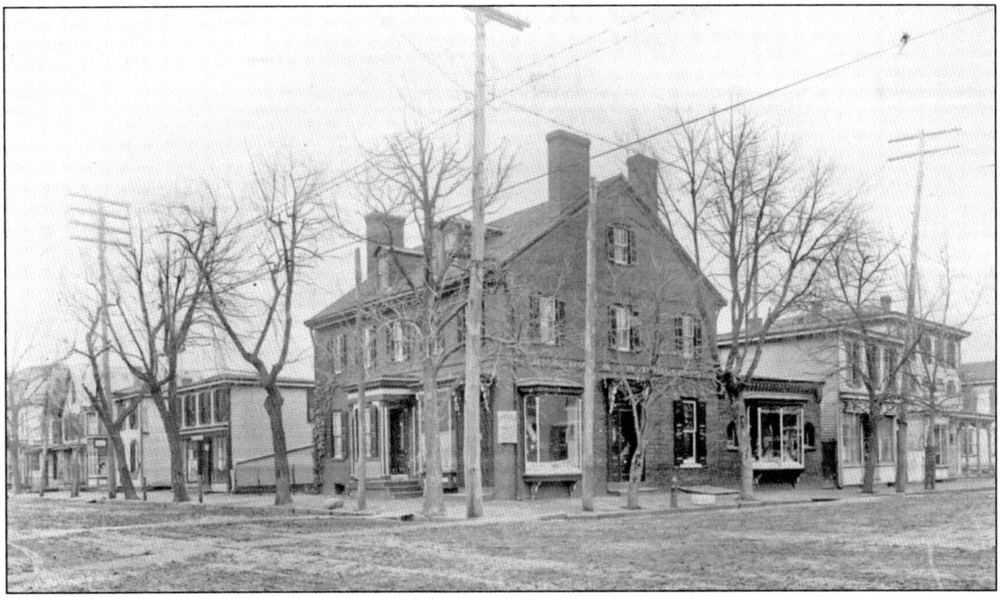

The building at 2 East Main Street, at the southeast corner of Main and Broad Streets, is one of the town's oldest structures. It was originally a farmhouse that was possibly built in the 18th century. Richard Lockwood purchased the home in 1837 and transformed it into a store. The deed states it was a brick dwelling, kitchen, smokehouse, stable, granary, store, and tavern lot. The building continued to be used as a store, with dwelling rooms above and on the east side of the ground floor. By 1886, it was operated as a pharmacy under various names, including that of J. Gaylord Bragdon (shown above in the 1910s), Culver's, Gerald McNaughton's Liggett-Rexall drugstore (shown below in the 1970s), and Cappeau's (in the 1970s). The structure was gutted by fire in 1960, leaving only the exterior walls, which were retained when it was rebuilt. (Above, courtesy of Middletown Historical Society; below, courtesy of Delaware Public Archives.)

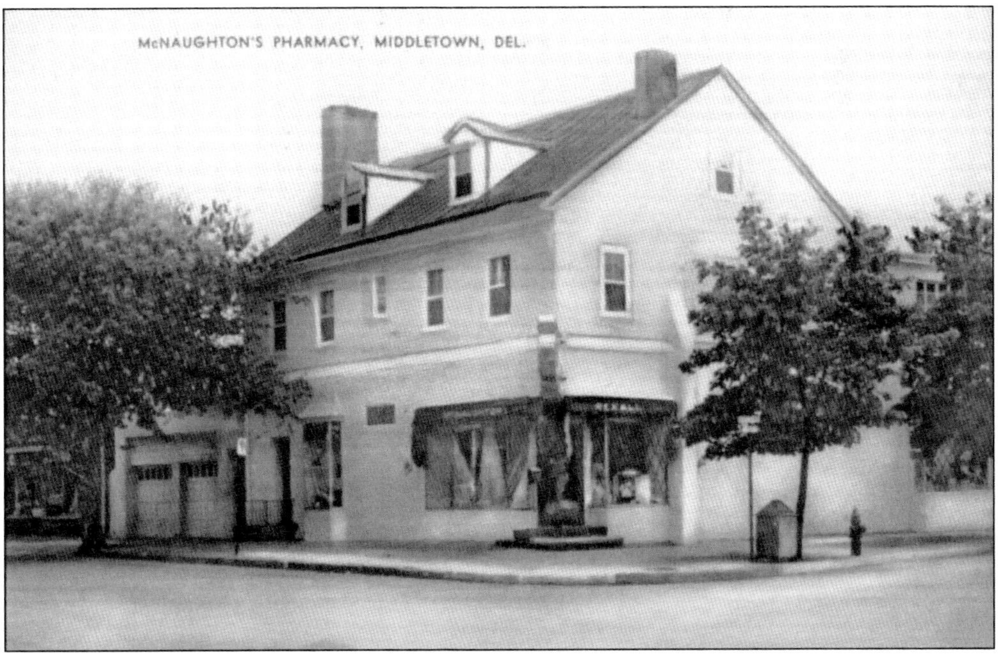

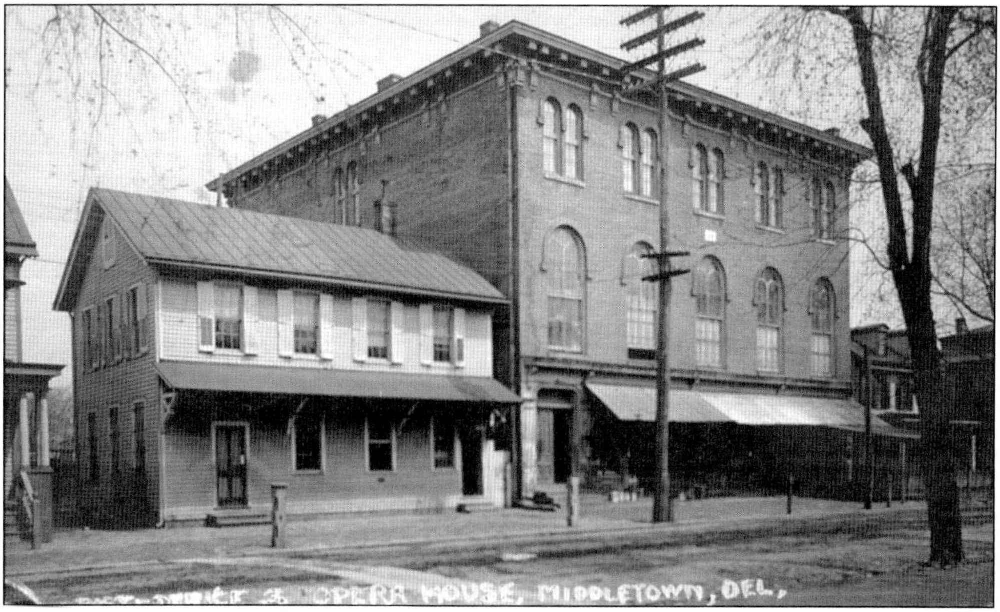

The Middletown Town Hall Company, founded in February 1867, planned for a new community building (above), which opened in January 1869 with three stores and the town hall on the first floor, an auditorium on the second floor, and three rooms on the third floor that were utilized by the Masonic Lodge No. 5. The building was destroyed by fire on December 31, 1918. The town rebuilt it on the same spot, but in 1921, the new structure was also destroyed by fire. Concrete and plaster were used to construct the current building (below), which opened December 7, 1922, as the Everett Theatre. Advancing technology slowly made the Everett nearly obsolete, and its doors were closed in 1979. However, in 1983, concerned citizens formed Associated Community Talents, Inc. (A.C.T.), to reopen and eventually restore the town's beloved theatre. (Above, courtesy of University of Delaware Library, Special Collections, Delaware Postcard Collection; below, courtesy of Middletown Historical Society.)

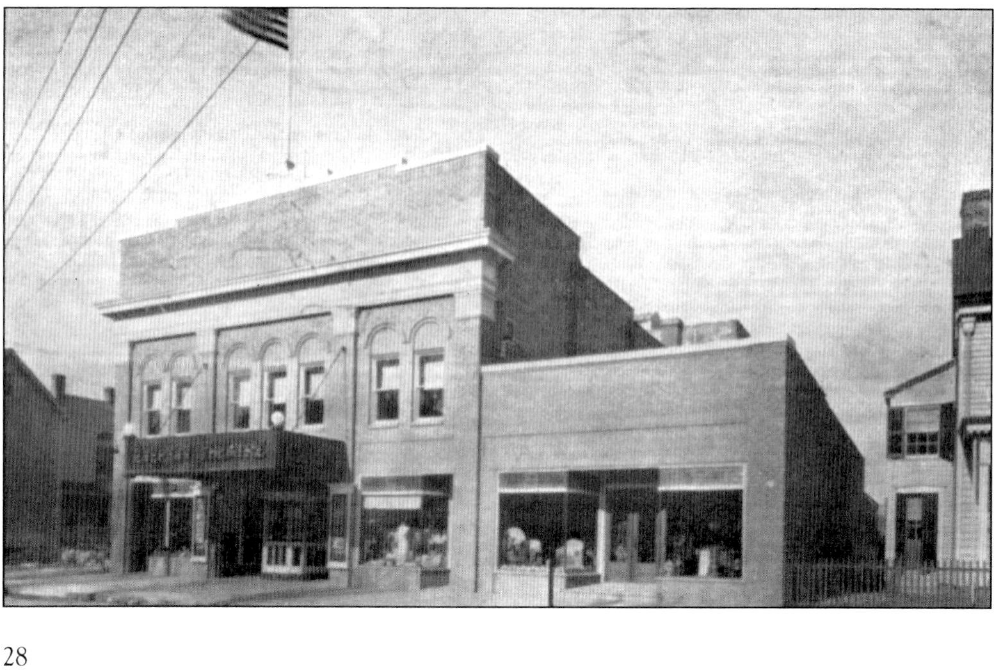

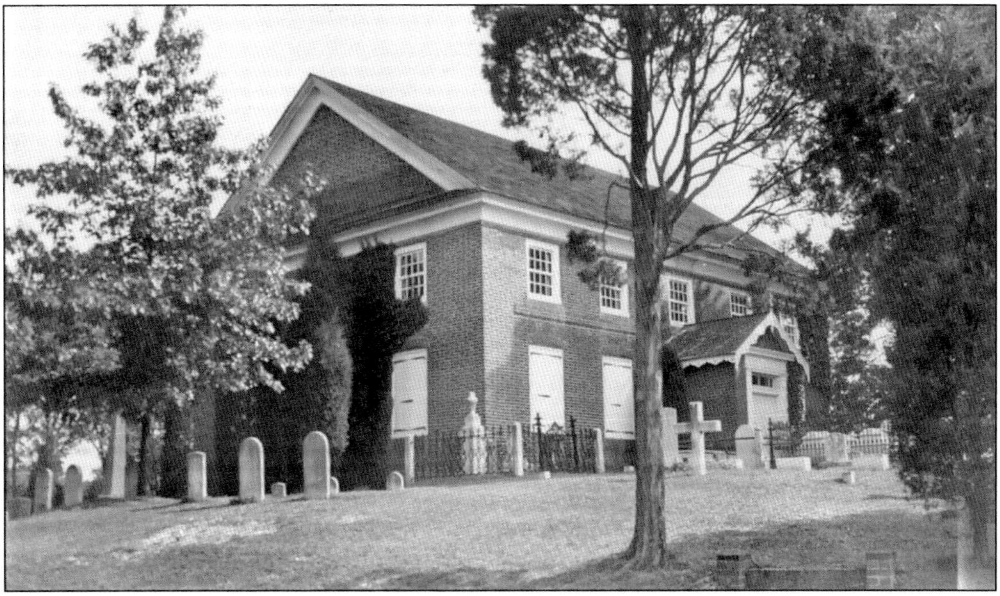

The roots of St. Anne's Episcopal Church can be traced to the early 1700s, when a log chapel was constructed just south of Middletown. Now called "Old St. Anne's," this structure on South Broad Street was built between 1765 and 1772. St. Anne's was named after England's "Good Queen Anne," who presented the church with an altar cloth that bore her initials, "A.R." for "Anne Regina." During the Revolutionary War, the Rev. Philip Reading, a Loyalist, locked the church doors to its congregants on August 25, 1776, because some were in favor of revolt. The church did not reopen until after Reading died in 1778, and services were sporadic until the 1830s. By 1872, the congregation outgrew this building and purchased land on East Green Street for a new place of worship. Old St. Anne's was restored in 1955 in time to celebrate the church's 250th anniversary. (Both, courtesy of Delaware Public Archives.)

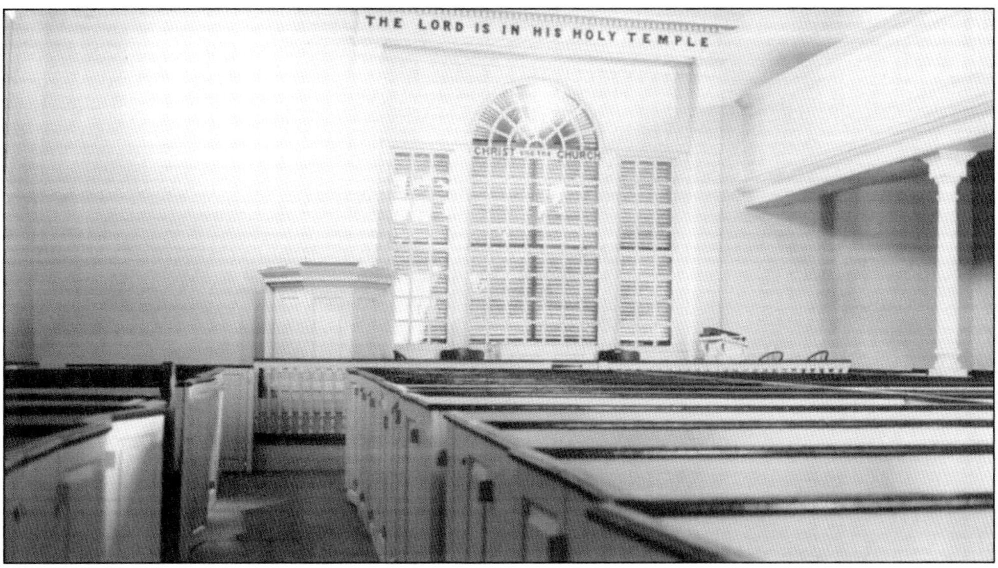

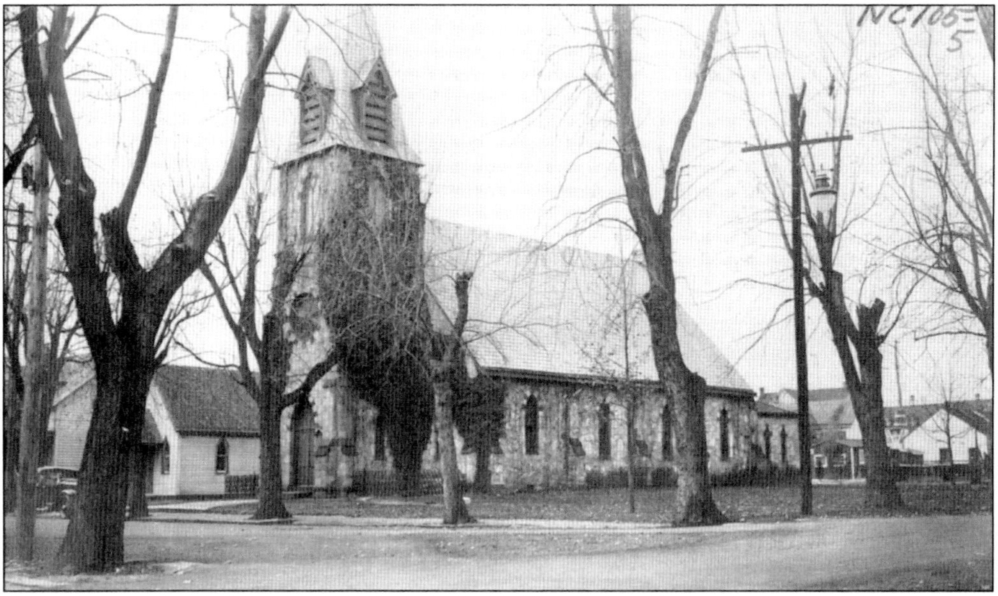

After purchasing this property at 15 East Green Street in 1872, the congregation of St. Anne's Episcopal Church erected a large, gothic-style serpentine stone structure that still stands at the quiet crossroads of East Green and Cox Streets. The location was more centrally located than the former church, which was dubbed "Old St. Anne's" upon completion of the building pictured above. The St. Anne's rectory, pictured in the c. 1865 photograph below, was originally located across from the Old St. Anne's Church cemetery just south of town limits. It was relocated by horses that pulled it into town in the late 1800s and set it down at 12 and 14 East Green Street, where it was eventually renovated and made into a duplex. (Both, courtesy of Delaware Public Archives.)

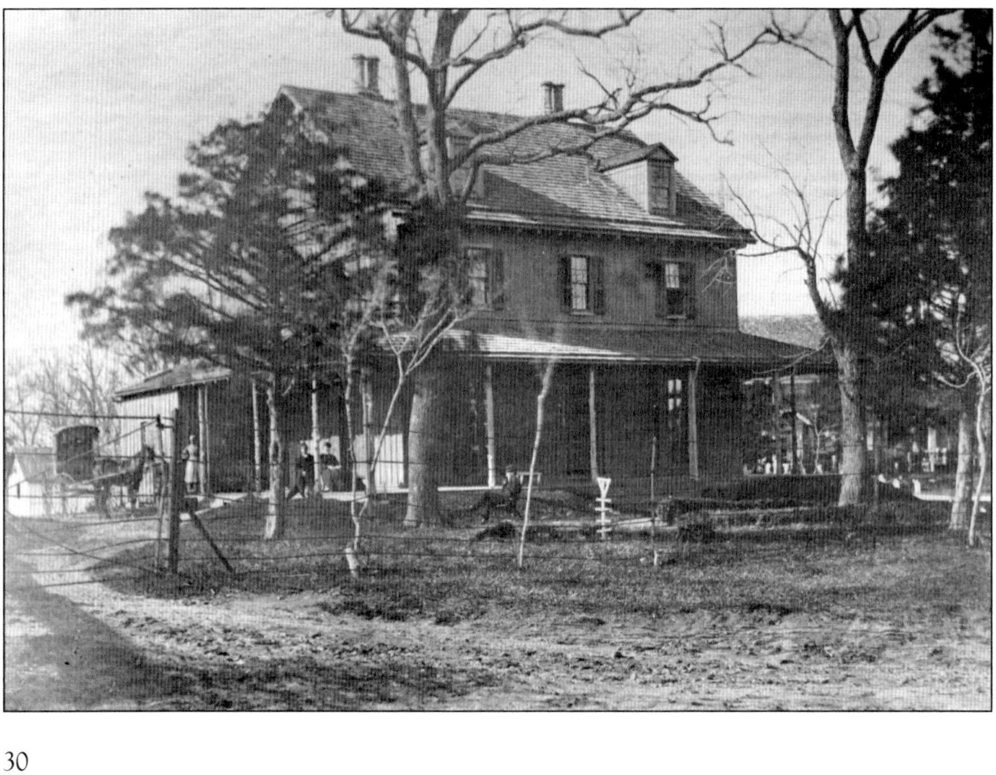

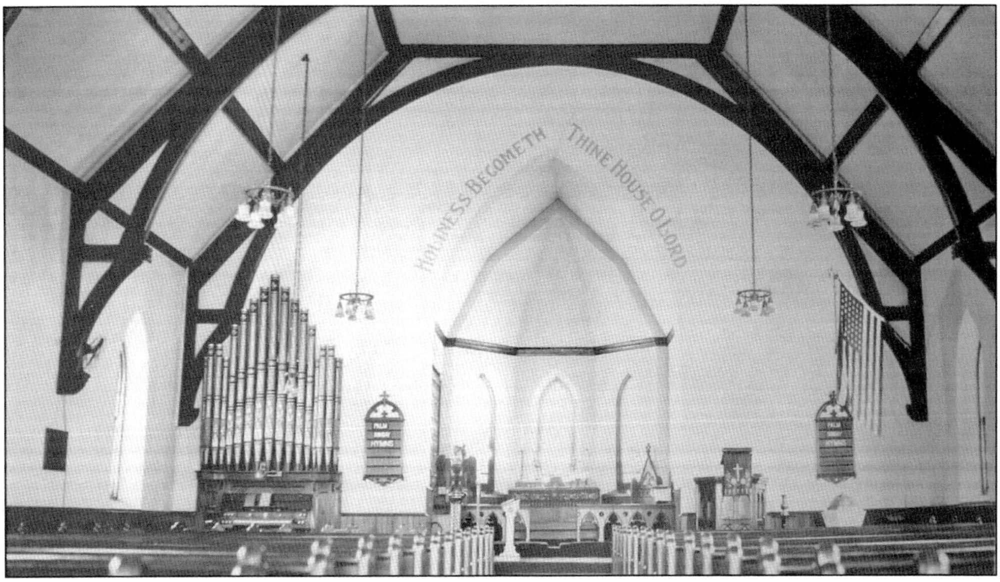

An 1882 fire that started at Cox Carriage Works on South Broad Street destroyed the decade-old St. Anne's Episcopal Church. The only remnants were the green stone walls. Luckily, the communion table covering donated by Queen Anne was saved. The longest-serving leader of the church was the Rev. Percy L. Donaghay, who served from 1908 to 1943. St. Anne's grew in membership and an addition to its Green Street building was constructed in 1949, which included a chapel, offices, a parish room, and a memorial to Dr. Martin Barr. Shown above and below are interior views of the church. St. Anne's continues to have a strong presence in Middletown and offers a free community meal every Thanksgiving. (Both, courtesy of Delaware Public Archives.)

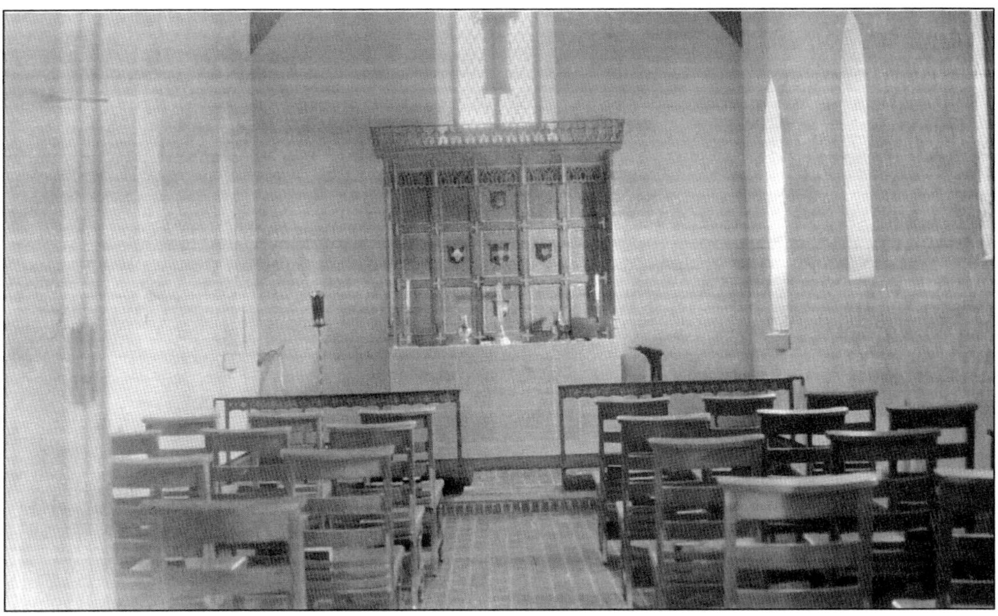

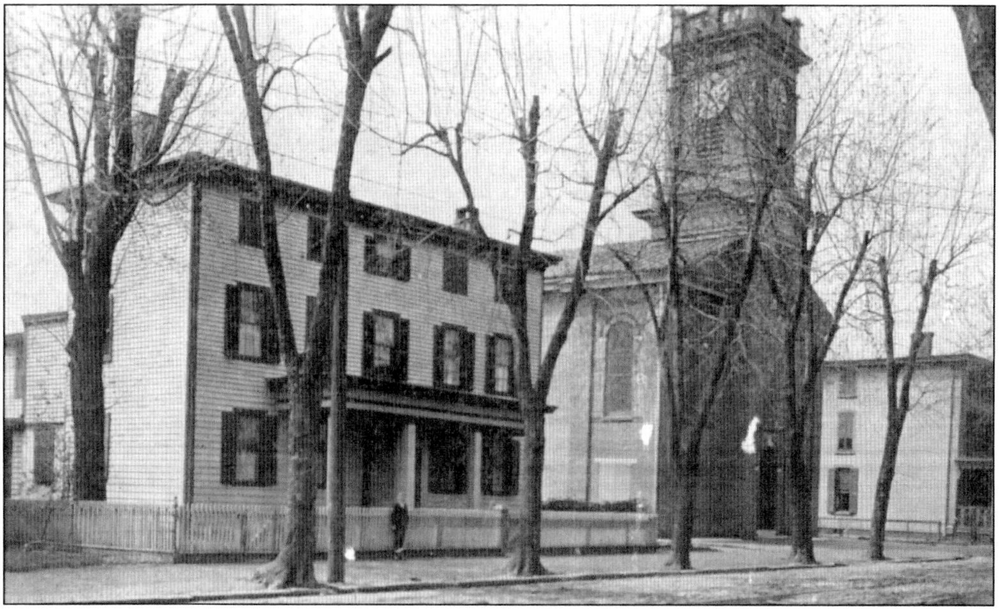

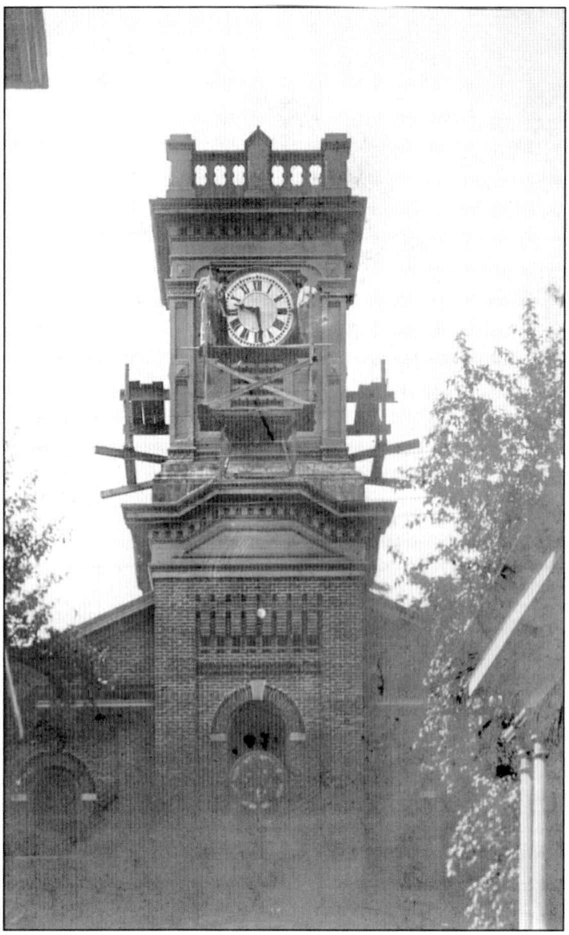

Presbyterians began to congregate in the area at least as early as 1711 at Drawyers Church, near Odessa, from which Forest Presbyterian Church arose in 1750. Members of the new congregation built a church on North Broad Street, where Forest Cemetery remains. The original building was demolished due to diminishing membership, but the congregation re-formed and erected this structure at 44 West Main Street in 1850. Also pictured is the church's manse, which no longer exists. The "town clock" atop the church was installed in 1906. It was donated by Frances Cochran Comegys as a memorial to her parents and is visible from many buildings along the street. (Both, courtesy of Delaware Public Archives.)

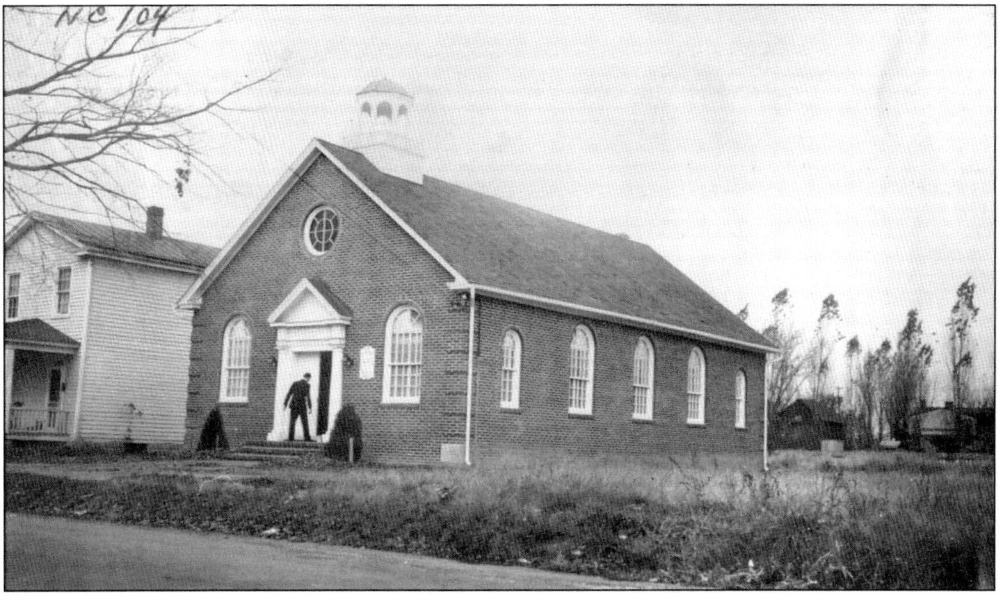

Grace Orthodox Presbyterian Church arose from a division among the congregation of Forest Presbyterian Church. Part of the congregation split to follow its own worship style at Grace Church, which was constructed in 1937 on Pennington Street. The Rev. F. Clarke Evans led the congregation for 20 years—from the 1950s through the 1970s. (Courtesy of Delaware Public Archives.)

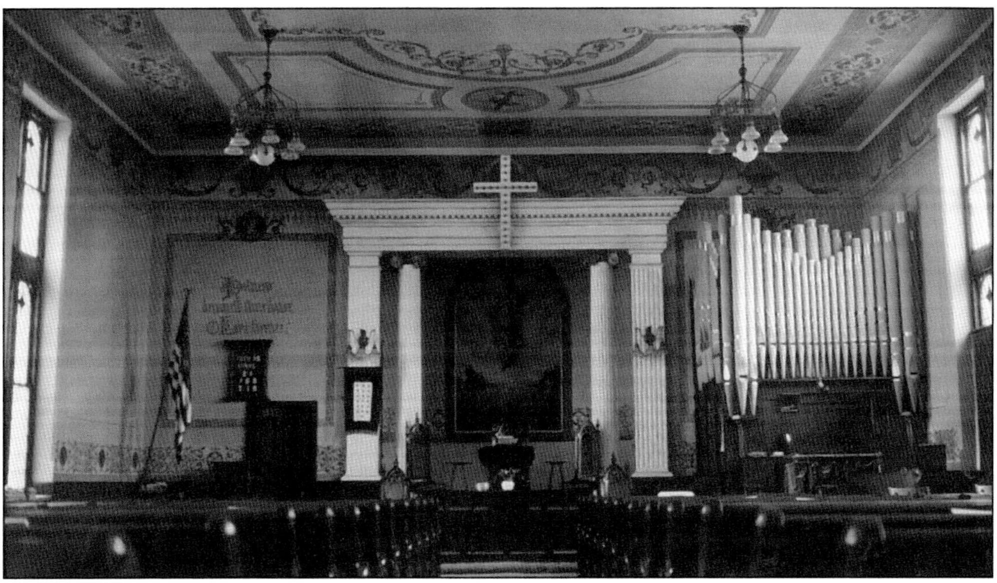

Bethesda United Methodist Church opened on East Main Street in April 1823. A cornerstone was laid for the building's first addition in 1849. In 1879, a rear extension, an organ recess, stained-glass windows, a double system of heaters, a gas generator for lighting, and the tower and steeple were added. New stairways and a gallery were built in 1910. Around 1950, Bethesda Hall was added to create more community space. (Courtesy of Delaware Public Archives.)

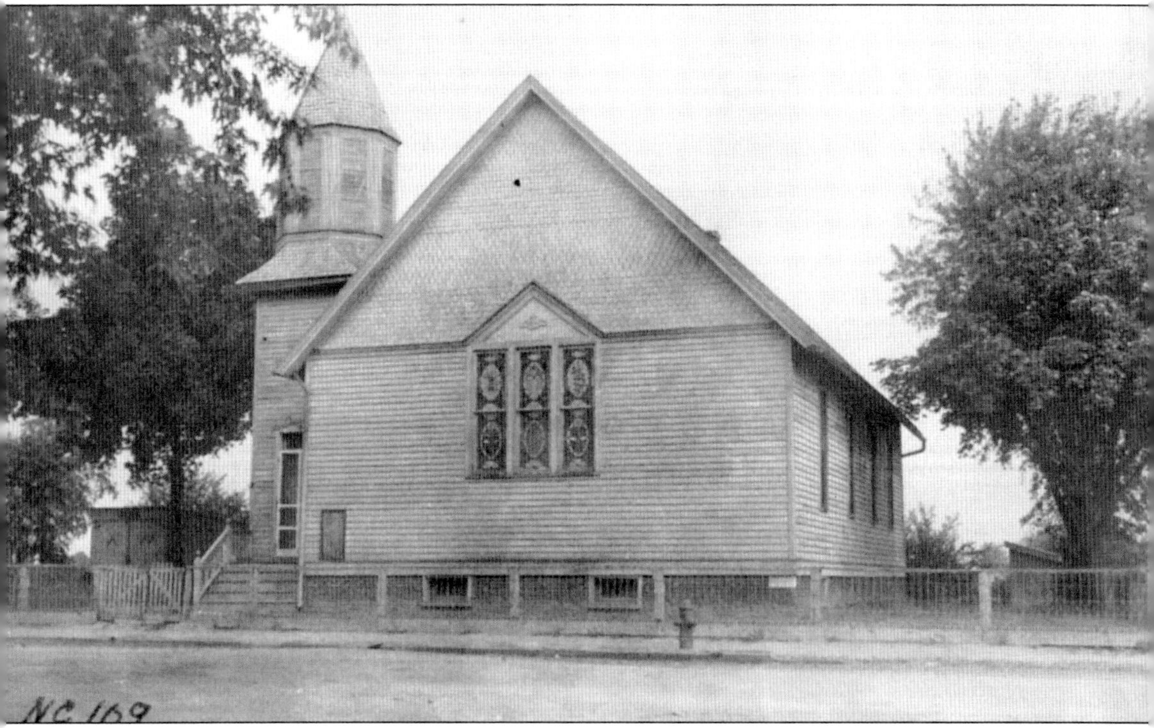

Dale United Methodist Church was built in 1894 on East Lake Street as a place of worship for black residents. The congregation previously worshiped at a New Street location purchased from Samuel Dale by the congregation's trustees on December 15, 1869. That parcel encompassed 3,700 square feet, a space that the church quickly outgrew. In 1886, Z.A. Pool sold a 6,000-square-foot parcel of land on East Lake Street to the church, allowing for an expansion. Mount Calvary Baptist Church, also founded for black worshipers, now exists on New Street, with Trinity AME Church a few blocks away on Lockwood Street. Current and former residents of the Lake Street area flock to local churches with friends and family for the annual camp meeting in July that pays homage to the religious founders and is a celebration among old friends. (Courtesy of Delaware Public Archives.)

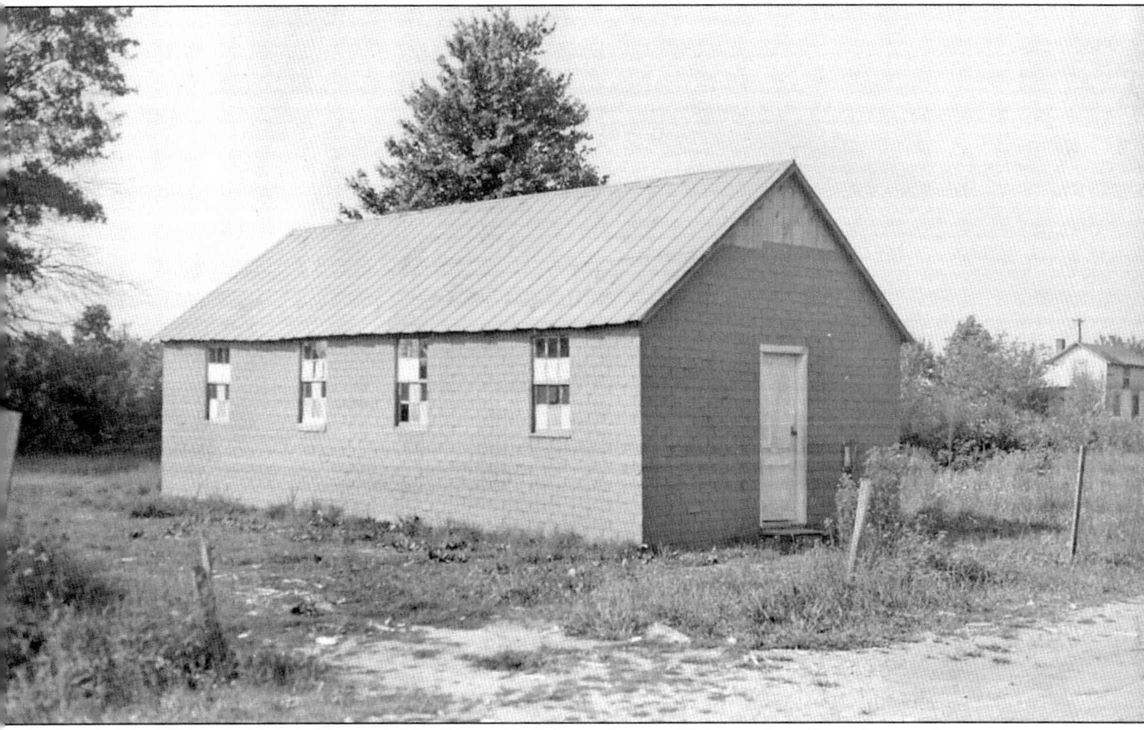

On the East Coast, many religious black people left traditional Methodist churches and united to form the African Methodist Episcopal (AME) denomination in April 1816 under the leadership of Delawarean Richard Allen. Intolerance of black people during that time often seeped into churches—among many other facilities and organizations—and caused a number of black worshipers to split from their congregations and join AME places of worship. Ringgold Chapel AME Church (pictured) was built in 1912 at 5017 Summit Bridge Road at the corner of Route 71/301 and Armstrong Corner Road. The quaint church draws a sizable crowd for worship services. Trinity AME Church, located at 27 Lockwood Street, was dedicated on October 18, 1885, by Bishop Cane and the Rev. Charles Ross. (Courtesy of Delaware Public Archives.)

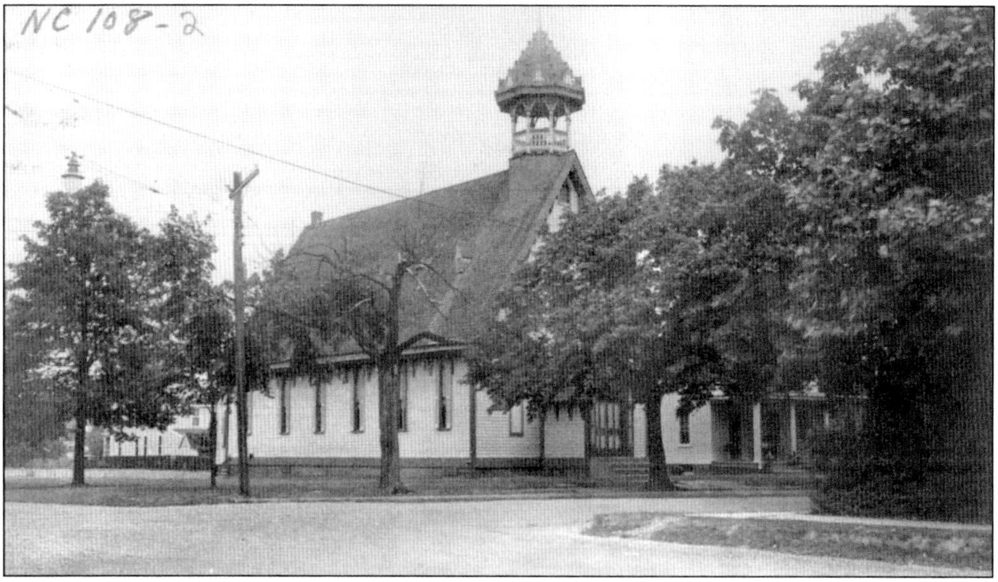

Until 1882, Catholics who lived in Middletown had no church building, instead attending mass in homes of the congregation and later in rented space in the Middletown Town Hall. The congregation grew to a size at which they were able to purchase a parcel of land on West Cochran Street in 1882. The cornerstone of St. Joseph Church, shown above, was laid in 1883 and was accompanied by the blessing of a 750-pound bell. Shown below is an interior view of the church, which cost $3,500 to build and was incorporated in 1906. The congregation gradually outgrew this building and relocated to East Main Street in 1993. (Both, courtesy of Delaware Public Archives.)

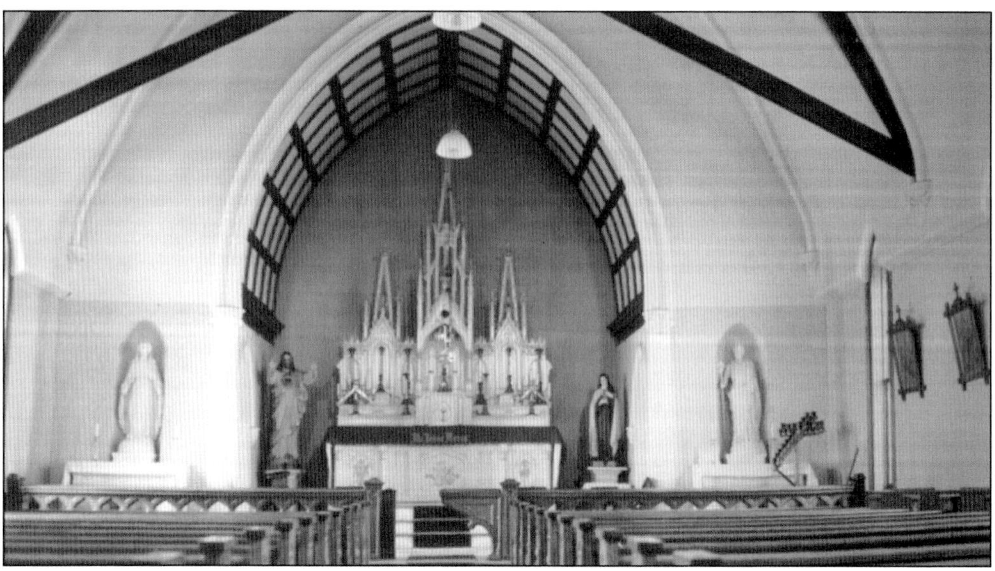

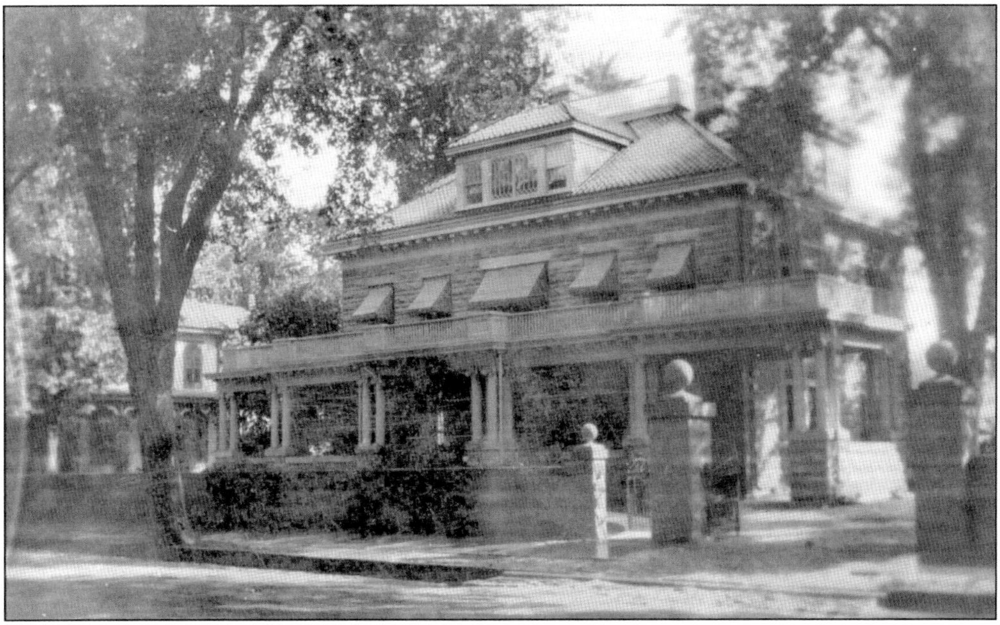

The original brick structure of the house at 217 North Broad Street—known as the "Grande Dame of Middletown"—is believed to have been built around the 1840s. That house lies within the building pictured here, as residents Dr. Dorsey Lewis and his wife, Mary, expanded the home by constructing a large stone addition around the original house in 1907. (Courtesy of Middletown Historical Society.)

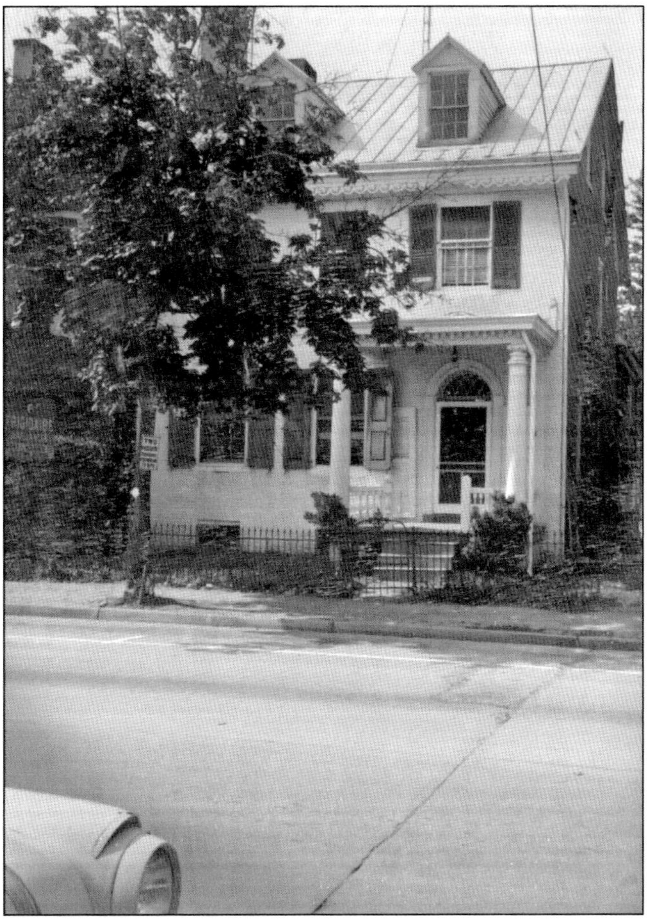

This house on East Main Street is also one of the town's oldest. It was built around 1800, possibly by a member of the prominent Lloyd family. The original interior included double-paneled cabinets with butterfly shelves in the dining room, five fireplaces, and a walk-in fireplace in the kitchen that was used for cooking. (Courtesy of Middletown Historical Society.)

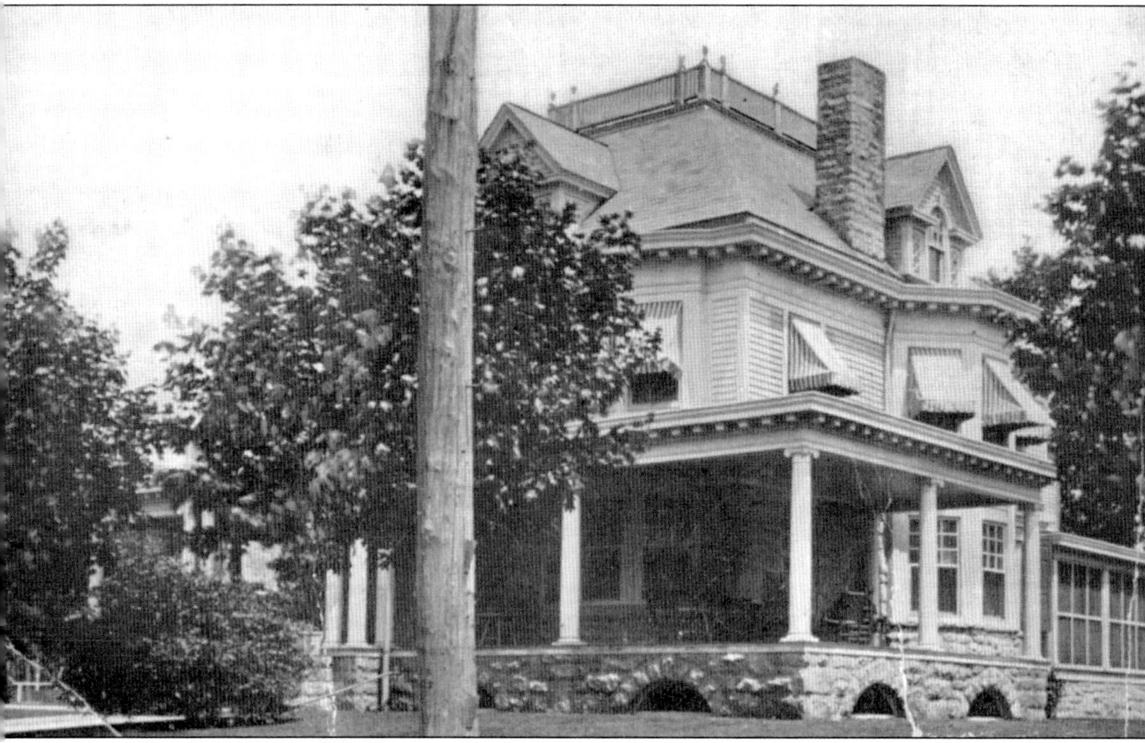

Middletonian Jesse Lake Shepherd and his wife, Temperance Elizabeth Caulk Shepherd, who was from nearby Sassafras, Maryland, built this residence at 105 South Broad Street in the late 19th century. The couple, who named the home Greystone, was very active in the church and the community. Jesse became successful early in life when he founded his own fertilizer and grain business at just 28 years old after working and saving money for 15 years. He was elected to the Middletown Citizen's National Bank board in 1899 and was vice president of the bank after it was sold to the Delaware Trust Company. Jesse remained in the banking business for 50 years and also served on the Middletown School Building Commission, on which he voted to approve funding for the public school building on South Broad Street in 1927. (Courtesy of the author.)

Three

COMMERCE

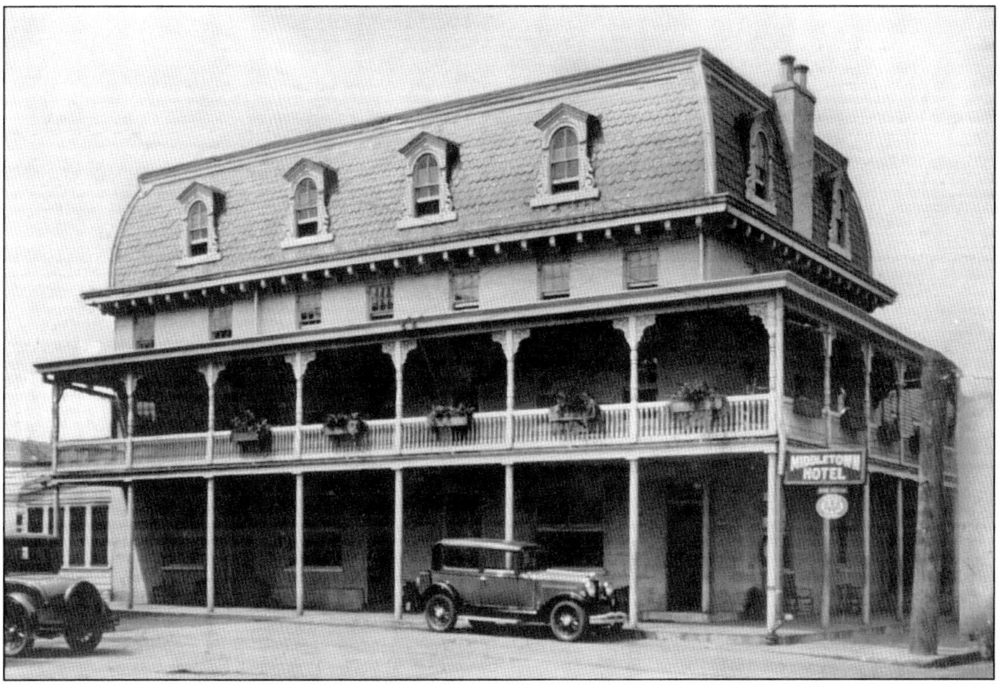

David Witherspoon built the Witherspoon Inn in 1761. Witherspoon was born in County Londonderry, Ireland, and died in Middletown in 1763. Early famous visitors included Caesar Rodney, in 1777, and Gen. George Washington in 1783. The inn has had many owners, one of whom was Robert Cochran, who purchased the property in 1844 and gave the entire southeast corner of the intersection at Main and Broad Streets the name Cochran Square. The building has been renamed several times over the years, and at one point was called the Middletown Hotel. Stories of disorderly patrons have been passed down as legends, including one in which well-known duelist James Knight entered the tavern drunk and raucously demanded to be served. Third owner David Witherspoon, a relative of the founding David Witherspoon, decided Knight was drunk enough and refused. The enraged gunfighter pulled a double-barreled pistol and tried to fire both barrels at Witherspoon, but the weapon misfired, and Witherspoon reached up to a shelf over the bar, drew one of two large "horse pistols," and fired a fatal shot at Knight. (Courtesy of Delaware Public Archives.)

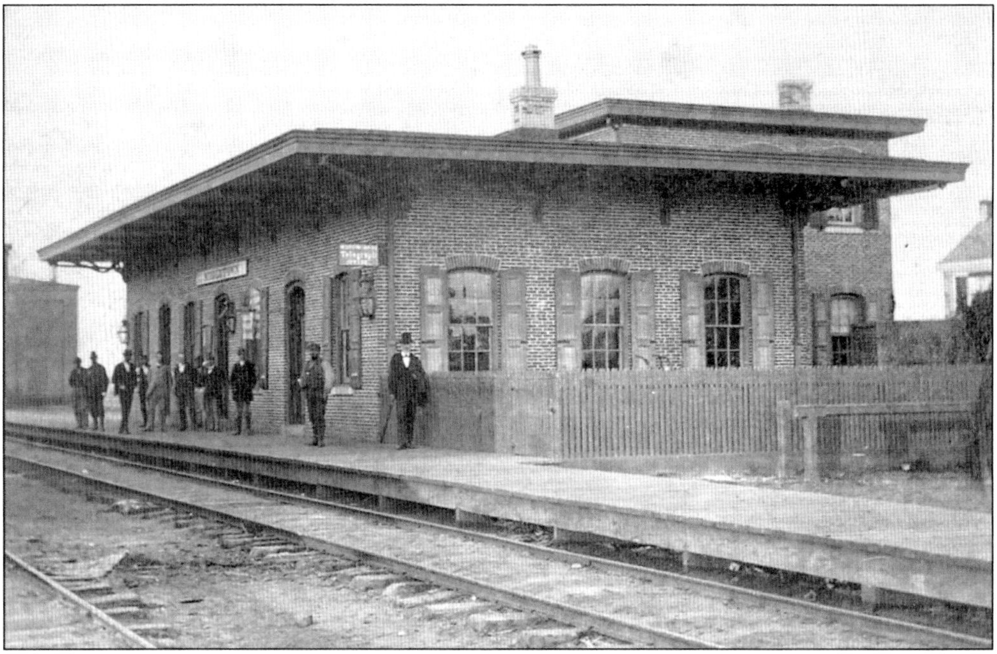

Middletown owes much of its prosperity to the railroad at the western end of town, which opened in 1855 and drew the center of trade and travel away from nearby Odessa. The Delaware Railroad was initially proposed for Odessa, which refused its construction. The line stretched from north to south and expedited agricultural trade and residential transportation on the Delmarva Peninsula. The depot was located between what present-day Peterson and Wood Streets, but trains that currently run through Middletown only carry freight (with the exception of passengers during the Delaware State Fair each July). (Both, courtesy of Delaware Public Archives.)

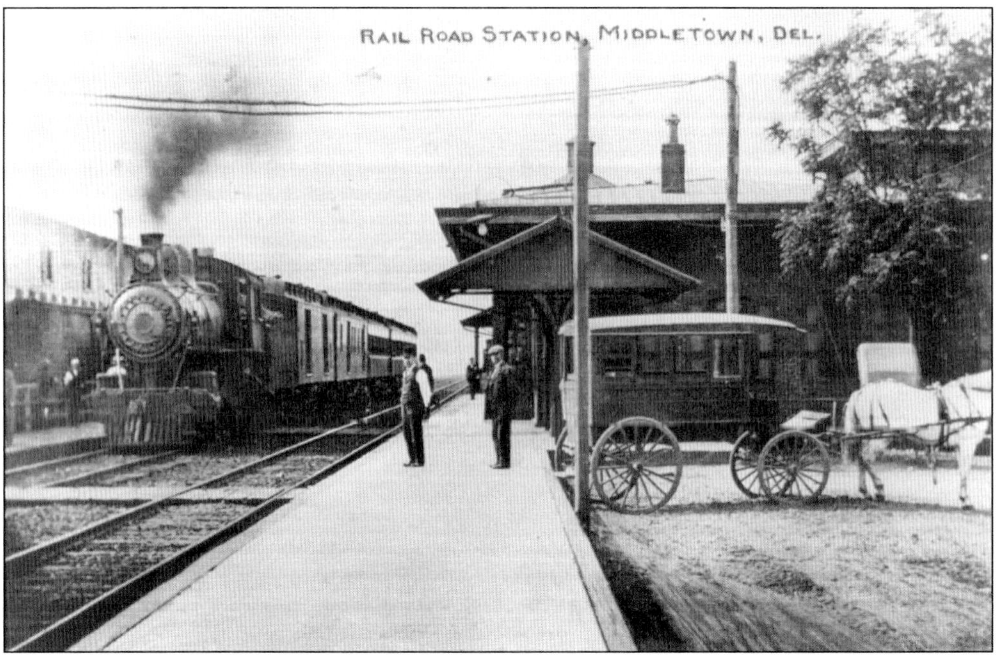

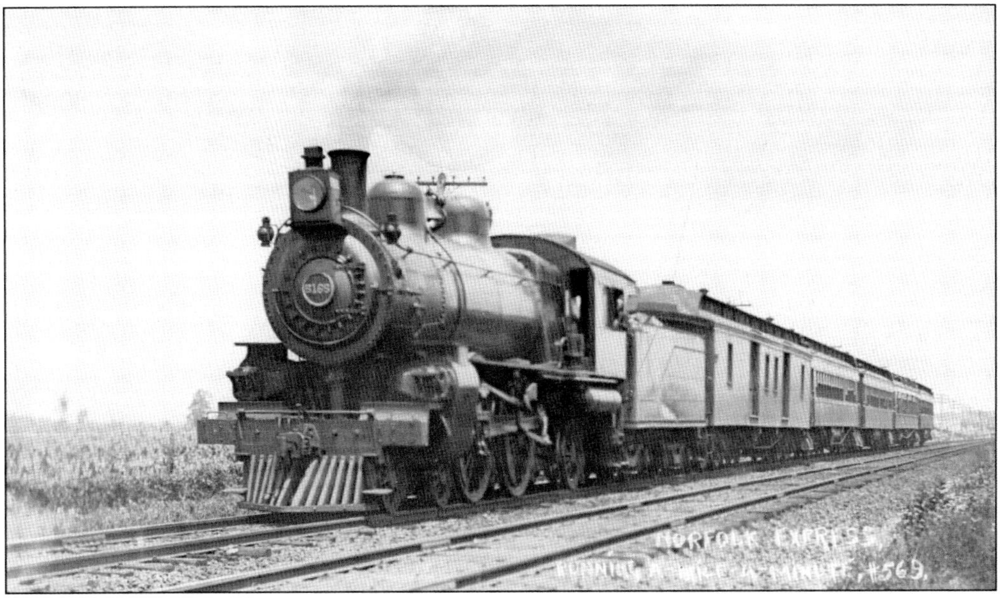

The railroad through Middletown has evolved along with the rest of the area. In the image above, the Norfolk Express steams through town limits. While Norfolk is more than 200 miles south of the town, its name is a familiar sight in the area, as the Norfolk Southern railroad, which includes the former Delaware Railroad, spans from the northeast tip of Delaware to well below the state's southern boundary. While local crops were once transported along the line, coal now travels from mines in Pennsylvania through Middletown. Shown below is a view of the railroad tracks past the former Middletown train depot. Only a single track runs through town now. (Above, courtesy of Scott Lawrence; below, courtesy of Delaware Public Archives.)

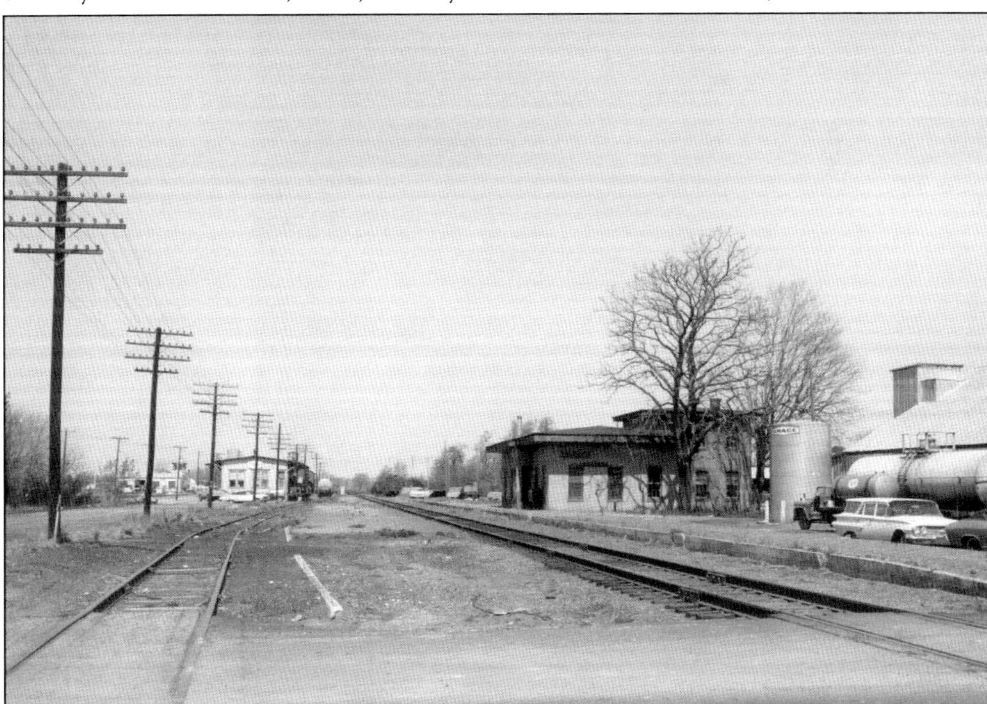

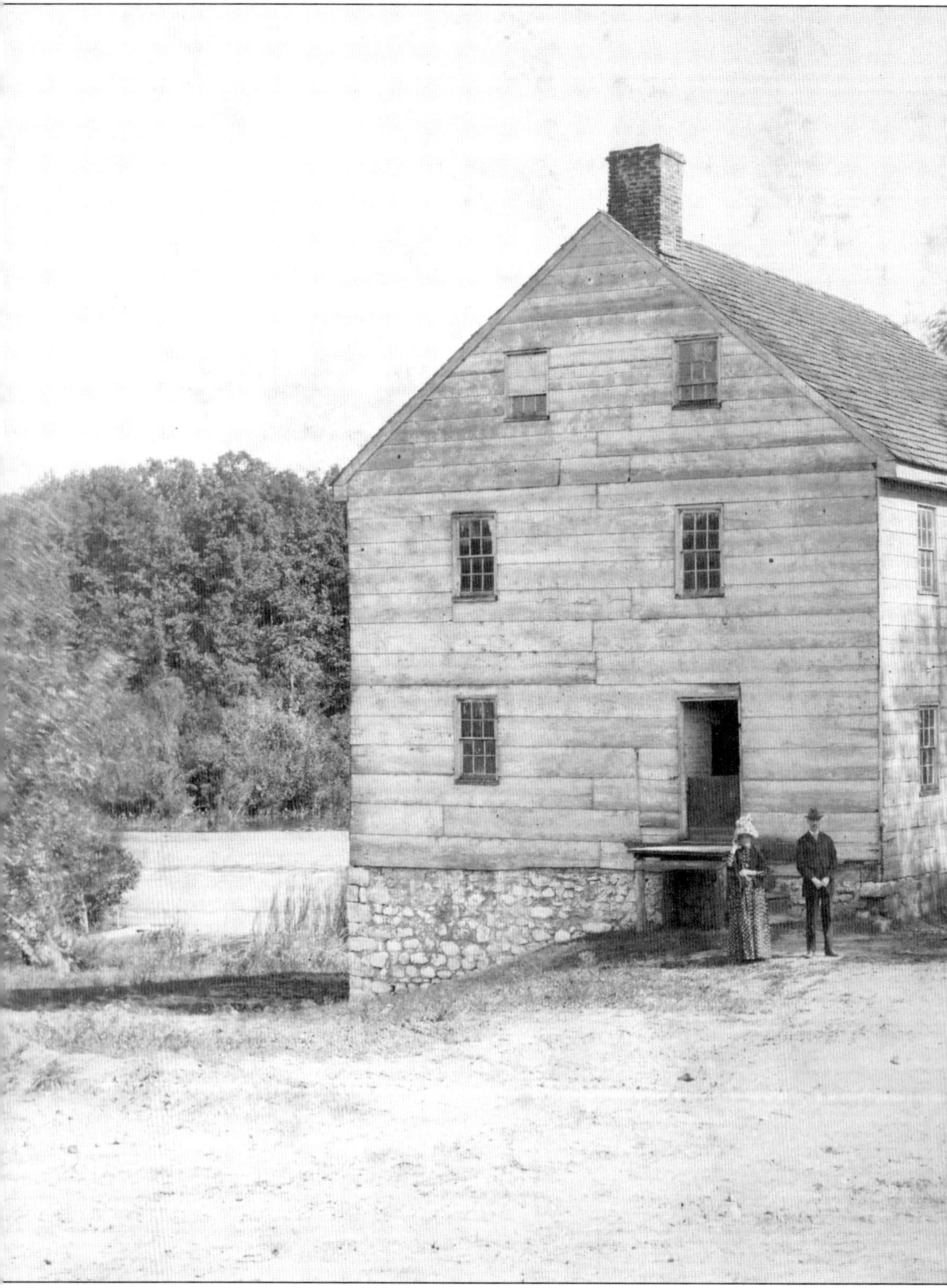

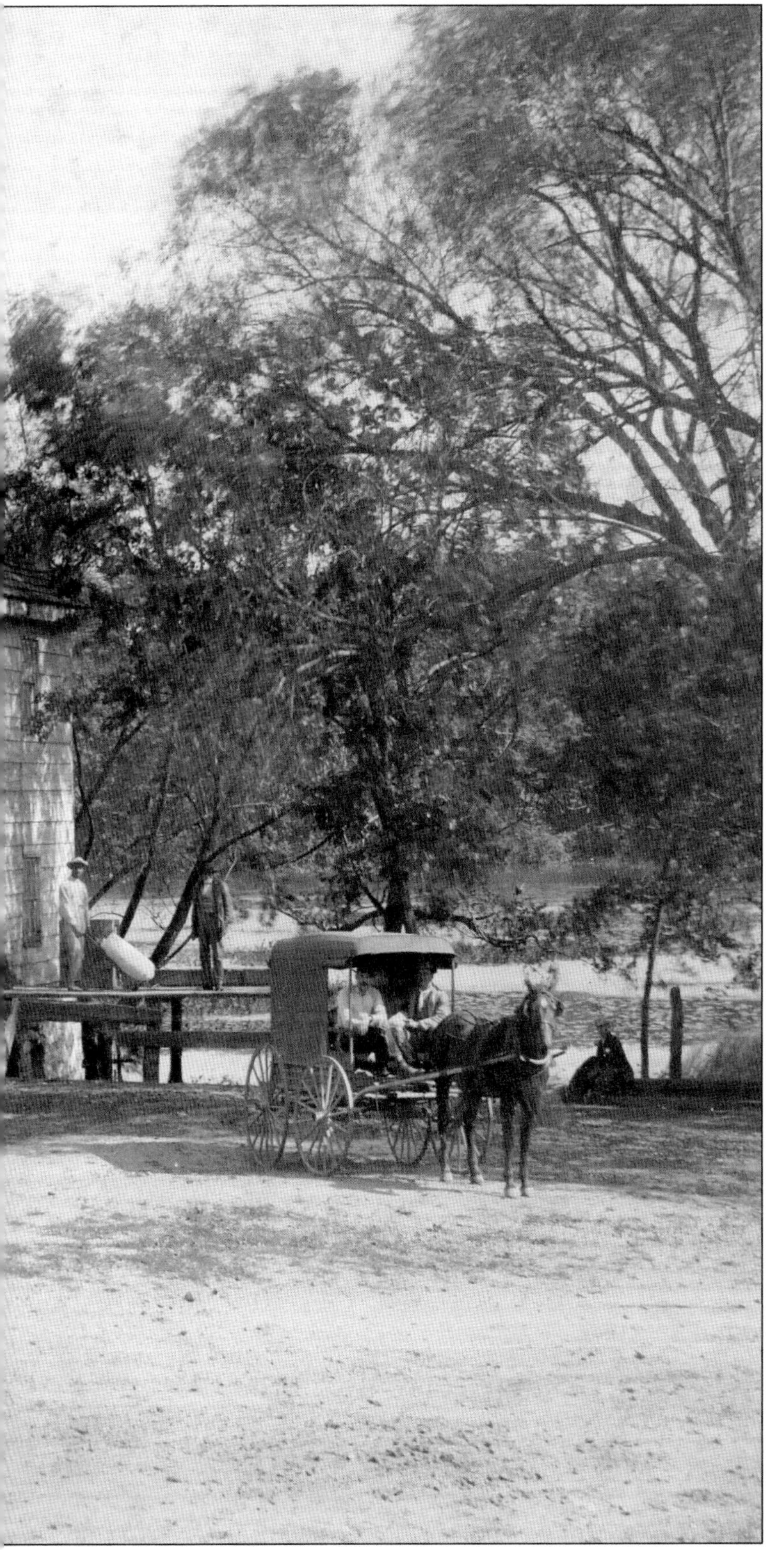

This 1870s photograph shows a Noxontown Road landmark—the Noxon Mill. Thomas Noxon operated at least three mills on the branches of the Appoquinimink Creek. The four-story frame building now known as Noxon Mill was constructed southeast of Middletown in 1740. The gristmill was used for merchant work, and its placement along the bank enabled ships to pull directly up to the structure for loading. Noxon died in 1743, but his mill retained great importance, as evidenced by Caesar Rodney's decision to march his Kent County militia to protect it from foraging by the British. After 1855, the operation became a custom mill. W.E. Evans purchased the property in 1870 and utilized the mill as a feed and agriculture implements business. W.D. Evans took ownership in 1901 and opened stores at the mill and in Middletown. (Courtesy of Middletown Historical Society.)

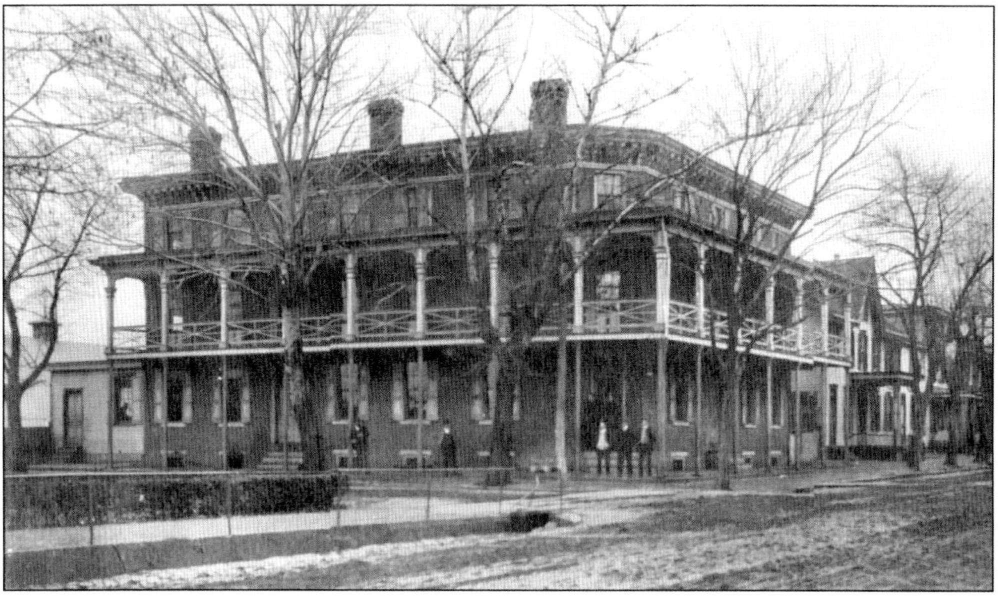

The National Hotel was born out of a mid-19th-century political division in Middletown. The main hotel, known as the Witherspoon Inn, was operated by Southern sympathizer L.C. Davis and was heavily patronized by Confederate sympathizers. Bitter and sometimes violent disputes among patrons caused local Union loyalists to form a joint stock company in 1862 and build a brick building by the rail station that became the 40-room National Hotel (above). This hotel was operated by Northerner John Lippincott and was a rival to the Witherspoon for years after the Civil War ended. The National Hotel building stood until the 1960s, when it fell into disrepair (below) and was demolished. (Above, courtesy of Middletown Historical Society; below, courtesy of Delaware Public Archives.)

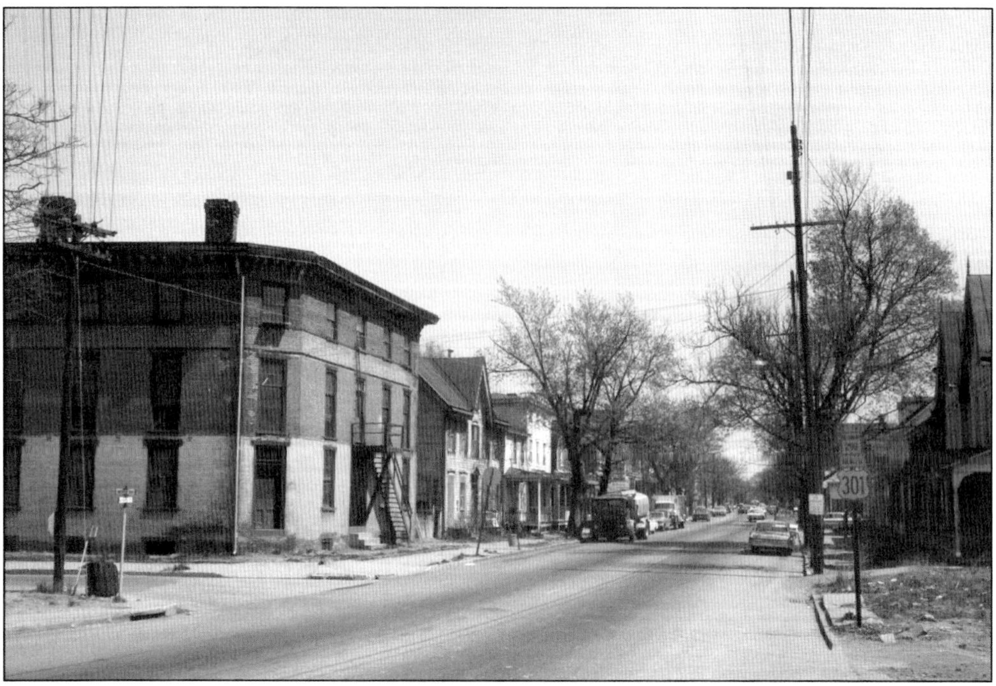

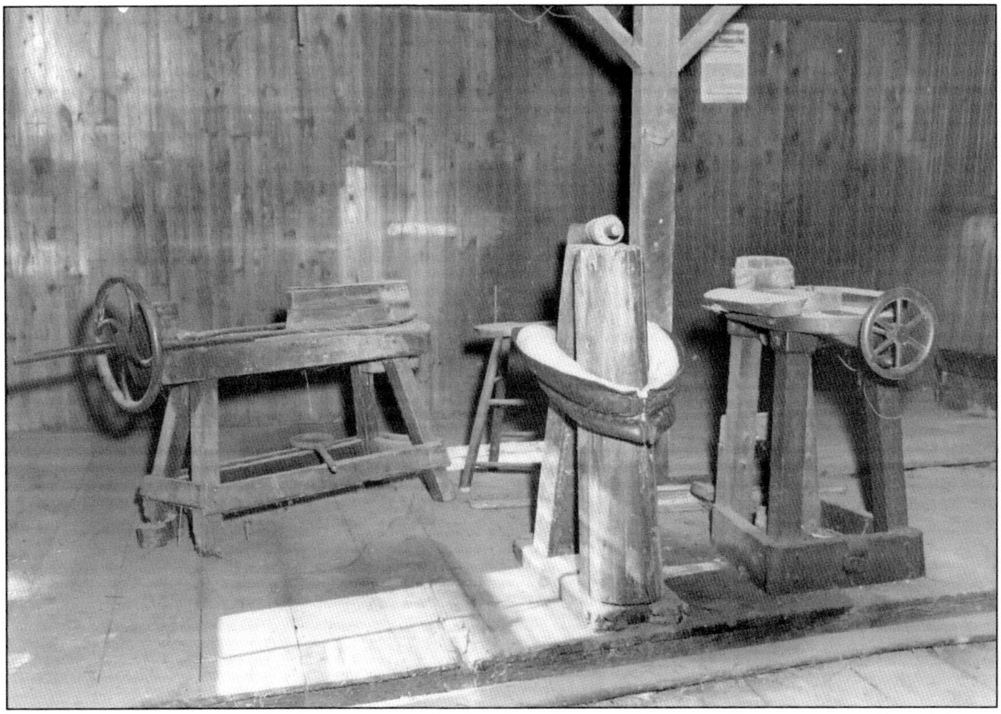

Adam Reed operated a shop on Anderson Street where he created handmade horse collars (above, center), which were attached to a harness and used to distribute weight around a horse's neck when pulling a wagon or plow. The collars allowed horses to use their entire strength and therefore work more efficiently. Below is a close-up of tools used in the shop. Reed sold his well-made collars to customers as far away as Fulton, New York. (Both, courtesy of Delaware Public Archives.)

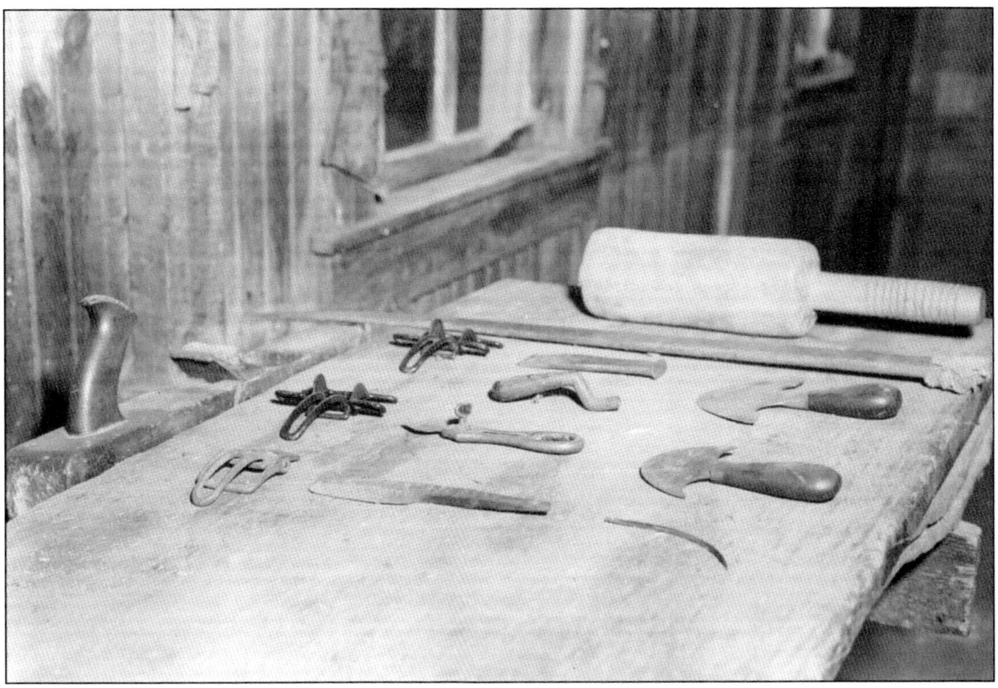

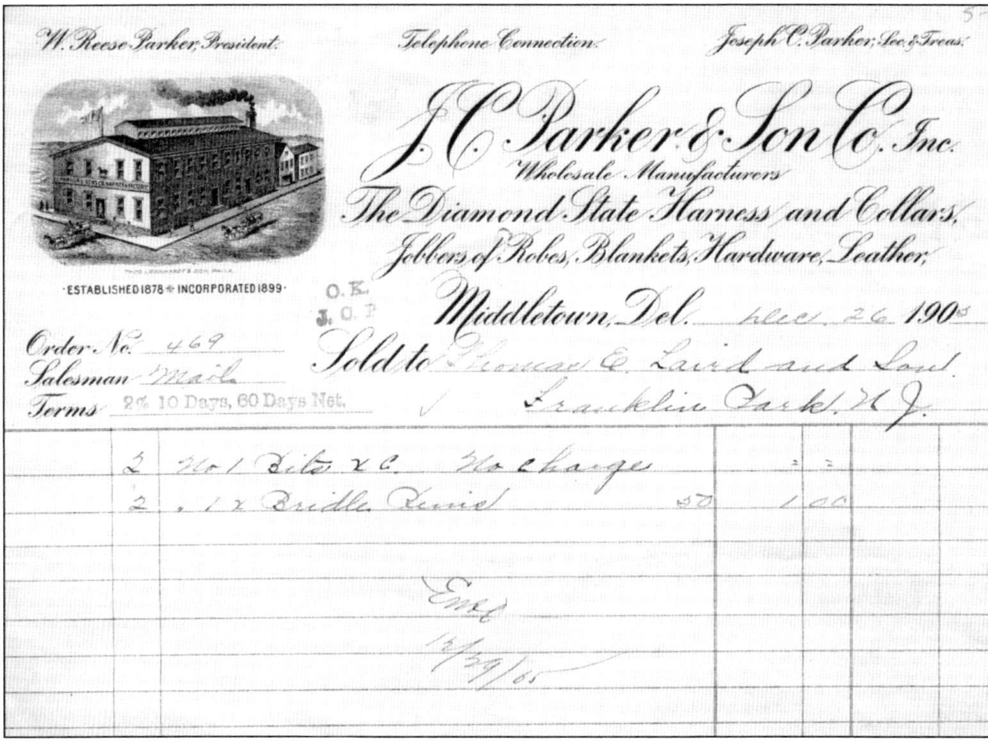
W. Reese Parker, President. Telephone Connection. Joseph C. Parker, Sec. & Treas.

J.C. Parker & Son Co. Inc.

Wholesale Manufacturers

The Diamond State Harness and Collars,

Jobbers of Robes, Blankets, Hardware, Leather,

·ESTABLISHED 1878 ✣ INCORPORATED 1899·

O.K. J.C.P.

Middletown, Del. Dec. 26 1905

Order No. 469

Salesman Mail

Terms 2% 10 Days, 60 Days Net.

Sold to Thomas E. Laird and Son

Franklin Park, N.J.

2	No 1 Bits X C No charge			
2	" 1 X Bridle Reins	50	1 00	

Ent 12/29/05

The J.C. Parker & Son Co. was established in 1878 and won acclaim for its harnesses, which were of superior quality and "honest workmanship." The business successfully grew, drawing important customers such as Barnum and Bailey. In 1911, the company began to assemble cars. (Courtesy of Middletown Historical Society.)

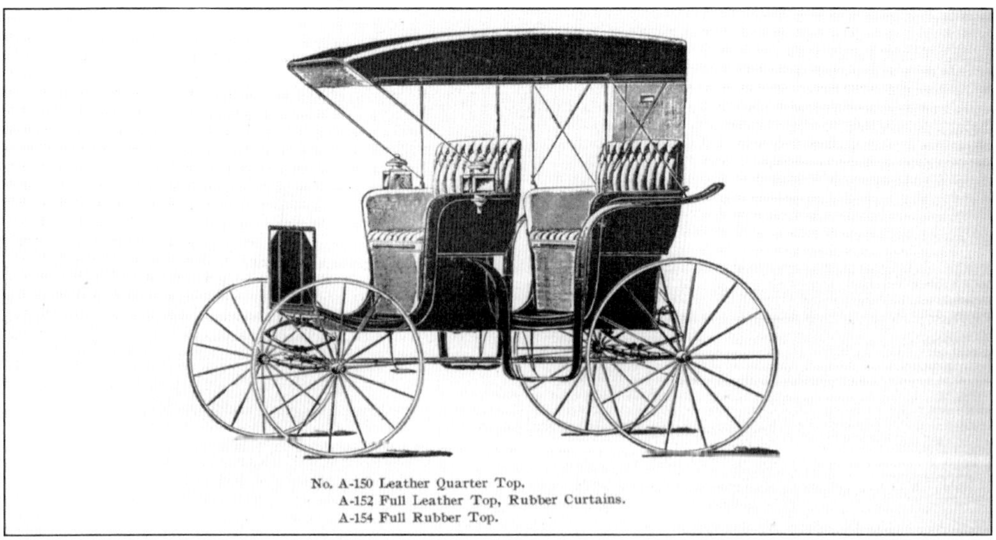

J. Frank McWhorter, who once served as a town commissioner, owned the J.F. McWhorter & Son store, which sold farming implements and stoves. A brochure—*Compliments of J.F. McWhorter & Son*—advertised a line of carriages for sale. The shop had a showroom and machinery hall downtown. The hall was popular for local dances and town meetings. (Courtesy of Middletown Historical Society.)

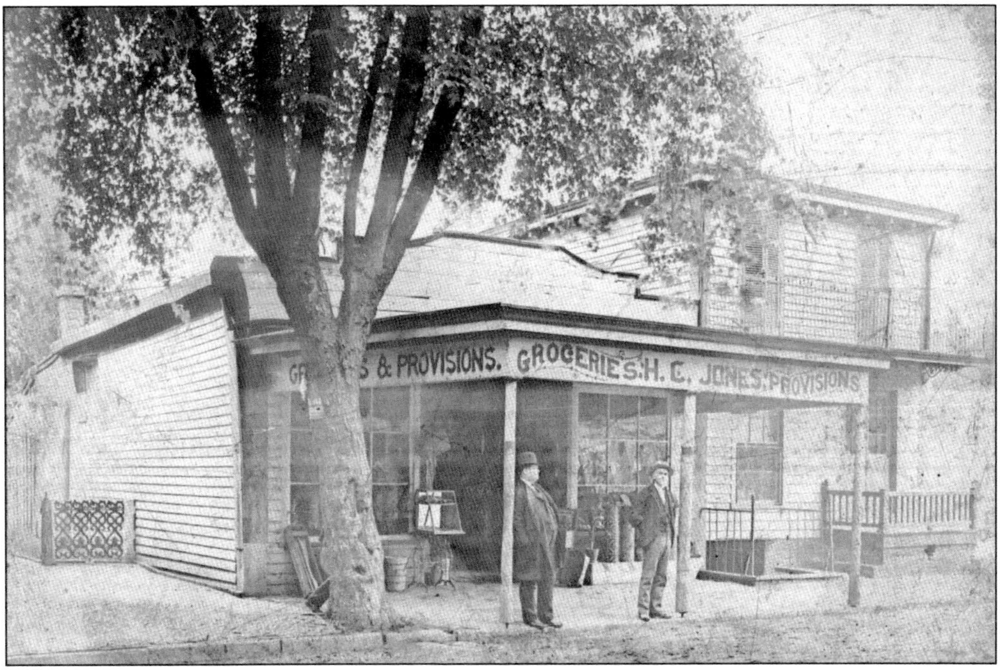

Store owners could often be seen standing outside their downtown shops during slow times. The H.C. Jones store (above) offered groceries and provisions at the corner of Anderson and North Broad Streets. A meat market (below) was located on West Main Street next to the current Everett Theatre Annex. (Both, courtesy of Middletown Historical Society.)

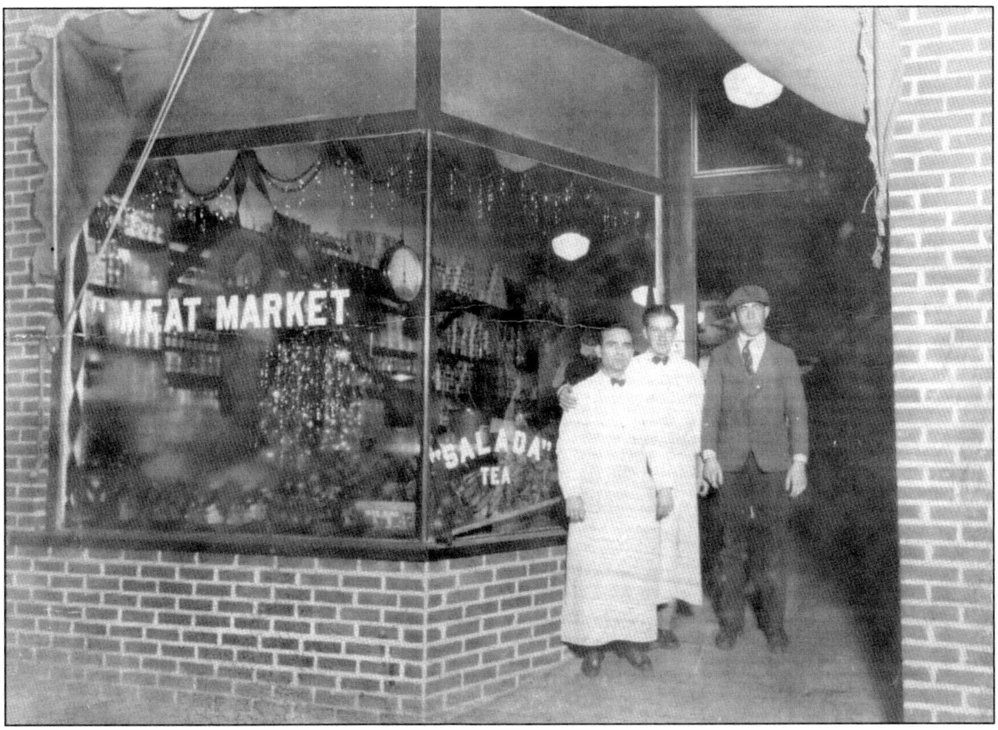

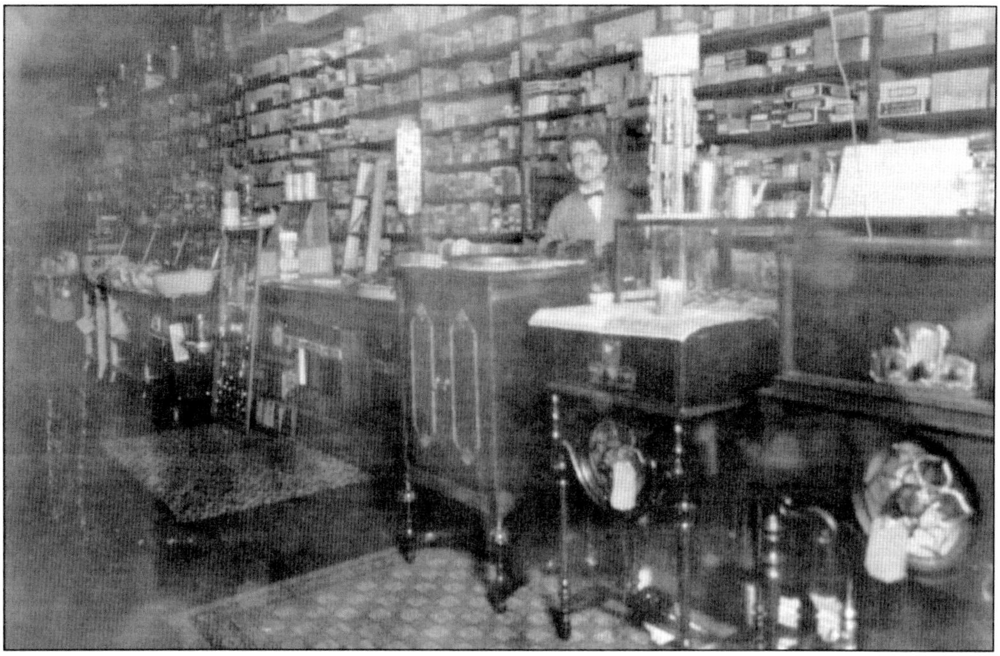

Roe S. Redgrave is pictured behind the counter of his store, Redgrave Bros., on West Main Street. Redgrave lived on Cass Street with his wife, Lena, who was a teacher. He sold retail hardware in his shop. Many local men made livings by selling goods in Middletown, while women often taught in area schools. (Courtesy of Middletown Historical Society.)

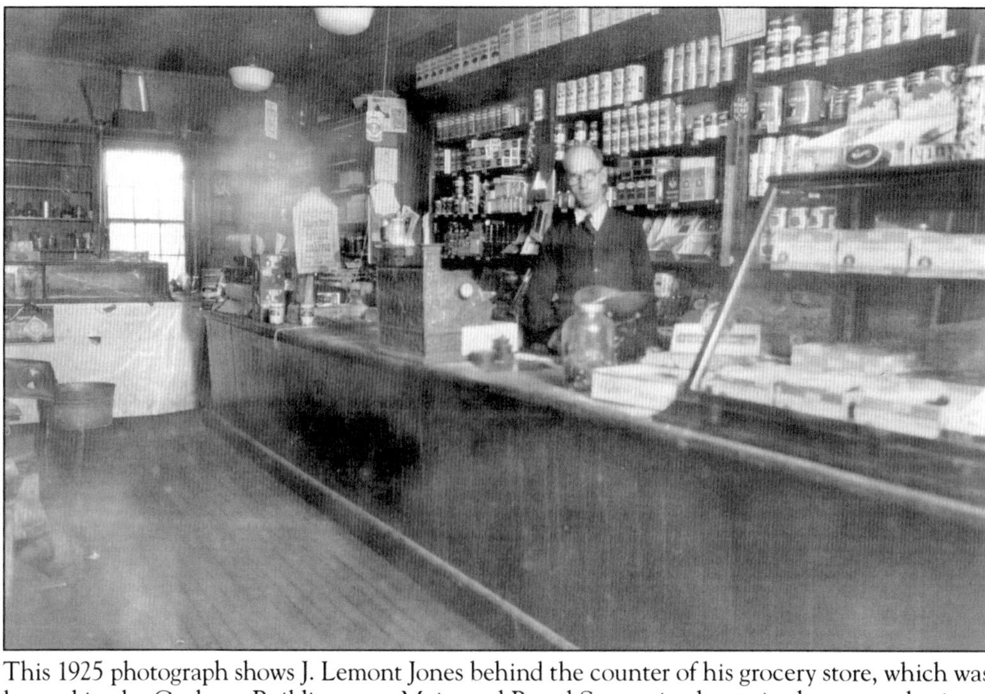

This 1925 photograph shows J. Lemont Jones behind the counter of his grocery store, which was located in the Cochran Building near Main and Broad Streets in the main downtown business intersection. Jones resided on East Green Street with his wife, Ethel, and was a driver on the mail route. (Courtesy of Middletown Historical Society.)

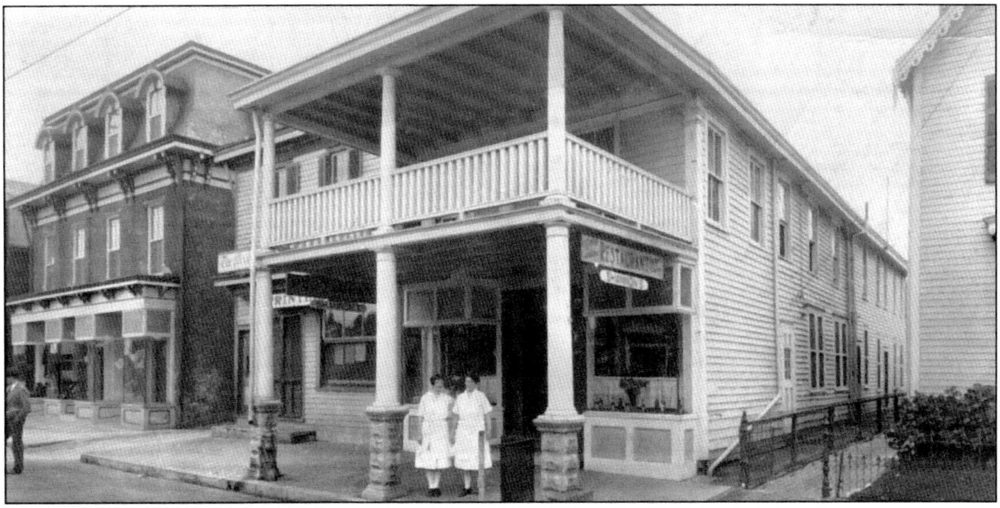

In the 1920s, Shannon's Restaurant was located at 26 West Main Street, next to the Middletown Transcript Building. Here, Jeannie McAllister (left) and Grace Dodds stand outside the eatery. The building has served various purposes since and currently houses the business of Shane O'Neill, a nationally acclaimed tattoo artist. (Courtesy of Scott Lawrence.)

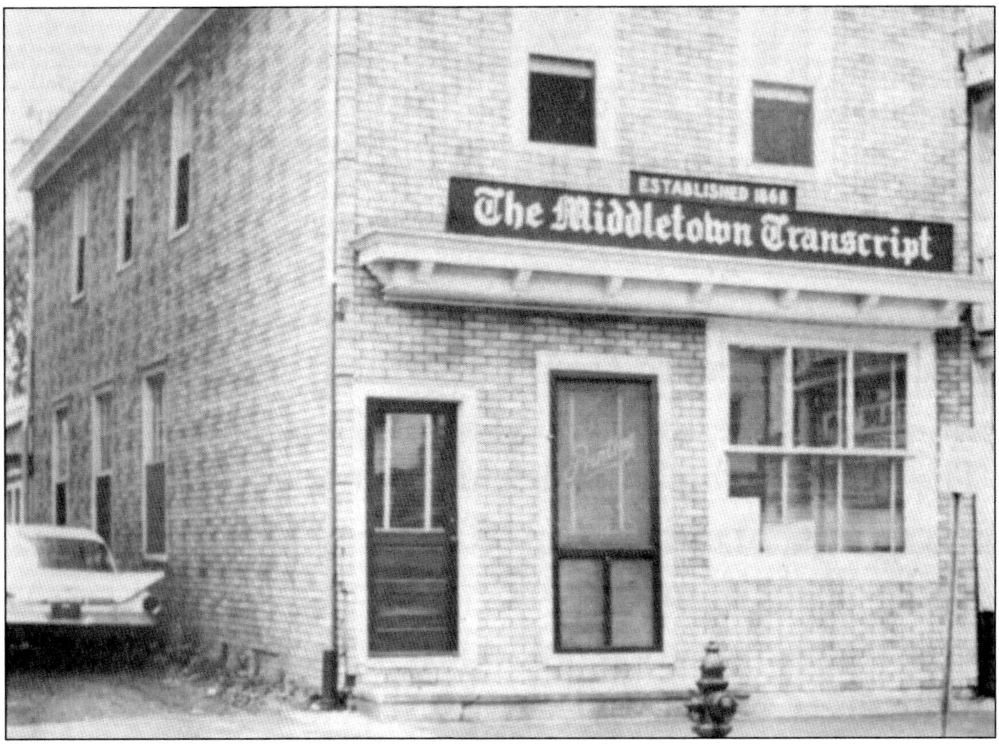

The *Middletown Transcript*, the beloved weekly newspaper for southern New Castle County, was first published on January 4, 1868, by Charles H. Vandeford in the basement of a West Main Street building. Vandeford produced the first edition on a Washington handpress with a capacity of one copy per minute. The paper had several homes until Thomas S. Fouracre purchased it in 1900 and, soon after, constructed this building—which still serves as the paper's office—at 24 West Main Street. (Courtesy of the author.)

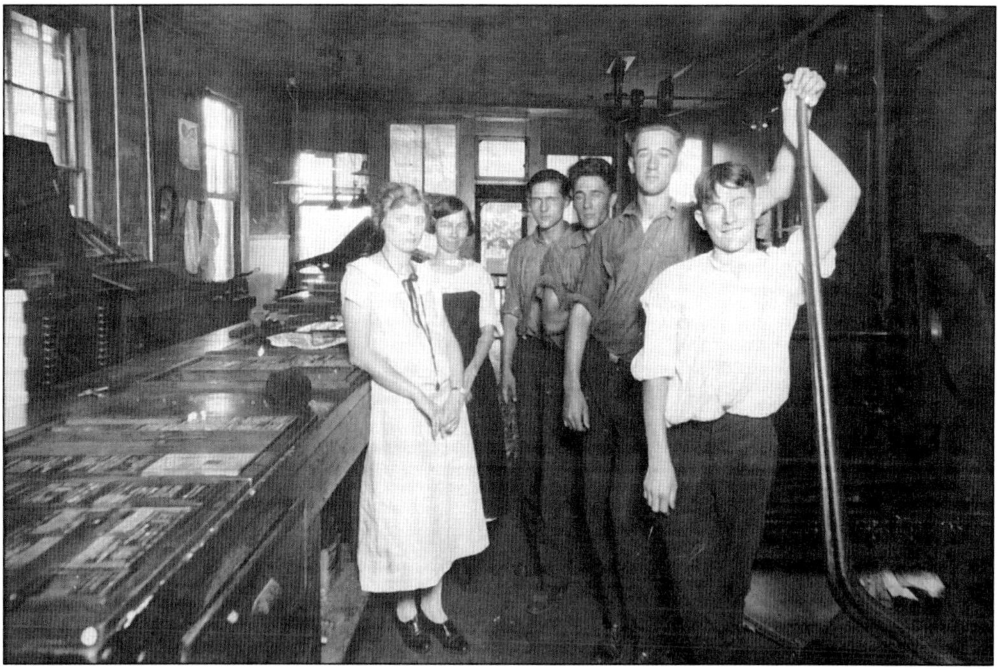

Early editions of the *Middletown Transcript* consisted of happenings in the town, region, state, and nation, along with prose submitted by faithful readers. A popular column, Those who entertained and have been away, was a frequent feature, as were comedic anecdotes such as the Poetic Trifles below that describes a rat found in a previous building in March 1871. In the image above, staff members stand in the 24 West Main Street office with now outdated equipment, much of which remained in the building for decades after the paper's production became modernized. The *Transcript* remained in the Fouracre family into the 1980s, and visitors often stopped by the West Main Street building to drop off community news, chat with staff, or pick up the latest edition of the newspaper. (Both, courtesy of the author.)

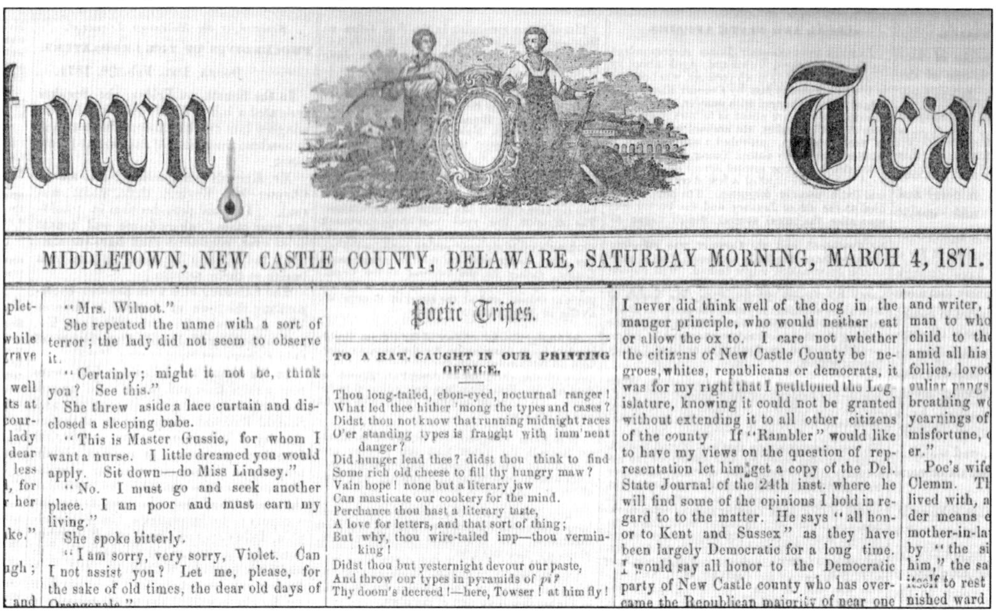

MIDDLETOWN, NEW CASTLE COUNTY, DELAWARE, SATURDAY MORNING, MARCH 4, 1871.

"Mrs. Wilmot."

She repeated the name with a sort of terror; the lady did not seem to observe it.

"Certainly; might it not be, think you? See this."

She threw aside a lace curtain and disclosed a sleeping babe.

"This is Master Gussie, for whom I want a nurse. I little dreamed you would apply. Sit down—do Miss Lindsey."

"No. I must go and seek another place. I am poor and must earn my living."

She spoke bitterly.

"I am sorry, very sorry, Violet. Can I not assist you? Let me, please, for the sake of old times, the dear old days of

Poetic Trifles.

TO A RAT, CAUGHT IN OUR PRINTING OFFICE.

Thou long-tailed, ebon-eyed, nocturnal ranger!
What led thee hither 'mong the types and cases?
Didst thou not know that running midnight races
O'er standing types is fraught with imm'nent danger?
Did hunger lead thee? didst thou think to find
Some rich old cheese to fill thy hungry maw?
Vain hope! none but a literary jaw
Can masticate our cookery for the mind.
Perchance thou hast a literary taste,
A love for letters, and that sort of thing;
But why, thou wire-tailed imp—thou vermin-king!
Didst thou but yesternight devour our paste,
And throw our types in pyramids of *pi?*
Thy doom's decreed!—here, Towser! at him fly!

I never did think well of the dog in the manger principle, who would neither eat or allow the ox to. I care not whether the citizens of New Castle County be negroes, whites, republicans or democrats, it was for my right that I petitioned the Legislature, knowing it could not be granted without extending it to all other citizens of the county. If "Rambler" would like to have my views on the question of representation let him get a copy of the Del. State Journal of the 24th inst. where he will find some of the opinions I hold in regard to to the matter. He says "all honor to Kent and Sussex" as they have been largely Democratic for a long time. I would say all honor to the Democratic party of New Castle county who has overcame the Republican majority of near one

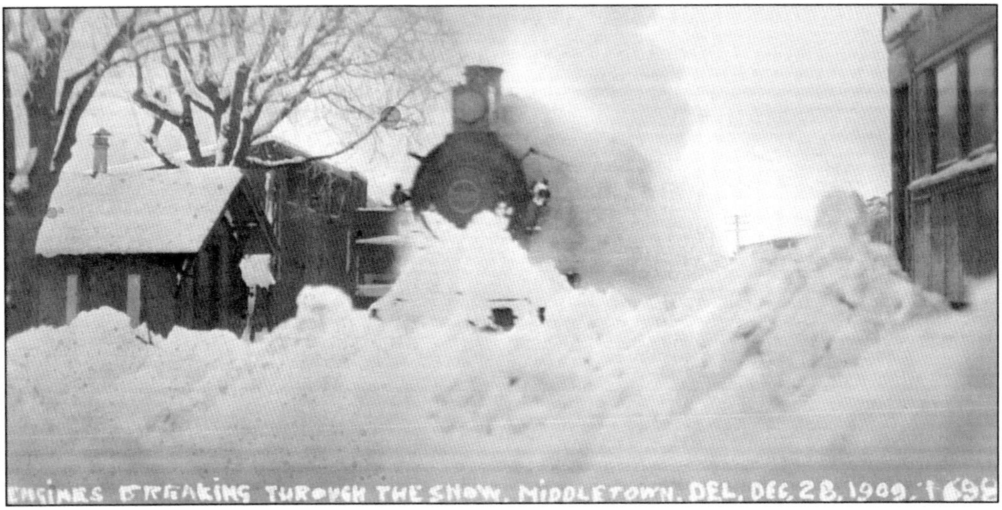

Snow days in Middletown were not necessarily a cause for staying indoors. The blizzard of December 26, 1909, did not halt business in Middletown, as evidenced by the train breaking through snow (above) and the efforts of a Mr. Williams to make milk deliveries (below). A February 1895 blizzard, however, did prove too much for the train; a snow-blocked railroad caused a passenger train to sit for several days before a relief train with five engines arrived to take the stuck train and its passengers to Middletown. About 100 railroad workers braved the elements to help clear the tracks. (Above, courtesy of Delaware Public Archives; below, courtesy of Richard and Marlene Green.)

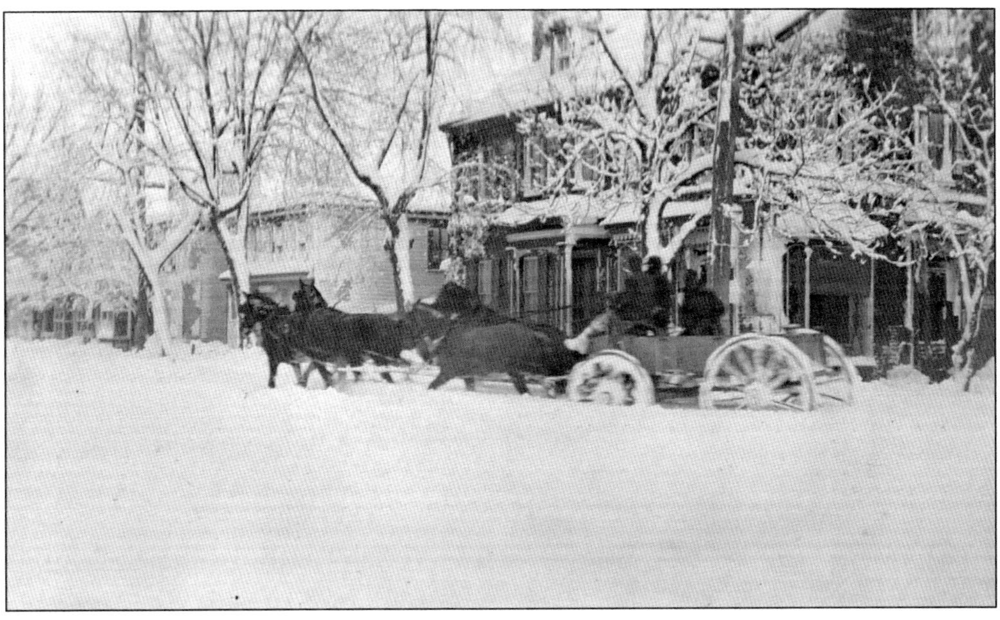

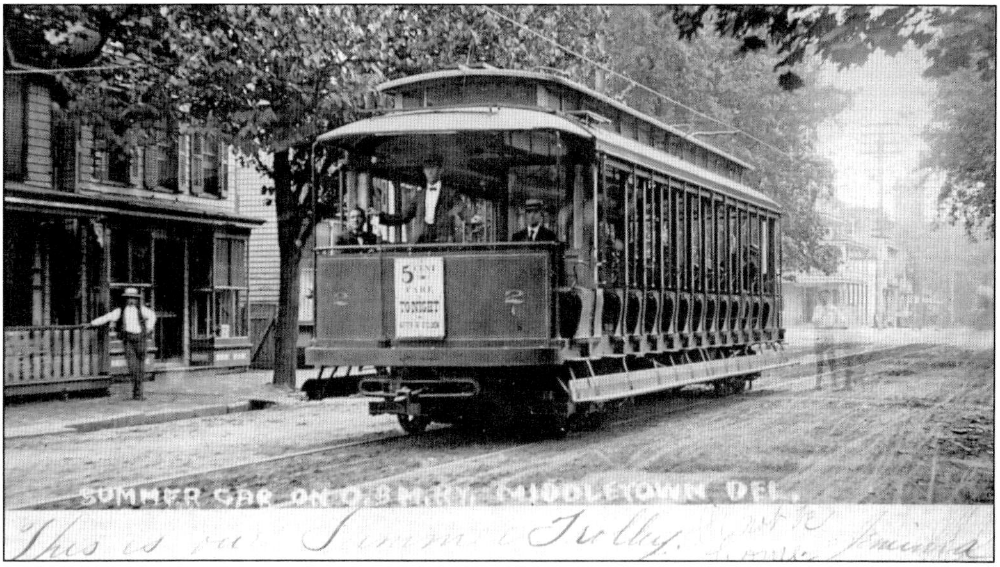

The Odessa & Middletown Railway was established after William R. Polk proposed a trolley line to connect the railroad in Middletown with Appoquinimink Creek in Odessa. The line was completed in 1903 and operated by electricity from the Middletown Electric Plant, with summer and winter passenger trolleys and a flatcar to haul freight. Plans were announced to extend the line to Smyrna. There was also talk of an extension to Cecilton and possibly Fredericktown, Maryland. While people walked from as far as Townsend to experience the trolley, the line was less profitable than expected and closed in May 1908. Removal of the rails began shortly thereafter. (Above, courtesy of Delaware Public Archives; below, courtesy of Middletown Historical Society.)

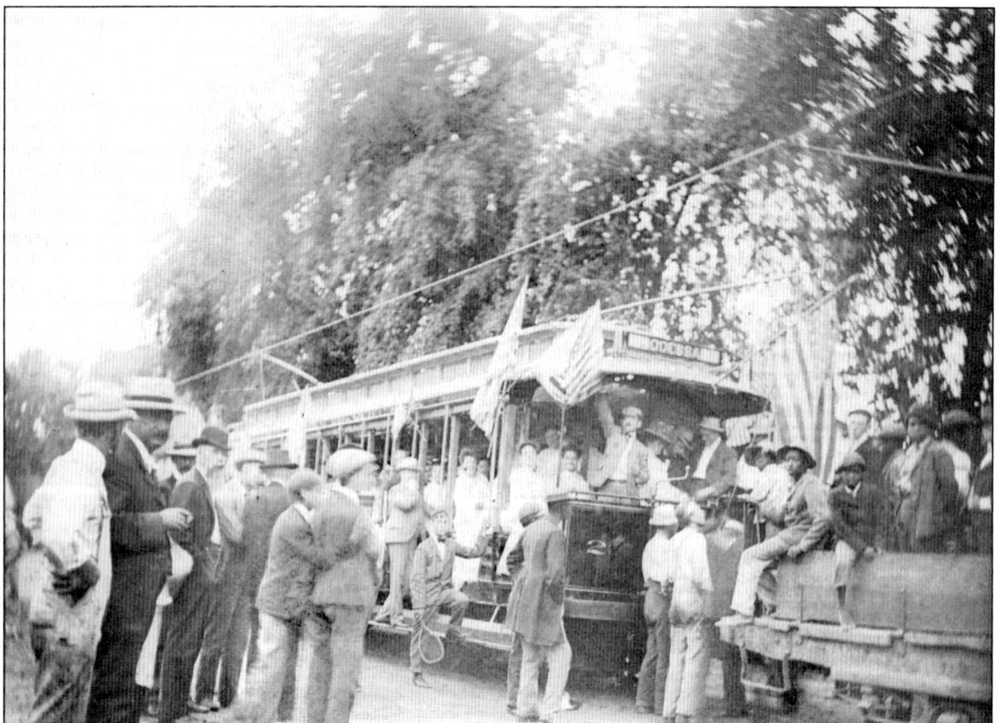

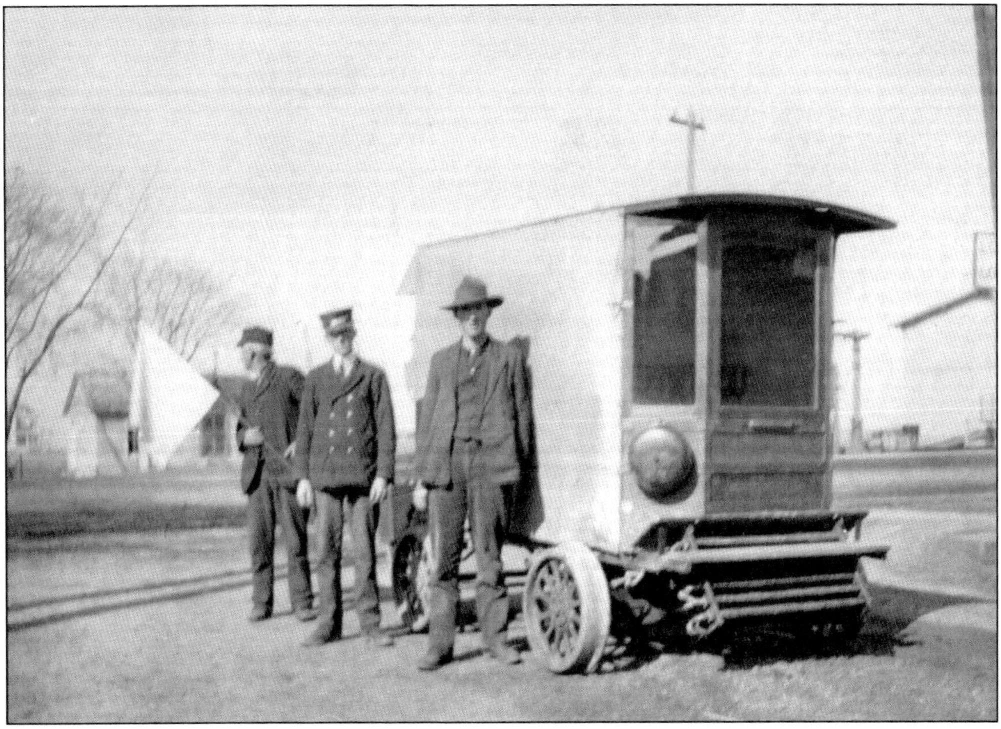

Walter S. Letherbury, a local hardware dealer, councilman, and first mayor of the town, served as superintendent of the trolley line, as seen on the schedule of travel below. The fare for travel was 5¢ after 6:00 p.m. on Sundays, Tuesdays, and Thursdays. A gasoline motorcar was used by the Odessa-Middletown Railway Co. in 1906 due to its cheaper cost of operation. It held nine passengers and was nicknamed the "peanut roaster" by local residents. A 1906 accident—the line's most serious—occurred when a trolley headed for Odessa crashed into a herd of cattle, killing three of them. (Both, courtesy of Middletown Historical Society.)

ODESSA & MIDDLETOWN RAILWAY---SCHEDULE OF CARS

IN EFFECT 7.20 A. M., NOVEMBER 28TH, 1904

LEAVE ODESSA	CONNECTS DELAWARE R. R. NORTHWARD	CONNECTS DELAWARE R. R. SOUTHWARD	LEAVE MIDDLETOWN
7.20 A. M.	* 7.48 A. M.	8.21 A. M.	* 7.55 A. M.
8.15 "			8.35 "
8.55 "	* 9.22 "	* 9.18 A. M.	* 9.25 "
9.55 "	*10.24 "		*10.30 "
11.00 "		*11.37 "	*11.40 "
12.30 P. M.			1.00 P. M.
1.20 "	* 1.40 P. M.		* 2.00 "
2.30 "		* 3.53 P. M.	3.00 "
3.30 "	4.17 "	4.31 "	* 4.00 "
4.30 "	* 6.01 "		5.00 "
5.30 "			* 6.00 "
6.30 "		7.42 "	7.00 "
7.30 "			8.00 "
8.30 "			9.00 "
9.30 "			10.00 "

ALL CONNECTIONS WITH TRAINS MEAN FROM ODESSA *CONNECT PROMPTLY AT MIDDLETOWN FOR ODESSA

W. S. LETHERBURY, SUP'T.

TRANSCRIPT PRINT

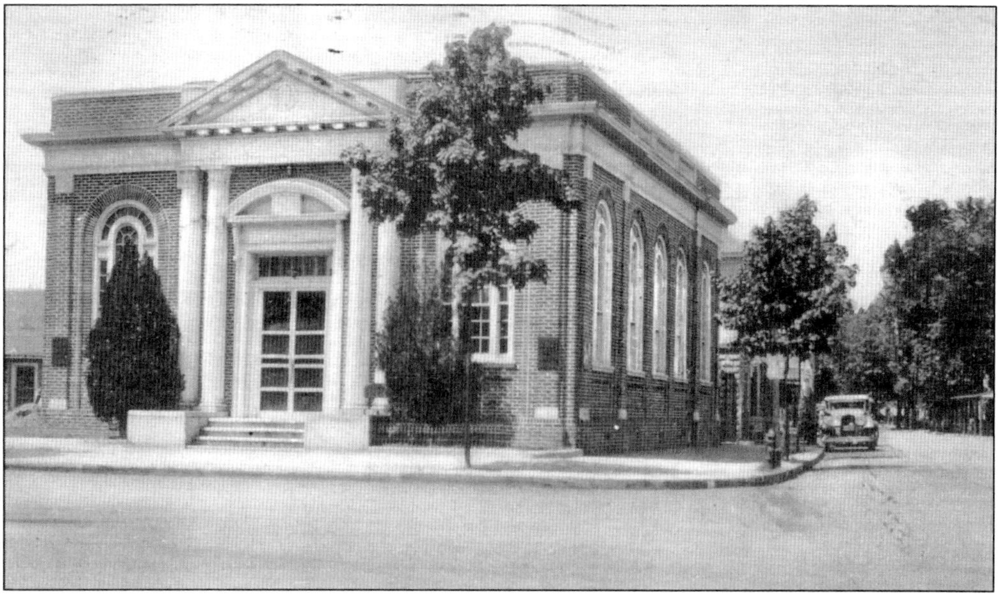

Citizens National Bank was incorporated in the mid-1800s at the northeast corner of Main and Broad Streets. The bank was relocated to the town hall on South Broad Street, and a more permanent home was constructed on the farm of Capt. Samuel Pennington at the northwest corner of Main and Broad Streets. It eventually became a national bank and was called the Delaware Trust Company of Middletown, the first of many name changes caused by company sales and mergers. The prominent 1923 structure in the center of town remained in operation as a bank until the early 2000s, when the bank relocated to a new facility on East Main Street. (Above, courtesy of Middletown Historical Society; below, courtesy of Delaware Public Archives.)

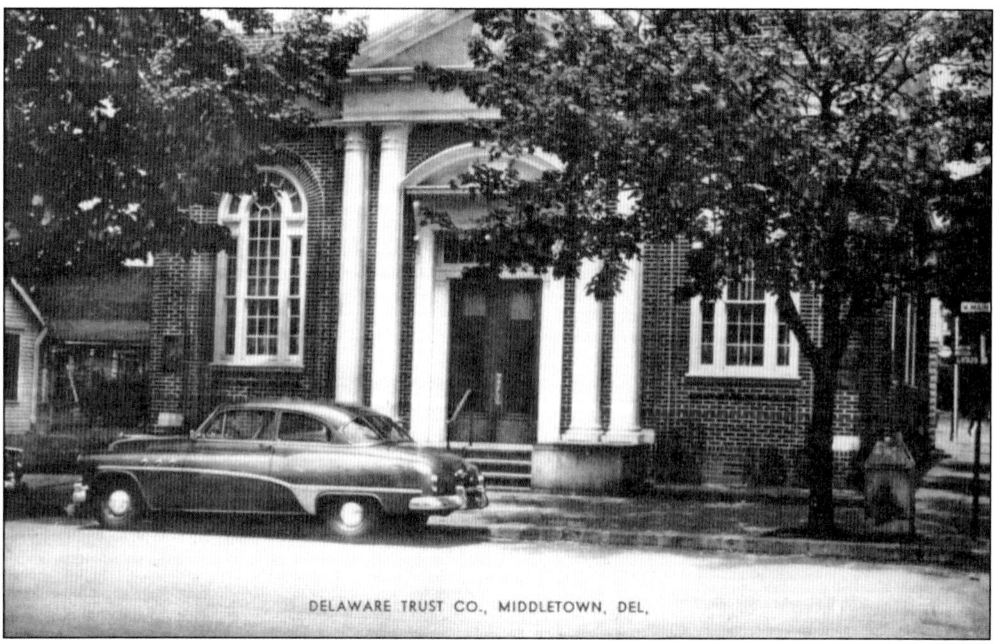

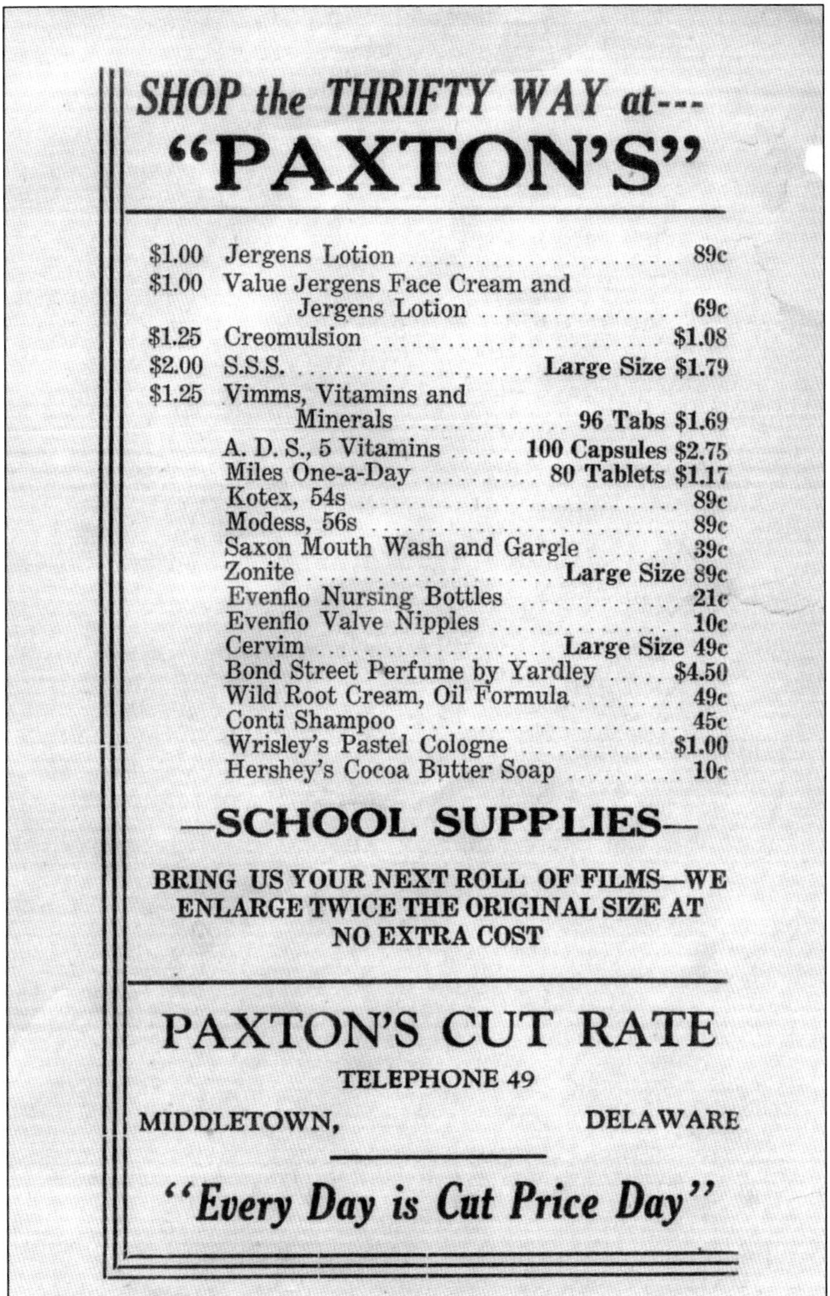

Paxton's—where "Every Day is Cut Price Day"—boasted great savings for shoppers in the downtown area. The store opened in September 1934 between the Everett Theatre and the former post office on Main Street. A 1934 advertisement from the *Middletown Transcript* shows Paxton's prices: Kleenex for 16¢, Listerine antiseptic for 59¢, and Woodbury's soap for 9¢, among other items. A 1942 advertisement in the *Transcript* lists Woodbury Face Powder for 43¢, Alka Seltzer for 49¢, Vicks VapoRub for 27¢, and Noxema for 19¢. Paxton's also advertised its "extra fine photograph finishing" and non-fade photograph printing services. The date for the ad pictured is not known. (Courtesy of Middletown Historical Society.)

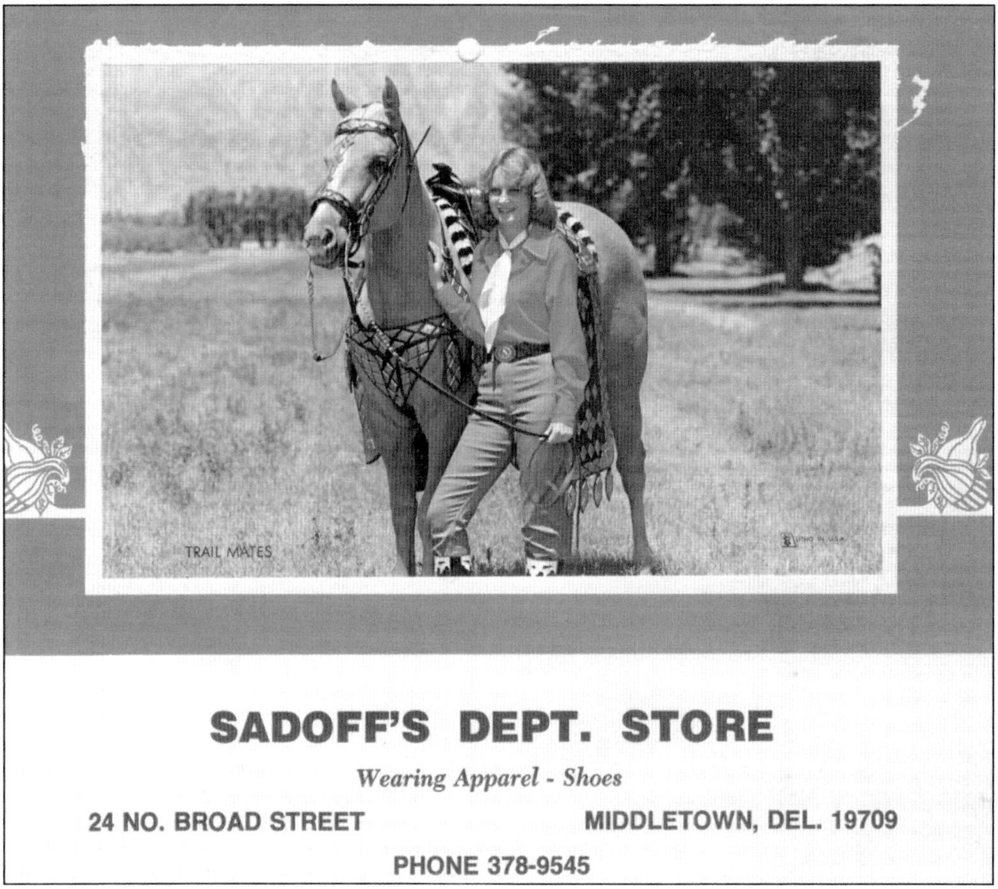

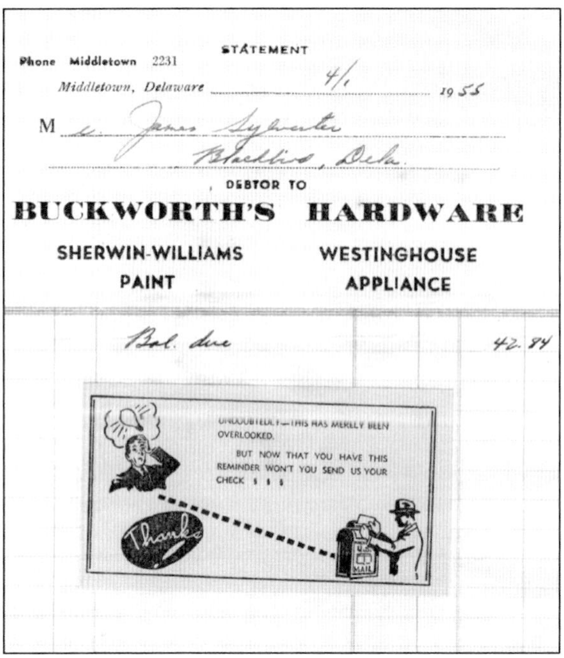
STATEMENT

Phone Middletown 2231

Middletown, Delaware 4/1 1955

M r. James Sylvester
Blackbird, Dela.

, DEBTOR TO

BUCKWORTH'S HARDWARE

SHERWIN-WILLIAMS PAINT

WESTINGHOUSE APPLIANCE

Bal. due 42.84

UNDOUBTEDLY—THIS HAS MERELY BEEN OVERLOOKED.

BUT NOW THAT YOU HAVE THIS REMINDER WON'T YOU SEND US YOUR CHECK $ $ $

Thanks

Sadoff's Department Store was located at 24 North Broad Street. It was founded and operated by Jewish immigrant Benjamin Sadoff, who had changed his original surname, Sadowsky. (Courtesy of Middletown Historical Society.)

In 1869, William Moore and James Culbertson founded a large general store at 21 West Main Street, which sold textiles, silks, linens, lace, fancy goods, notions, hosiery, clothing, groceries, carpets, and more. Beginning in 1888, the store was operated by Walter Letherbury, the town's first mayor, and his descendants until it was purchased by James Buckworth in 1948. It remained in the Buckworth family for more than 60 years. (Courtesy of Middletown Historical Society.)

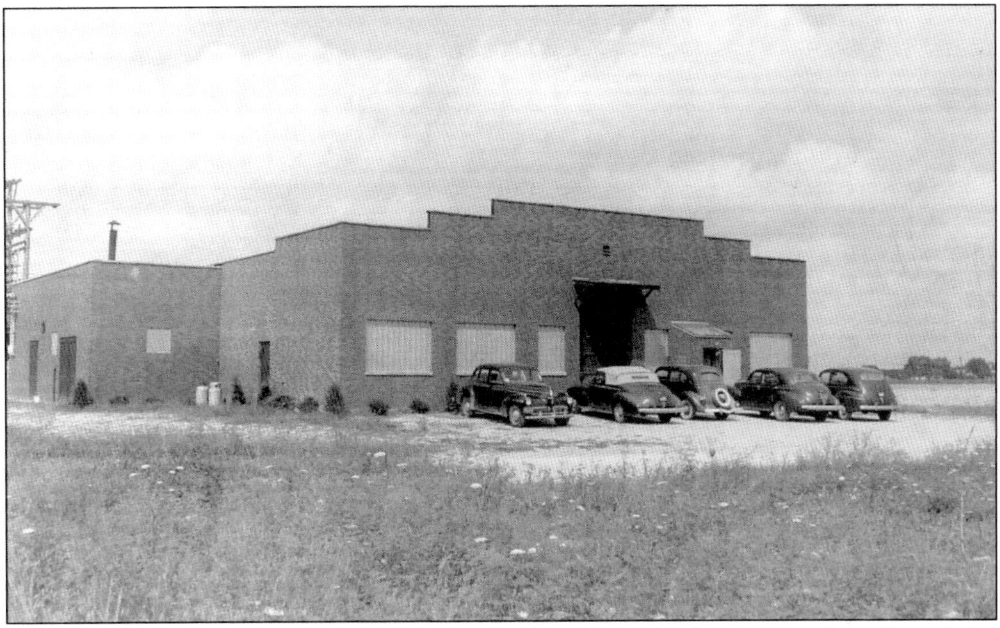

Middletown's economy began in agriculture and milling, but evolved and changed rapidly with the times. Tanners, distillers, and wheelwrights were some of the oldest businesses in town. Growth made way for foundries, blacksmiths, and makers of wagons and carriages. From the late 19th century until the 1970s, almost all necessities could be purchased in town. This photograph's description states that it shows a modern plant. (Courtesy of Delaware Public Archives.)

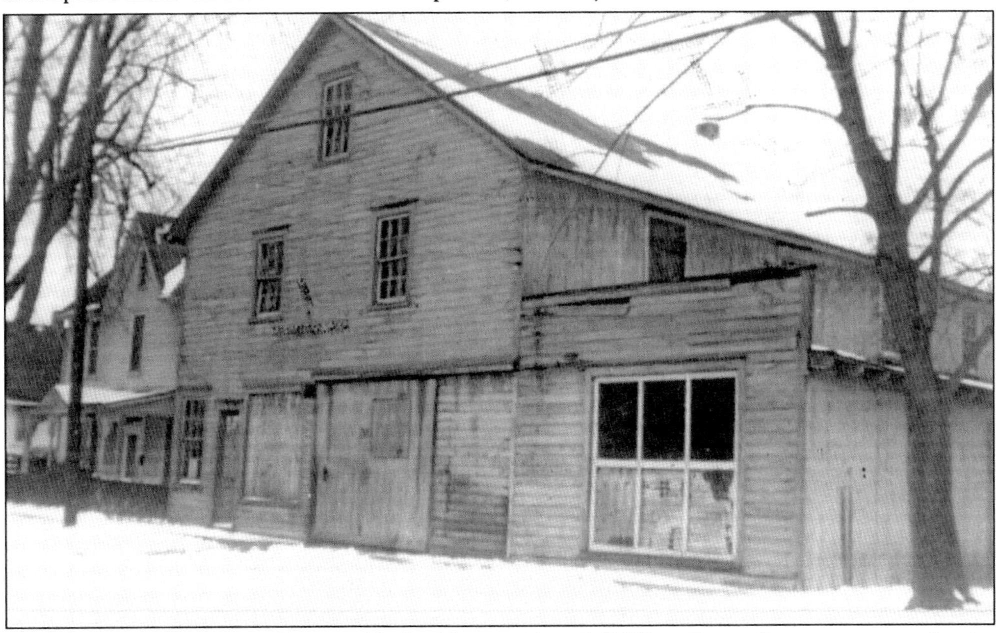

Shown around the 1920s, this wooden building at 10 and 12 West Green Street was once the site of the William Price and Son automobile dealership and repair shop. Next door, at 8 West Green Street, is a house built in 1891. Both structures still stand across from the current Middletown Town Hall, although the building pictured here was rehabilitated and is now nearly unrecognizable. (Courtesy of Middletown Historical Society.)

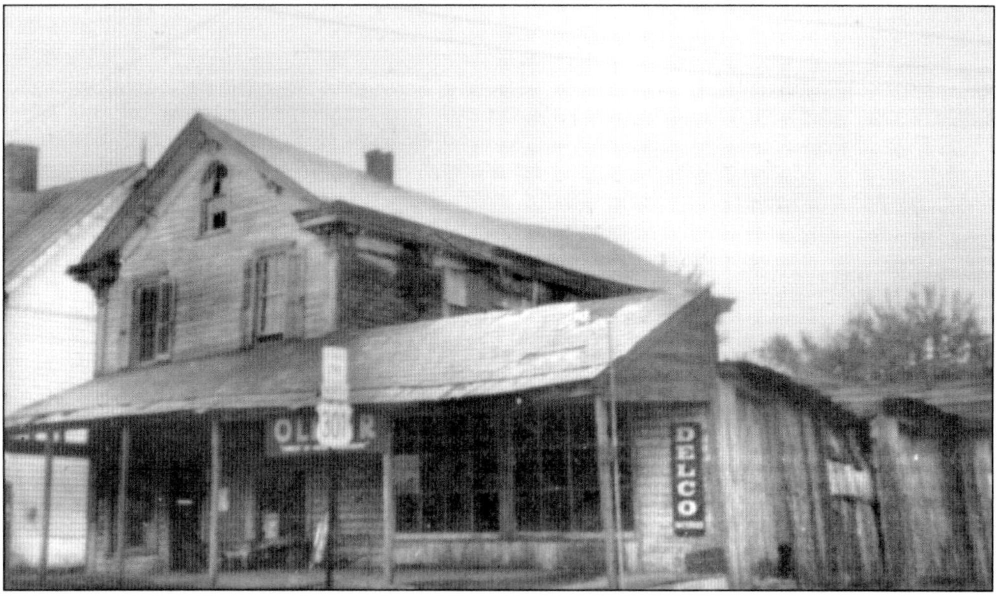

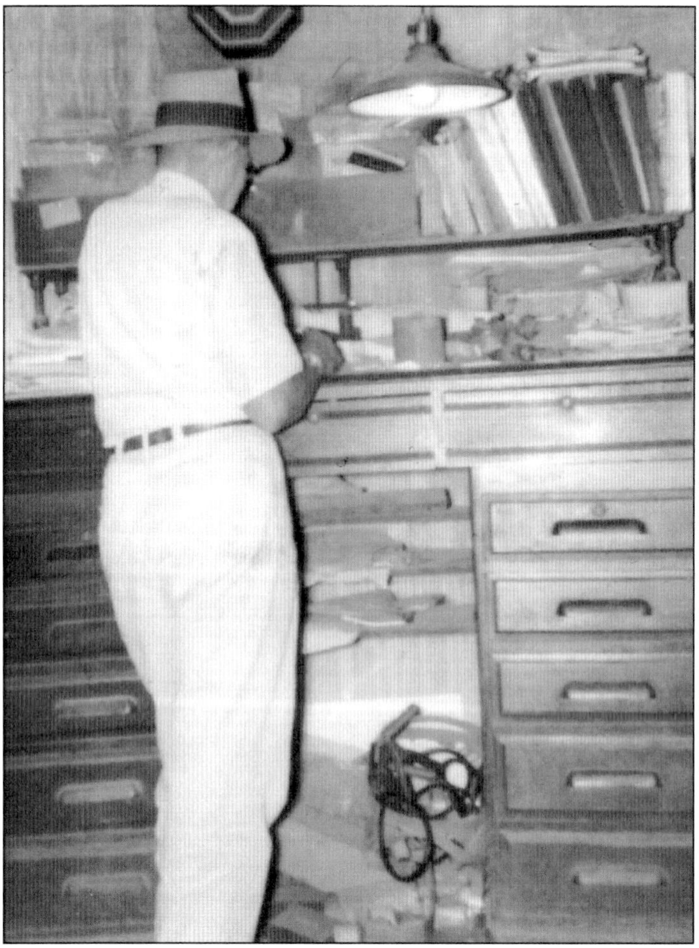

In 1895, Jesse Shepherd established a grain business, which was sold to Eugene Shallcross in 1918. These 1950s photographs show the building's exterior on West Main Street near the railroad tracks (above) and Eugene Shallcross in the area he used as an office (left). The Shallcrosses were one of the area's most influential families and largest employers, with a creamery, farms, and a car dealership in addition to the granary on West Main Street. Shallcross Place and Shallcross Lake Road are just two local landmarks bearing the family's name. (Both, courtesy of Louisa Price Zeh.)

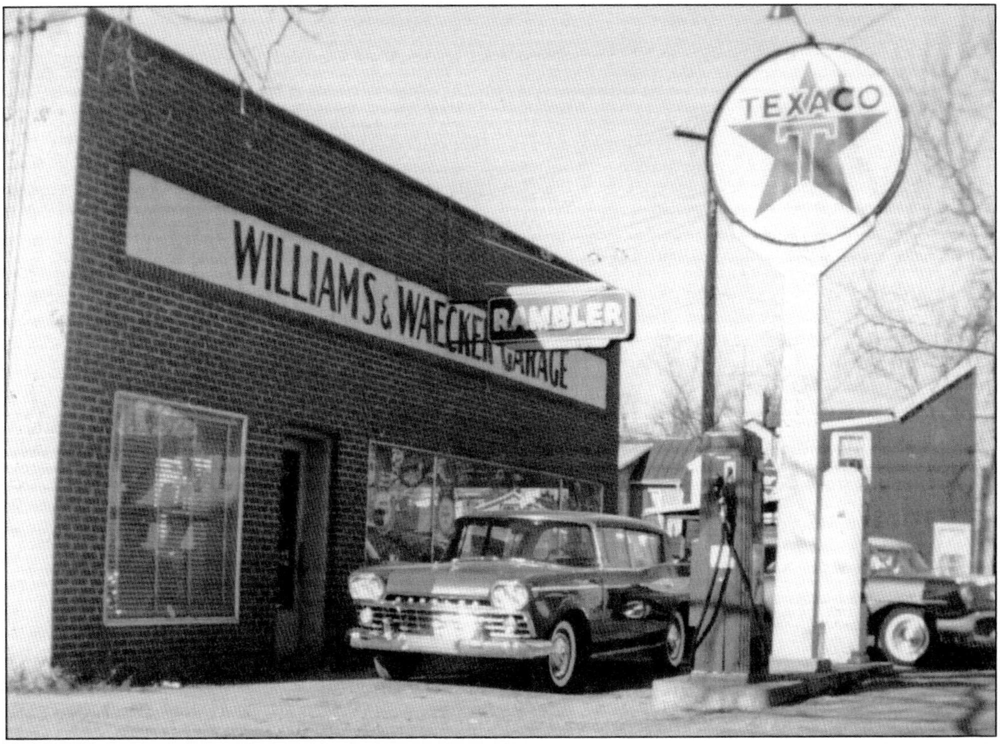

Williams & Waecker owned at least two Middletown businesses, including the Williams & Waecker Garage and Williams & Waecker Radio & TV Service on South Scott Street, which was demolished in the early 1970s. The December 1958 photograph above shows the garage and gas station. The photograph below shows the radio and television service that was operated out of a building at 16 South Scott Street that was purchased by James and Phyllis Waecker in 1972. The Volunteer Hose Company purchased it in 2001 when it relocated from South Broad Street to the corner of South Scott and West Green Streets. (Both, courtesy of *Middletown Transcript*.)

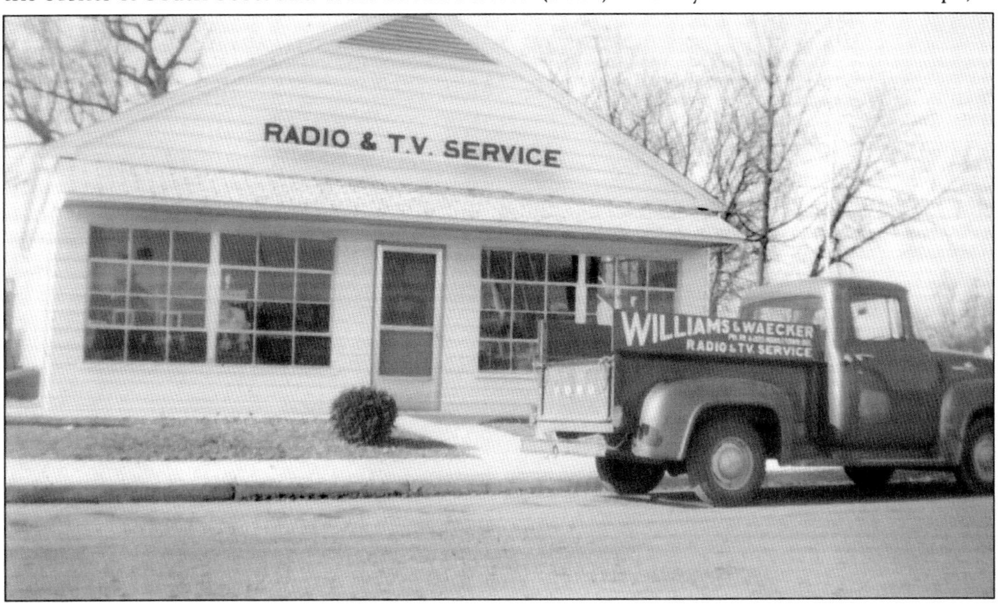

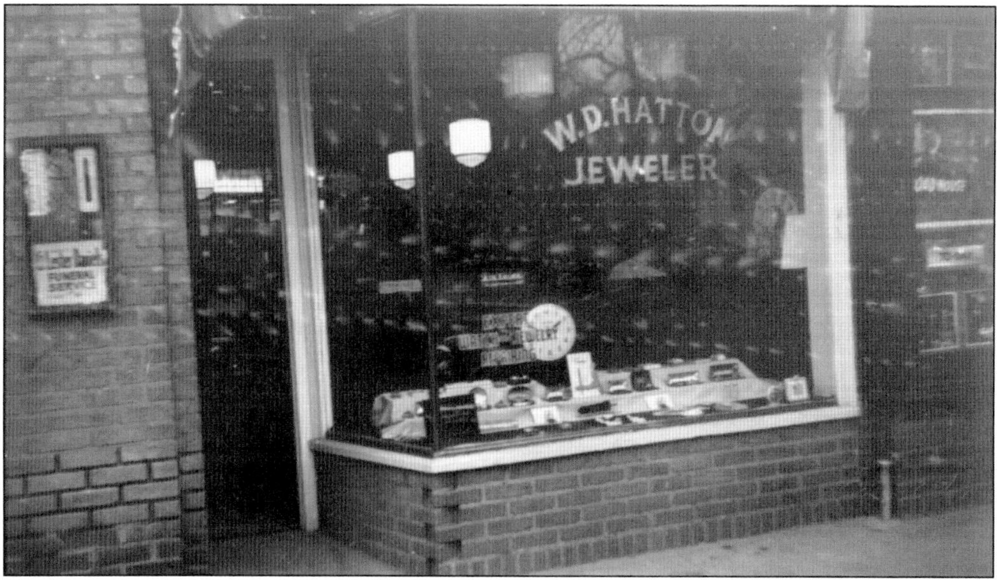

W.D. Hatton Watch, Clock & Jewelry Repair on West Main Street has been open longer than any other single-owner business on the street. Hatton purchased a shop (above) next to the Everett Theatre at 47 West Main Street in 1948, then relocated across the road to 22 West Main Street before settling at 19 West Main Street in 1979. Hatton grew up around the jewelry business and sold clocks, jewelry, lamps, and gifts until 1991, when he scaled back to only doing repairs. He celebrated 60 years in business in 2008. In the 1949 image below, Hatton is pictured with his assistant, Edna Buehm. (Both, courtesy of W.D. Hatton.)

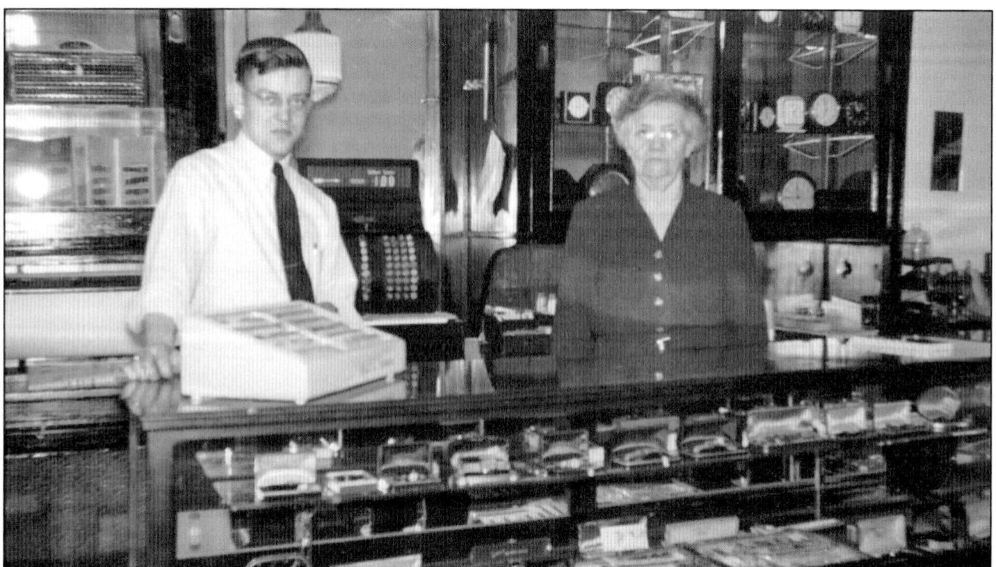

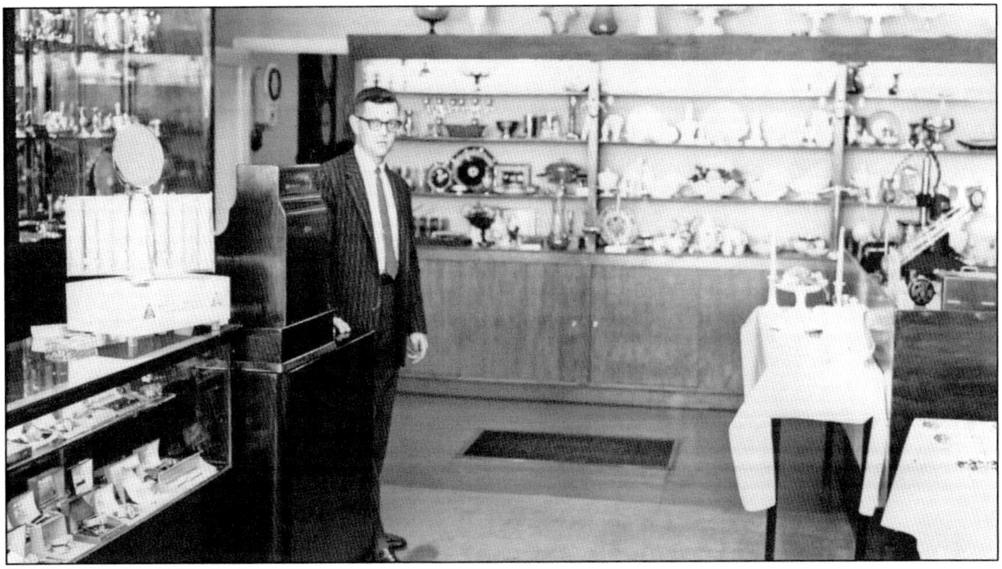

In 1979, W.D. Hatton purchased this store at 19 West Main Street, where it has remained since. He switched from selling jewelry, clocks, gifts, and lamps to repairs only after he was robbed twice—once with a gun and once with a knife. Upon the second robbery, Hatton chased the assailant through downtown Middletown until the police were able to make an arrest. Hatton—a veteran of the US Navy who, at the time of this publication, still lives with his wife, Jeanne, in Odessa at the time of publication—attempted to retire, but the repair business keeps him busy when he is not out on his sailboat. (Both, courtesy of W.D. Hatton.)

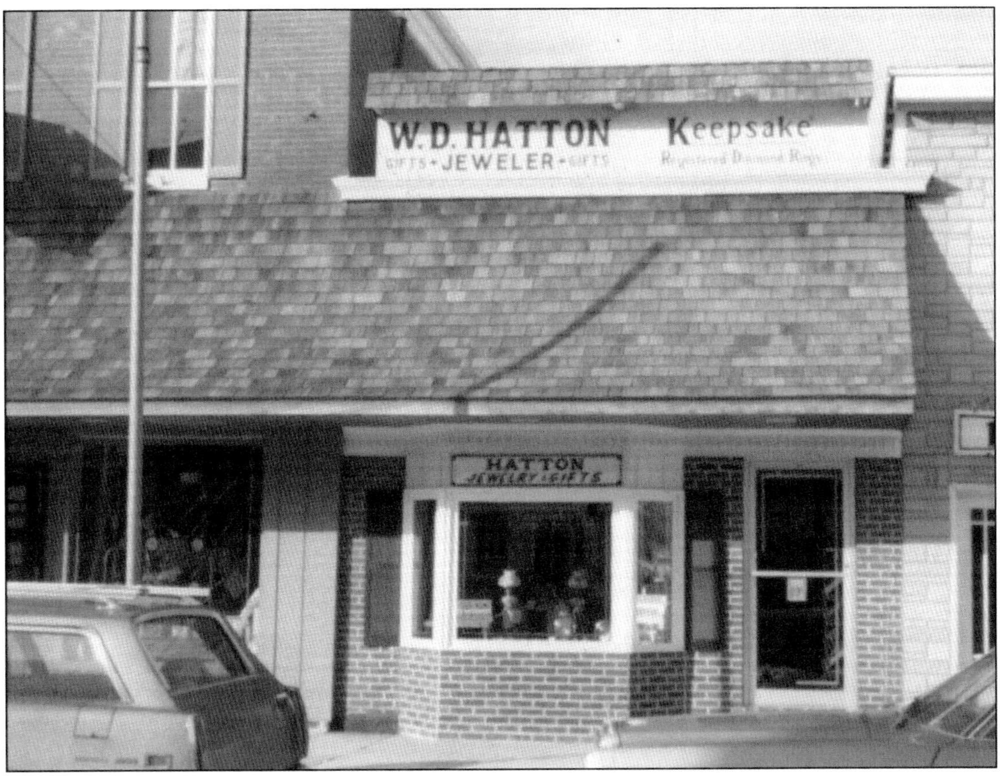

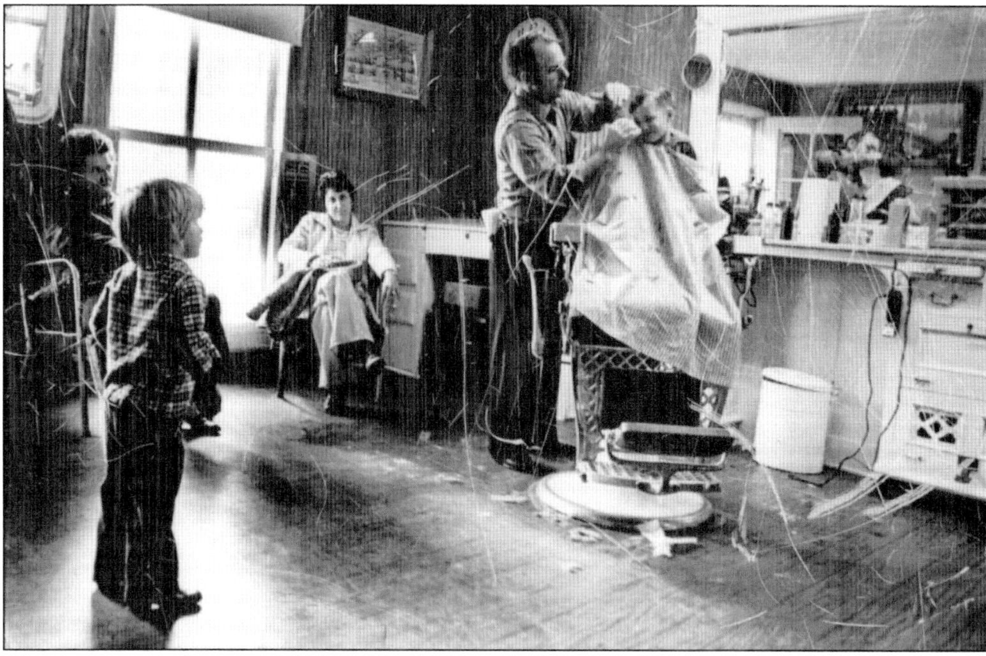

Charlie Biggs has been Middletown's best-known barber since he opened the Towne Barber Shop in 1956 on North Broad Street. He later moved to 15 West Main Street, which had long been a barbershop, where he is still cutting hair at the time of this publication. Biggs first took an interest in barbering when he was 14 years old and later went to school for his trade. In the 1970s, young men who were brought to his shop by their parents gave him the name "Chopper Charlie" after watching their long locks fall to the floor. Biggs has two sons with his wife, Madeline, and has long been active in the community. (Both, courtesy of Charlie Biggs.)

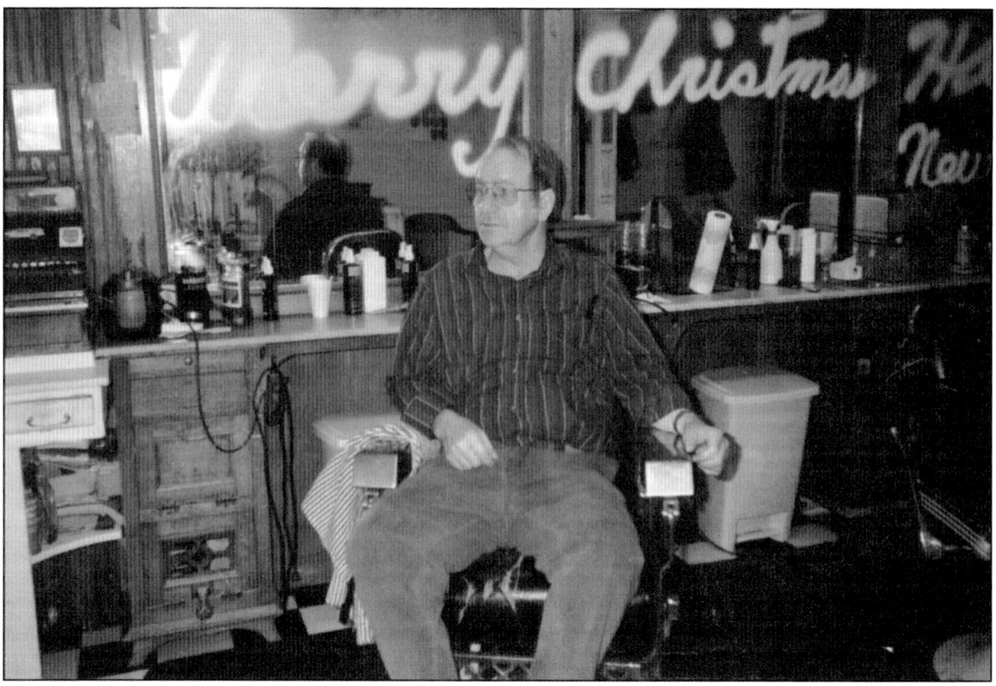

Four

AGRICULTURE

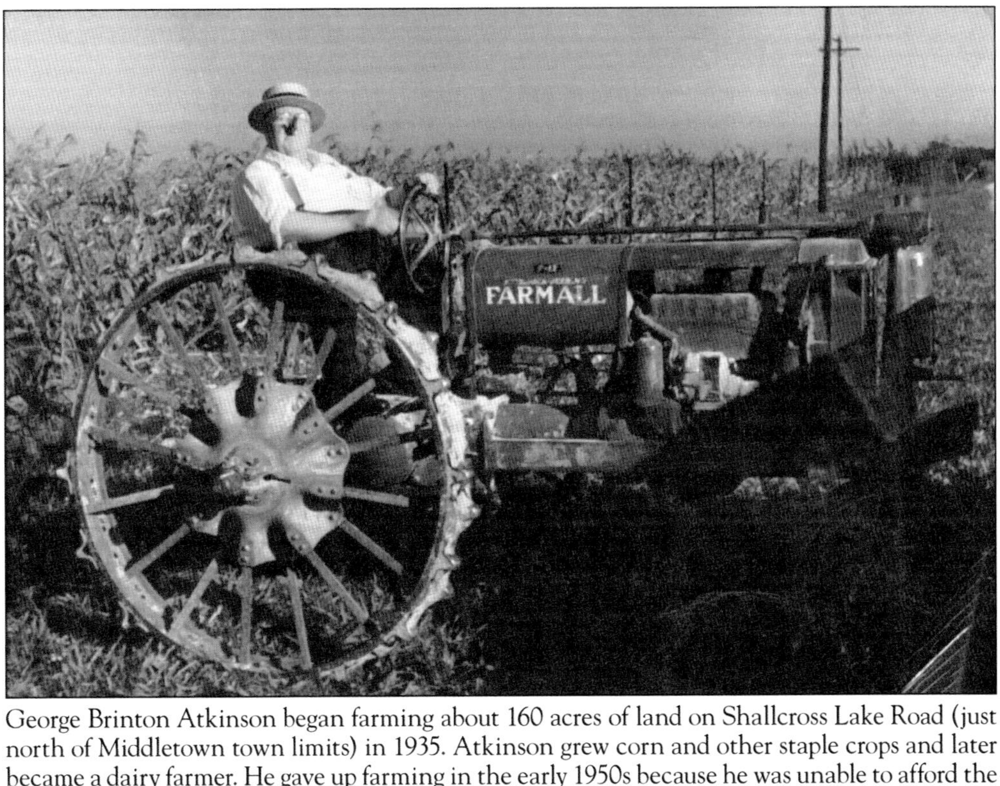

George Brinton Atkinson began farming about 160 acres of land on Shallcross Lake Road (just north of Middletown town limits) in 1935. Atkinson grew corn and other staple crops and later became a dairy farmer. He gave up farming in the early 1950s because he was unable to afford the upgraded equipment mandated by new regulations. Although he never married, he adopted his nephew and niece and became the family patriarch. (Courtesy of George and Julie Atkinson.)

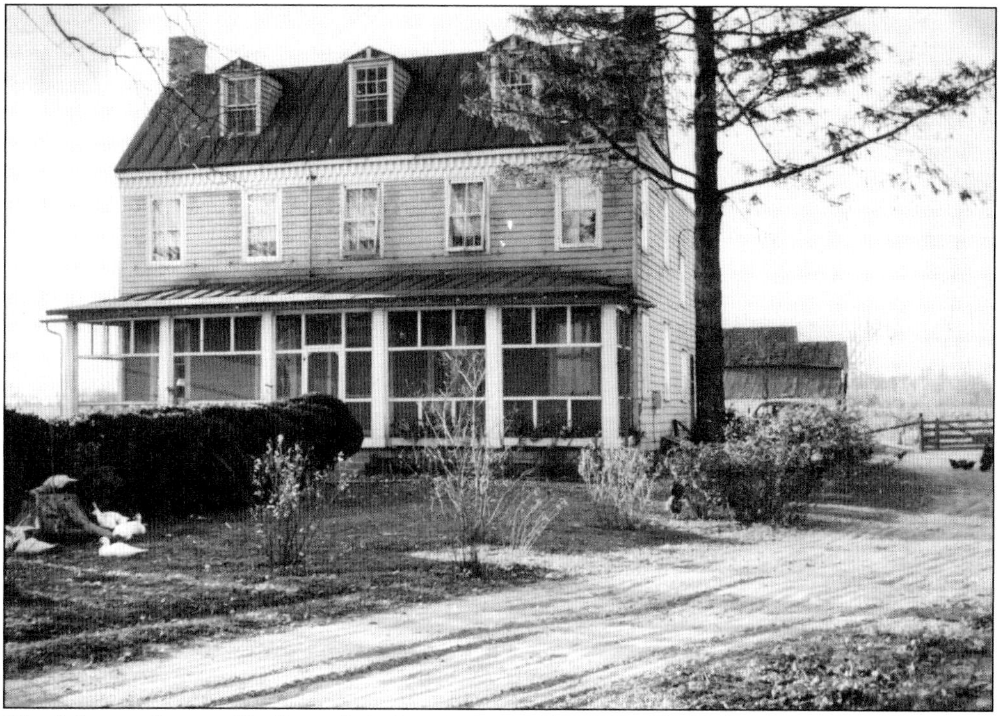

The Atkinson farm on Shallcross Lake Road was once known as the Perkins farm, after its previous owners. The Hirons and Morton families also owned the land at one time. George Atkinson, great-nephew and adoptive grandson of George Brinton Atkinson, resides in this c. 1860s home with his wife, Julie, at the time of this publication. Both George and Julie Atkinson retired as teachers from Middletown High School. (Courtesy of George and Julie Atkinson.)

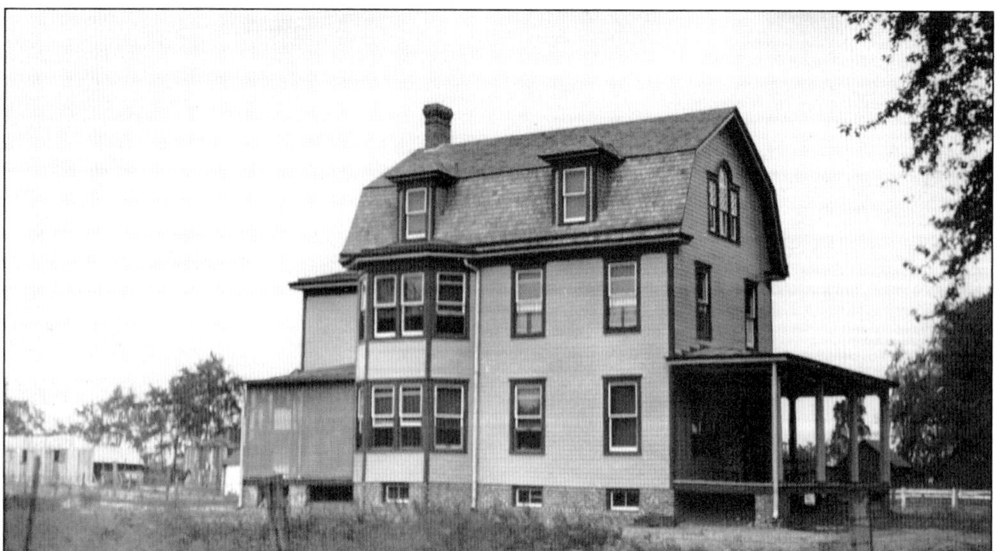

The Ingleside farmhouse at 201 East Main Street was owned by the Green family and situated on land that was once home to Middletown's first recorded business, the Philip Reading tannery. (Courtesy of Richard and Marlene Green.)

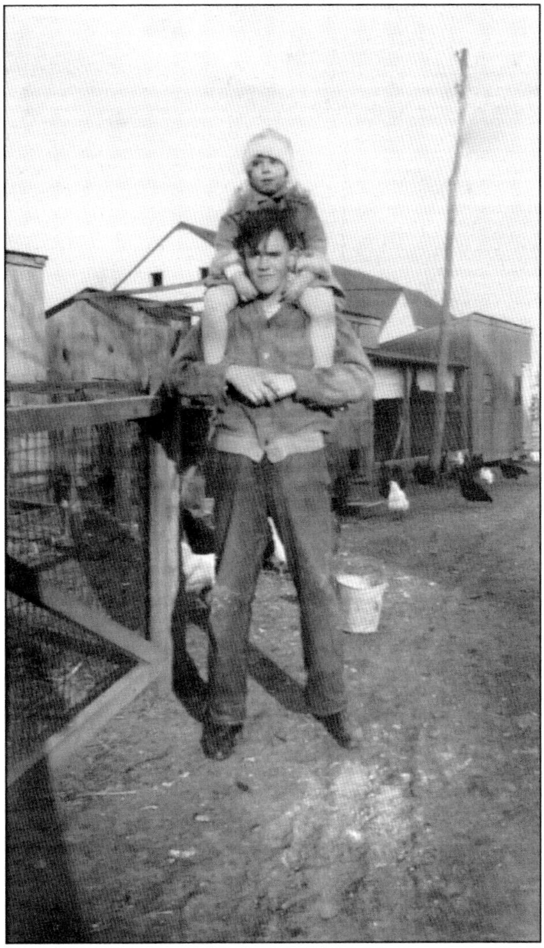

The Green family farmed land that spanned east of Broad Street and both north and south of East Main Street. A brick building at the farm was once used as a bark house for the Philip Reading tannery. The Green family continued to farm the land until Richard and Marlene Green sold it to a developer at the start of the 21st century. In the image at right, John C. "Jack" Green and his niece, Jenny Louise Lockwood, are pictured on the farm. In the photograph below, from left to right, James Chas, Victor Green, Adelaide Green, and Jack Green are pictured at the Green farm. (Both, courtesy of Richard and Marlene Green.)

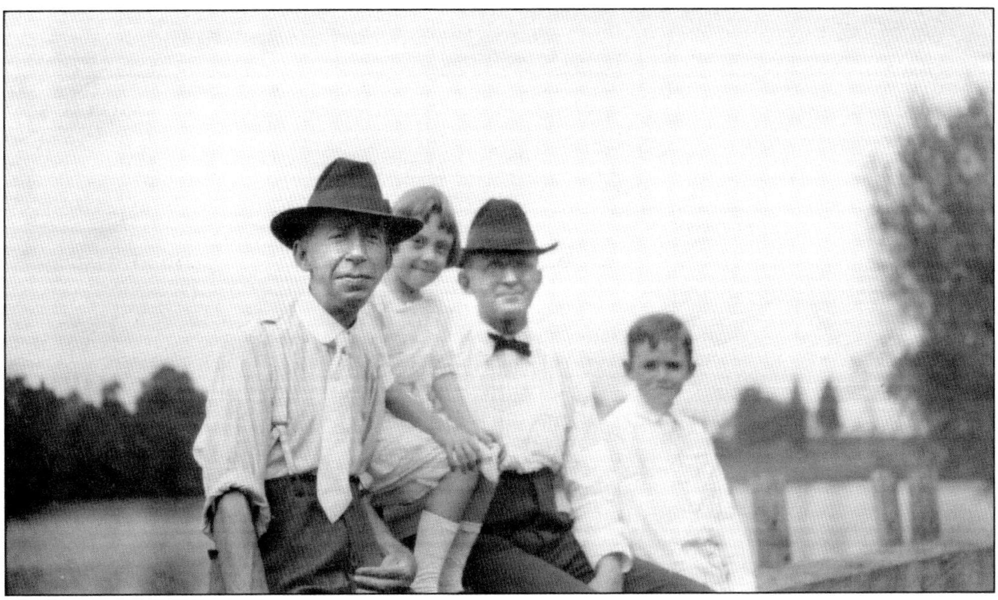

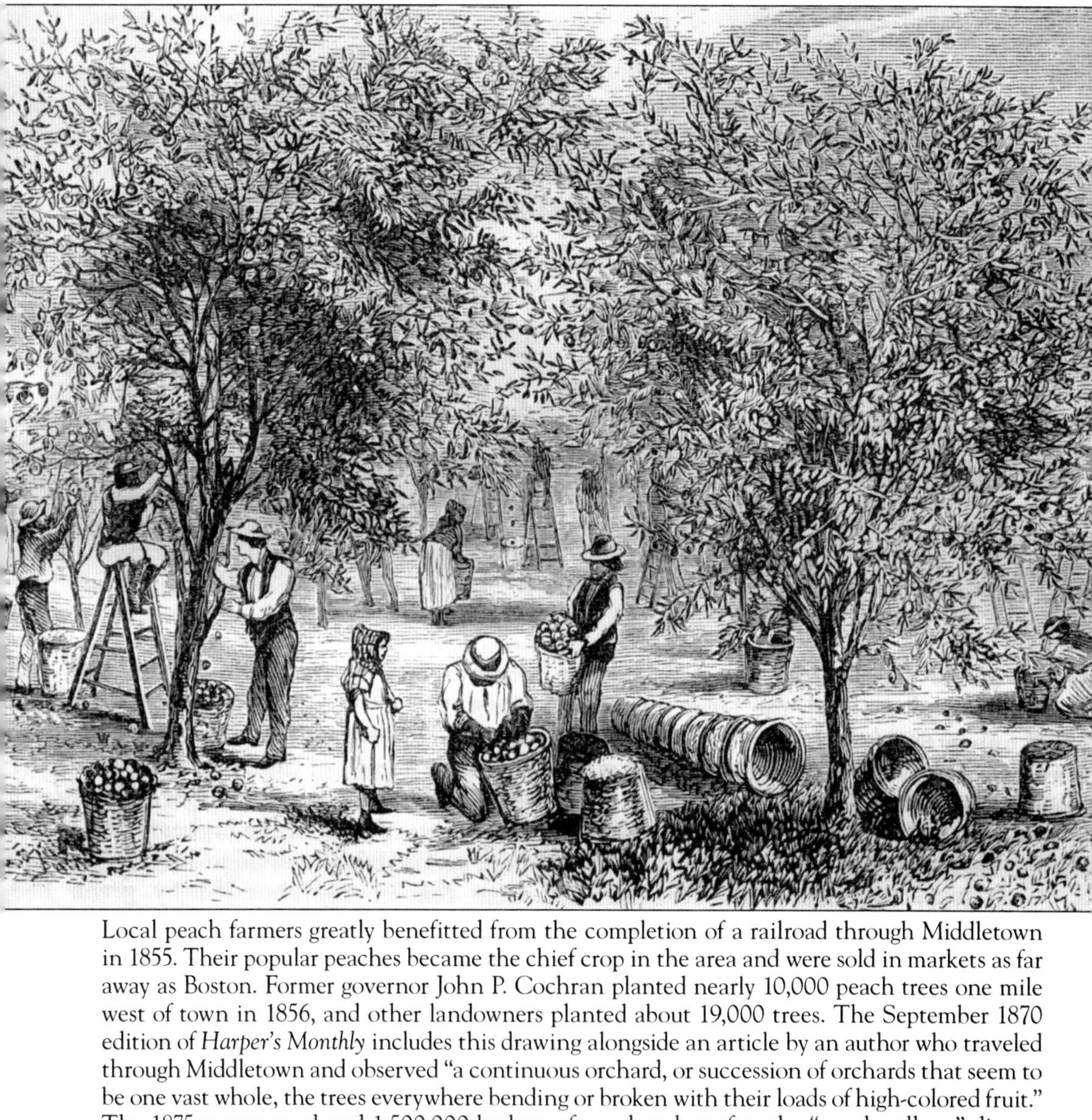

Local peach farmers greatly benefitted from the completion of a railroad through Middletown in 1855. Their popular peaches became the chief crop in the area and were sold in markets as far away as Boston. Former governor John P. Cochran planted nearly 10,000 peach trees one mile west of town in 1856, and other landowners planted about 19,000 trees. The September 1870 edition of *Harper's Monthly* includes this drawing alongside an article by an author who traveled through Middletown and observed "a continuous orchard, or succession of orchards that seem to be one vast whole, the trees everywhere bending or broken with their loads of high-colored fruit." The 1875 season produced 1,500,000 baskets of peaches, but after the "peach yellows" disease infested the crops in the 1890s, local growers turned to other plants. (Courtesy of Middletown Historical Society.)

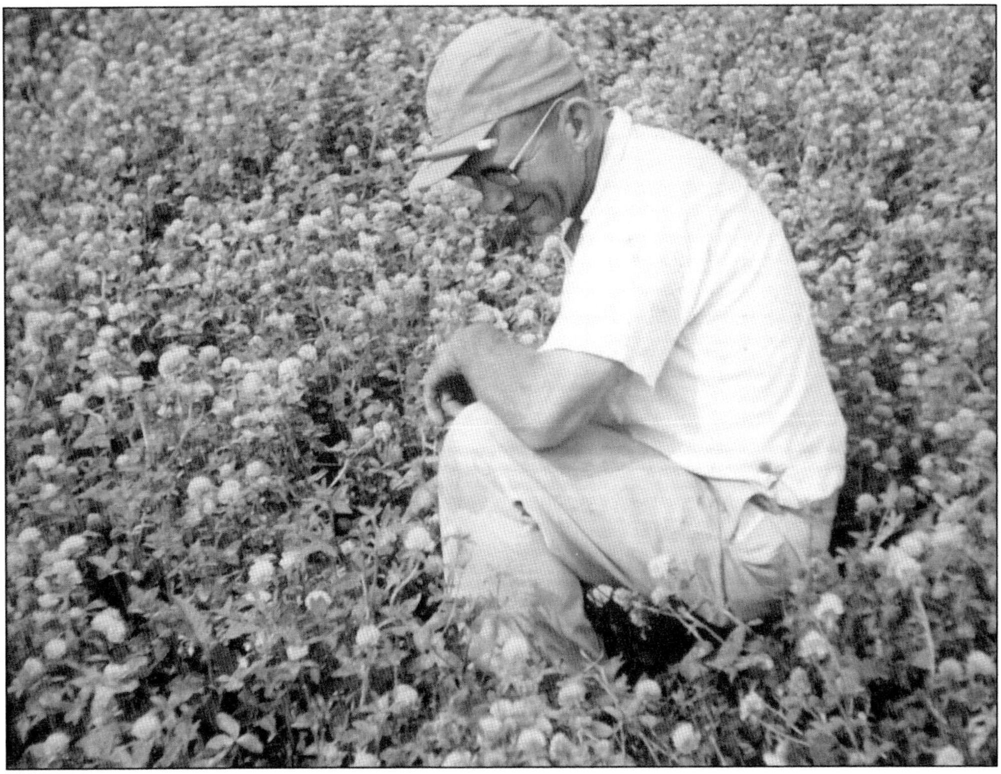

William Alfree (above) of Middletown Farms takes a moment to admire the red clover that would soon became high-quality hay at the University of Delaware Hay Research Farm on Bunker Hill Road. Red clover, hay from which was used as a protein source for cows, had a perennial lifespan of one to two years, and crops could yield 2 to 2.5 tons of the clover per acre. It was abandoned for alfalfa, which could yield 3 to 5 tons per acre. Alfree was the manager of the research farm, where emphasis was on the production and marketing of heat-cured hay for horses. In the image below, local cattle stand in a clover field. (Both, courtesy of Delaware Public Archives.)

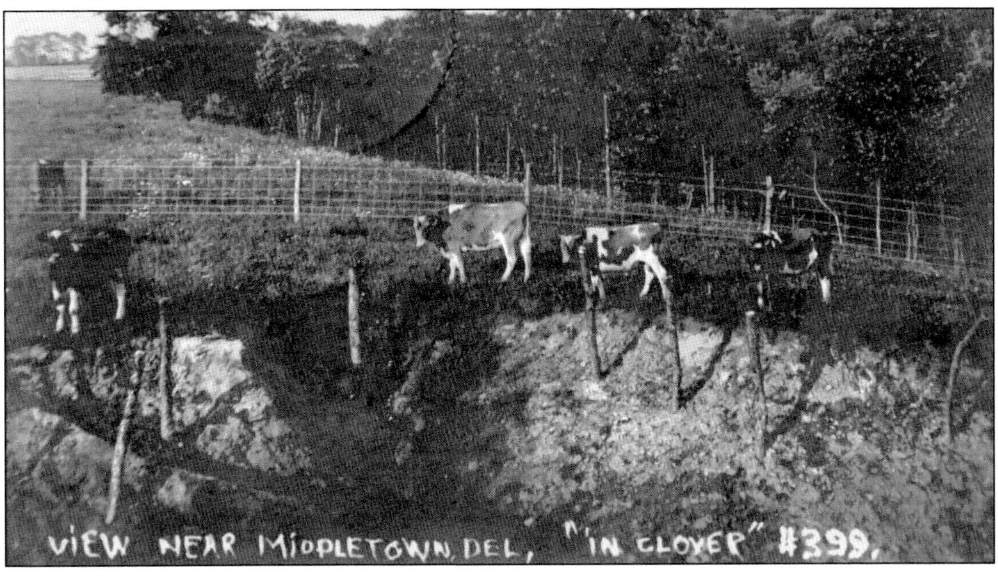

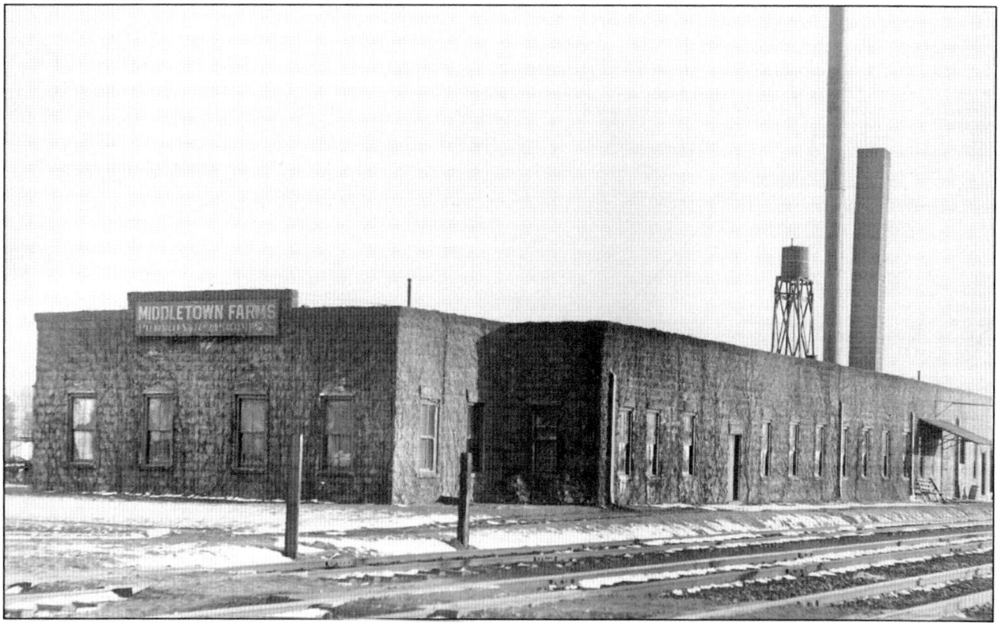

Middletown Farms was a creamery that processed milk from local dairy farms. It was located near the present-day site of the Middletown High School football stadium. After the original facility was destroyed by fire in 1906, the business was rebuilt to be bigger and better. The new building, constructed of stone and concrete, included facilities for making casein, cheese, ice cream, and ice. The creamery's products were sold at a retail store in Wilmington and a summer store in Ocean City, Maryland. Middletown Farms went out of business in 1932. (Both, courtesy of Delaware Public Archives.)

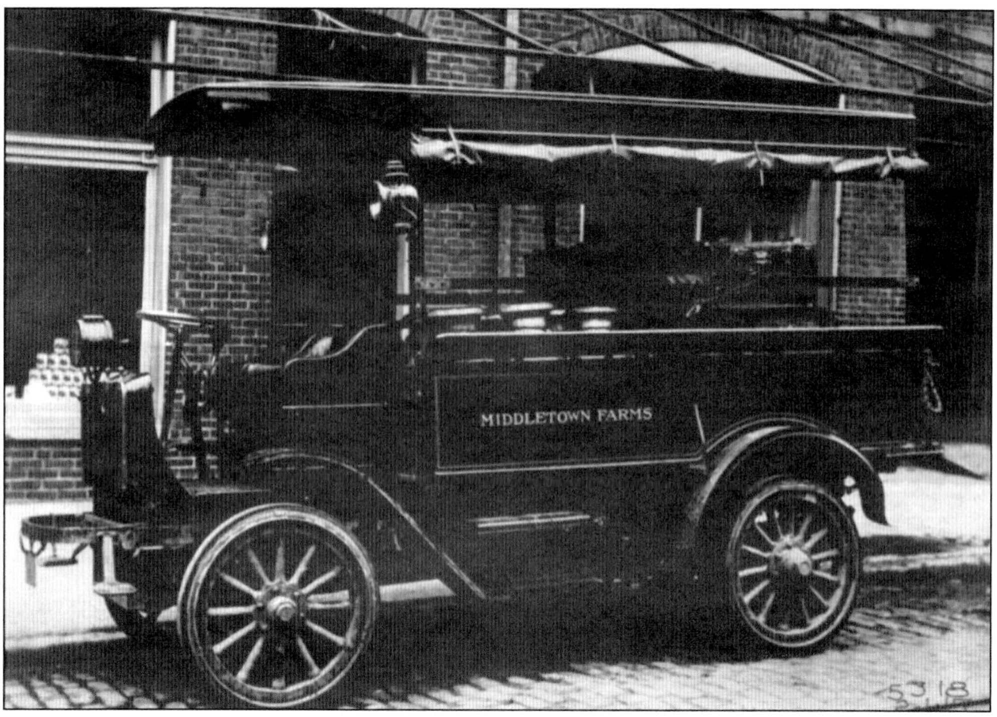

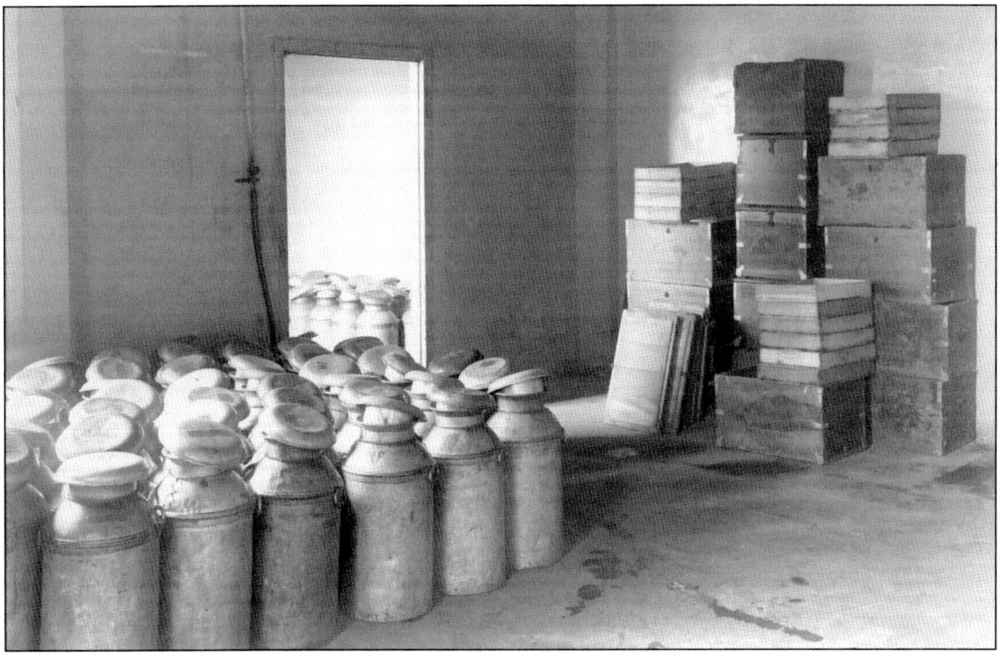

After the original Middletown Farms building was destroyed by fire in 1906, the new facility utilized the most modern technology of the time for milk production, including pasteurization, and distribution. The photograph above shows a portion of the can room with clean cans and boxes ready for use. The photograph below shows a section of the churning room, with its hermetically sealed vats and a sanitary cream pump. Milk processes became increasingly safer after the establishment of pasteurization in the late 1800s. Middletown's veterinarian, Dr. Louis Levinson, lobbied for a state bill to test Delaware cows for tuberculosis. His discovery lowered incidences of tuberculosis in humans. (Both, courtesy of Delaware Public Archives.)

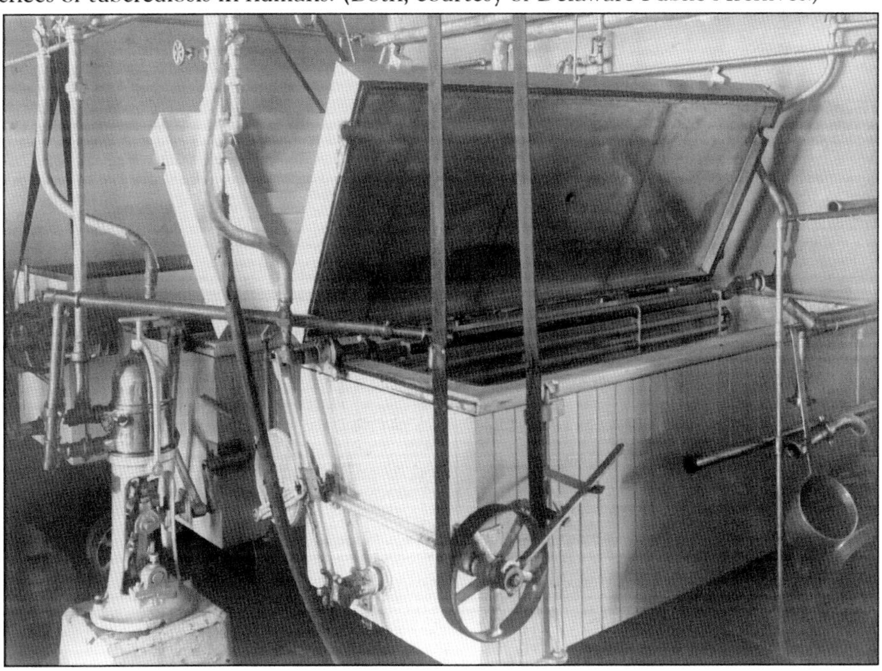

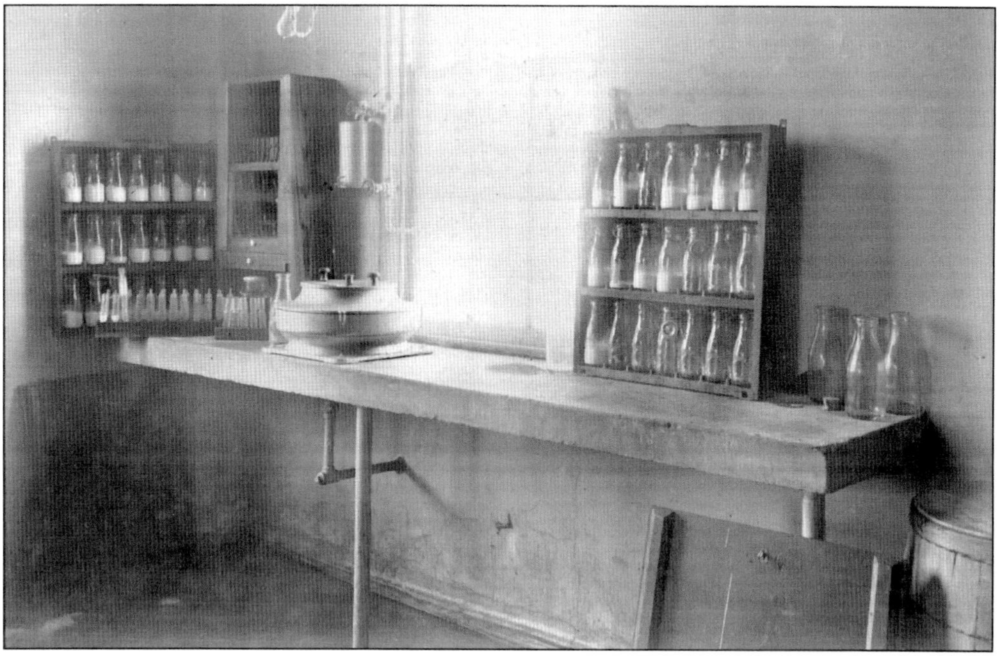

The Middletown Farms facility included a testing room equipped with sample bottles, testing tubes, and a mechanism used to test milk and cream prior to distribution. The company became one of the largest manufacturers of milk products on the East Coast and had a capacity of more than 1,000 gallons of ice cream per day. (Courtesy of Delaware Public Archives.)

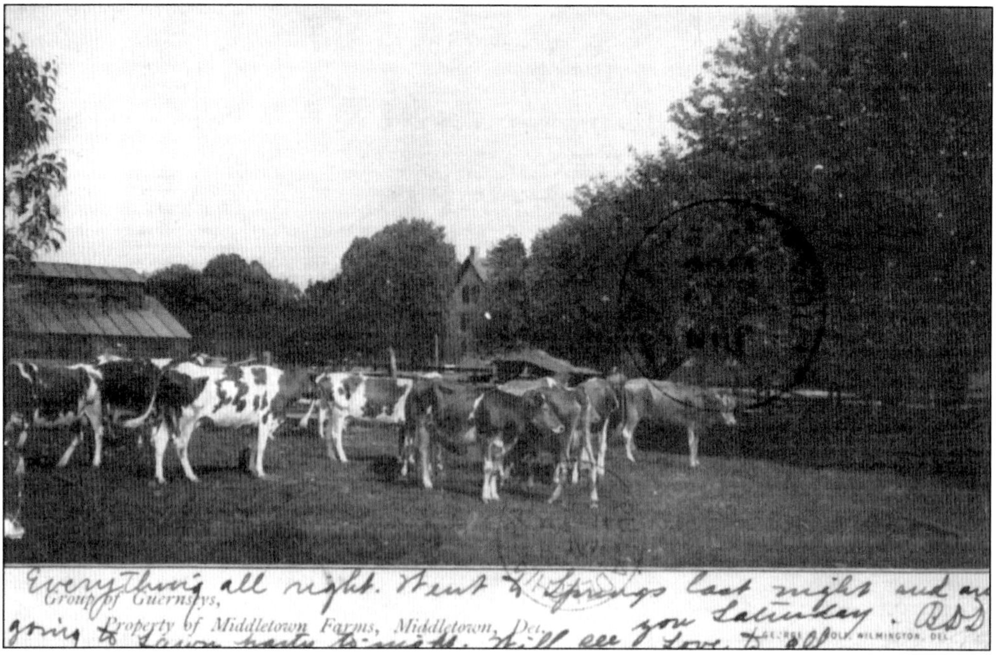

Herds of cattle were once a common sight in Middletown and the surrounding area. In the 1930s, more than 12,000 cows were milked annually in New Castle County alone. At that time, a cow in Delaware produced 4,200 pounds of milk per year on average, and farmers earned $1.60 per 100 pounds of milk. (Courtesy of Delaware Public Archives.)

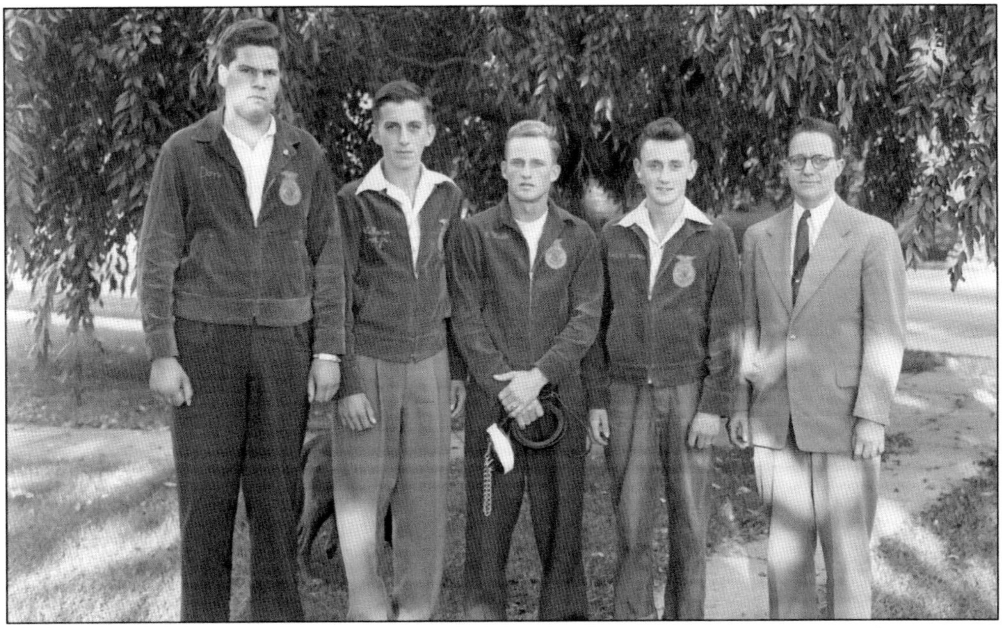

This Delaware Future Farmers of America dairy-judging team competed on October 2, 1950, in Richmond, Virginia. Pictured here are, from left to right, Donald Lerch (A.I. duPont High School), Wallace Cook Jr. (Middletown High School), Milbourne Webb (Caesar Rodney High School), Charles Savidge (A.I. duPont High School), and coach S.F. Simmons (A.I. duPont High School). (Courtesy of Delaware Public Archives.)

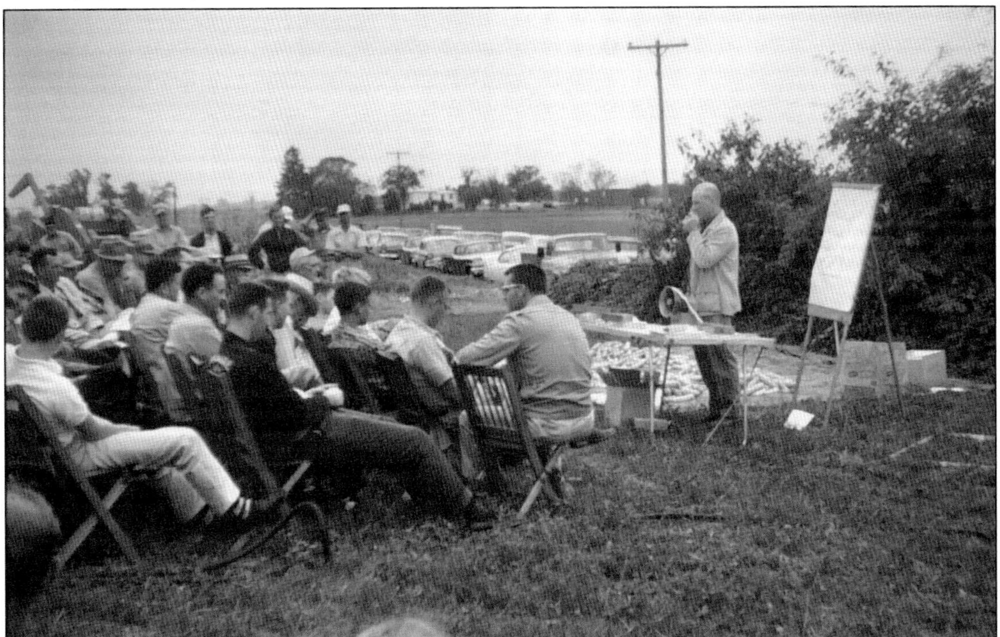

William Brady was a Middletown farmer and a leader in the agriculture industry. Brady spoke to many farm groups, including this one in Smyrna, to share his knowledge of agriculture. Corn production demonstrations and field classrooms were well received by farmers. (Courtesy of Delaware Public Archives.)

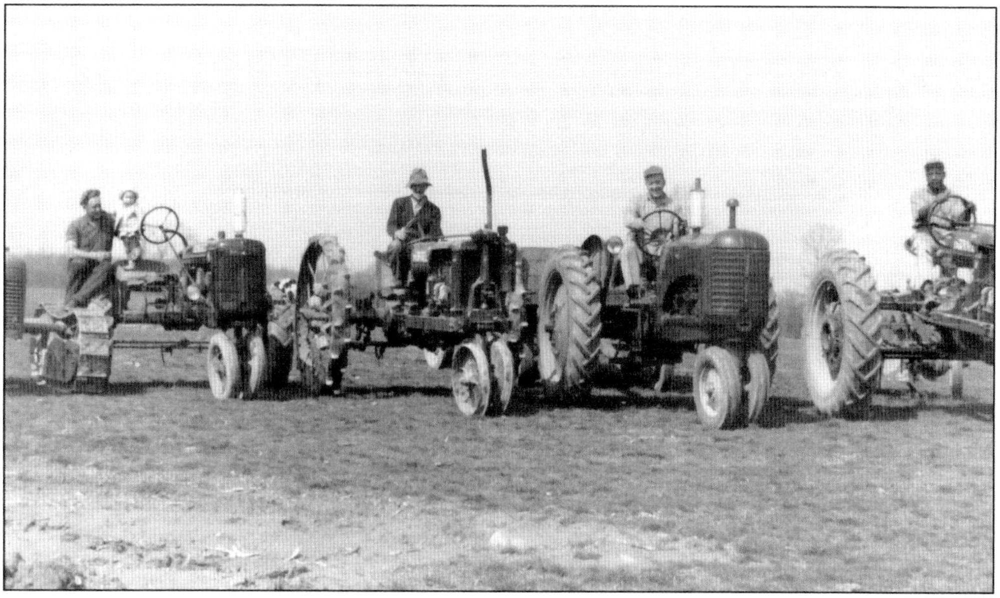

For 27 years, Corbit Collins grew everything—from corn to beans to wheat—on about 500 acres along Marl Pit Road after moving to Middletown from Townsend in 1949. These 1947 photographs of Collins and his family were taken on the farm owned by his father, William Morris Collins Sr., on Union Church Road in Townsend. Morris farmed several hundred acres. Above, from left to right, Corbit Collins holds his daughter, Terri, while William Morris Collins Sr., William Morris Collins Jr., and James Jackson pose on other tractors. Terri is also pictured below with her mother, Inez M. (Pierson) Collins, Anna (Shahan) Cummins, and William Morris Collins Sr. in front of tractors owned by Corbit. Corbit was an active volunteer and one of the founding members of the Delaware Agriculture Museum. He was also president of the New Castle County Farm Bureau and Federal Land Bank, which loaned money for farmland. (Both, courtesy of Delaware Public Archives.)

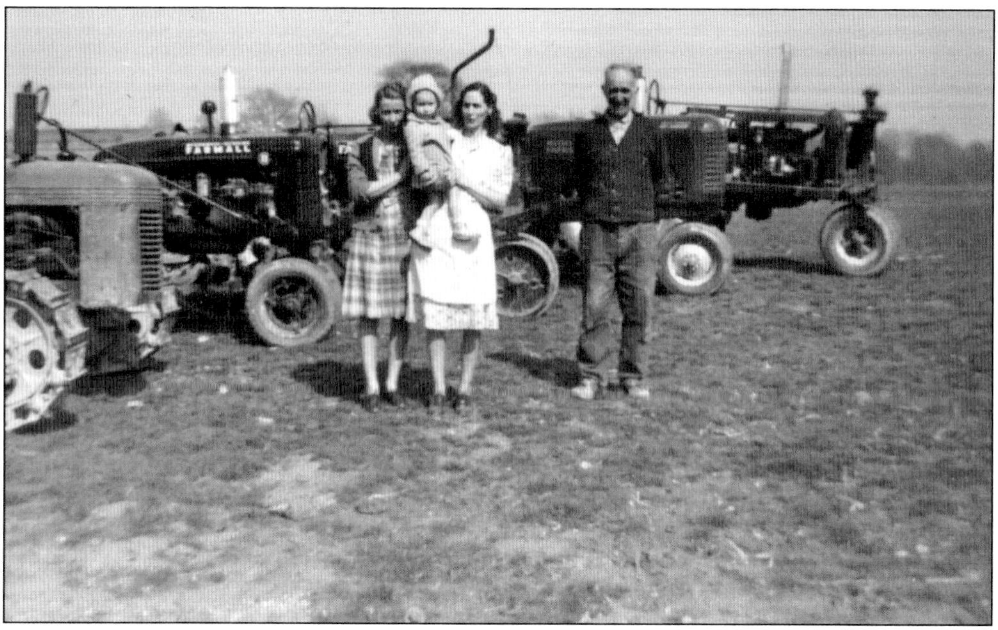

Five

Residents and Community

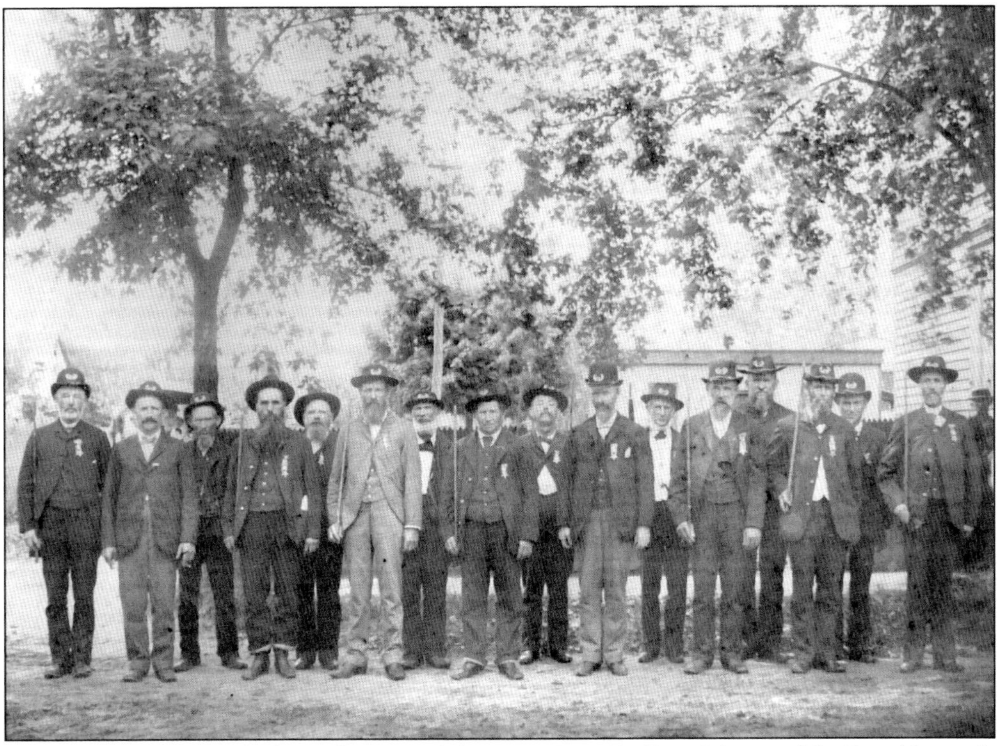

This c. 1900 photograph shows the Major John Jones Post 22, Grand Army of the Republic, with soldiers including Richard Lockwood, George Echenhofer, a Major Gore, Michael Greminger, John Dickinson, a Mr. Sharp, Kumpel, a Mr. Wilson, Barney Naudain, a Captain Pennington, Joseph Dekind, William Wilson, D. Denny, John Goller, and Dan Dunning. (Courtesy of Middletown Historical Society.)

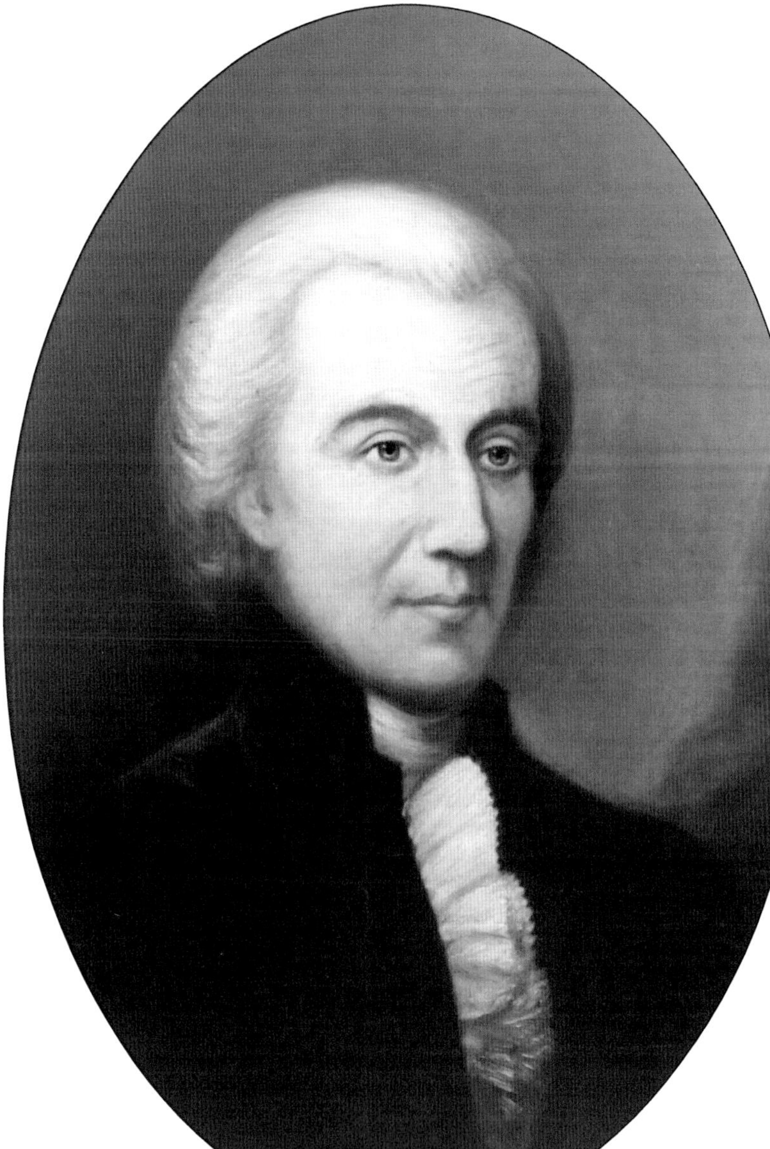

Middletown doctor Joshua Clayton served as president of Delaware starting in 1789, when the Delaware General Assembly selected the state's leader, then known as the president. Citizens were given the power to elect a governor under Delaware's Constitution of 1792, and the residents of Delaware elected Clayton as their first governor. Clayton got his start in politics as a Congressional delegate from 1782 to 1784. Prior to his time as president and governor, he was elected to the Delaware House of Representatives in 1785 and 1787, then served on the Court of Appeals and was elected as state treasurer in 1786. During his time in Delaware politics, cockfighting, shooting contests, and horse racing were outlawed; extra relief was approved for the impoverished; and the requirement of owning property in order to vote was repealed. His term as governor ended in 1796, and he went on to serve at the national level when he was elected to the US Senate in 1798. (Courtesy of Delaware Public Archives.)

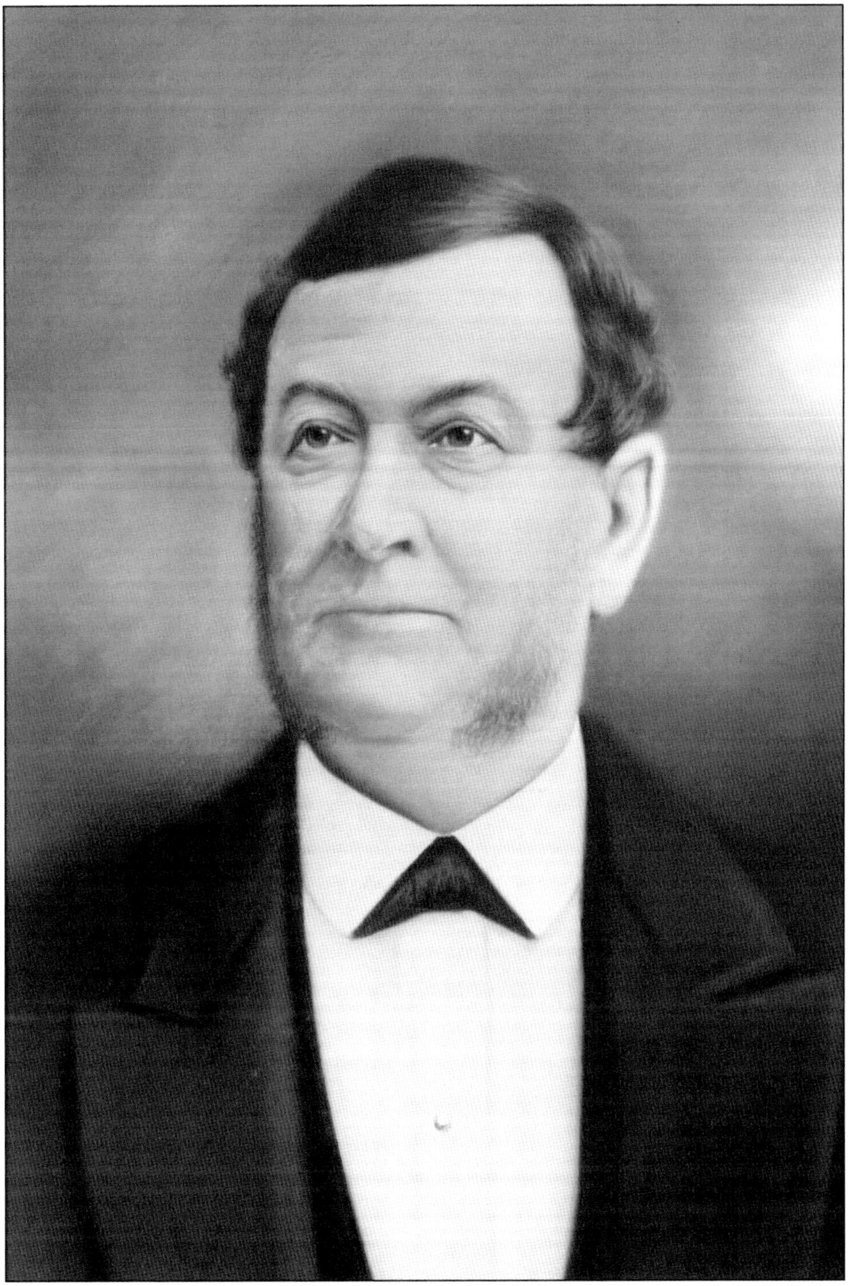

Middletown resident John P. Cochran, of the large Cochran family from Cecil County, Maryland, was Delaware's 43rd governor. He served on the New Castle County Levy Court from 1838 to 1846, and when he became governor in January 1875, he was the first New Castle County resident to do so in 30 years. He was born in Appoquinimink Hundred and became a prominent farmer and peach grower. He owned a great deal of land in the area, much of which is now home to modern commercial industry. While he was a devoted Democrat and active in politics, he held relatively few offices. He did, however, influence an amendment that helped with the creation of Delaware's free public school system. After his term as governor, he spent his remaining years on his gorgeous estate until he died at age 89. (Courtesy of Delaware Public Archives.)

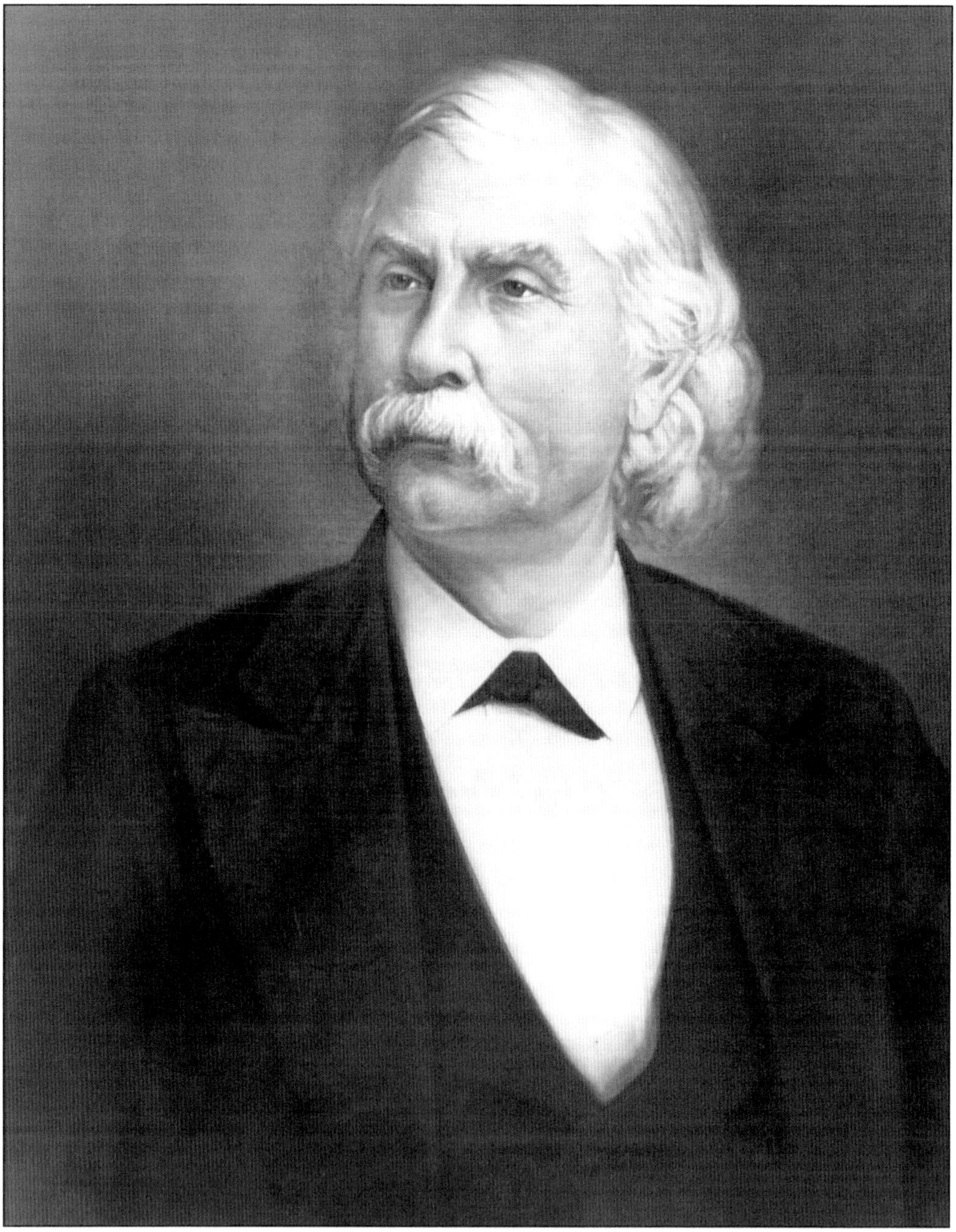

Middletown resident Benjamin Thomas Biggs, born in 1821 near Summit Bridge (just north of Middletown), became the 48th governor of Delaware. His start in politics came in 1853, when he served as a member of the Delaware Constitutional Convention. He served in the US House of Representatives from 1869 to 1873 and served as a delegate at the 1872 Democratic National Convention and as director of the Kent and Queen Anne's Railroad. Biggs was elected governor in November 1886. During his time as governor, he signed a bill that both created a hospital for the insane and mandated that husbands provide support for their wives and children. (Courtesy of Delaware Public Archives.)

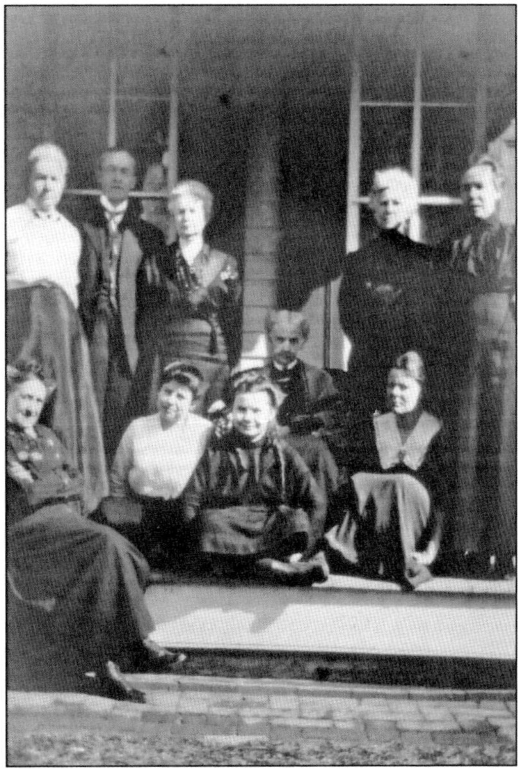

At one time, the Lockwood family resided at 102 South Broad Street; the family was most likely the namesake for Lockwood Street. The Lockwood family farmed around the area, including by Old St. Anne's Episcopal Church cemetery and the nearby "Levels." William Kirkly Lockwood married Elizabeth Watson Griffith in 1851, and they had nine children. Elizabeth is pictured in this early-1900s photograph with a few of her children, including Lizzie, William, Ida, Mollie, and Agnes Irene. Elizabeth, who was born in August 1830 by Cooch's Bridge (near Newark), sat with a pillow under her feet, as shown in the image below, due to her short stature. She was known for her "fancy work," including sewing, tatting, and crocheting. (Both, courtesy of Louisa Price Zeh.)

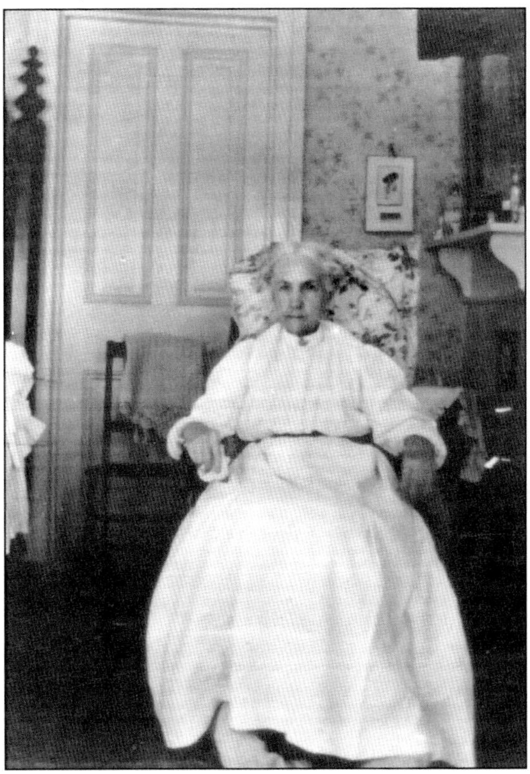

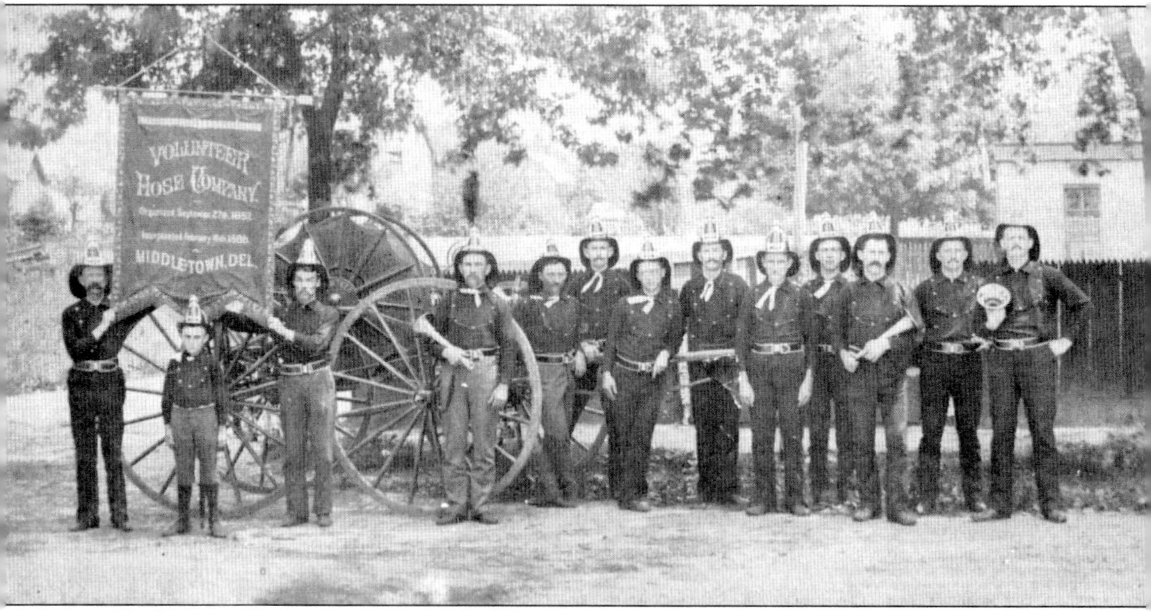

The Volunteer Hose Company of Middletown dates back to 1887, making it the second-oldest in New Castle County. An 1882 fire destroyed an entire block in the vicinity of Green Street, and another in 1886 claimed several homes on West Main Street. The town then installed its first water system. In 1887, citizens founded the Volunteer Hose and Ladder Company of Middletown, named after that year's America's Cup winner, the American *Volunteer*, which the beat British challenger, *Thistle*. Members of the fire company shown in this 1888 image are, from left to right, Joseph A. Svydam, William Gear, James C. Hall, E.S. Jones, George Pinder, John Ed Ginn, Joseph C. Jolls, Jacob Maxwell, John Gears, Andrew Kiepatrick, Harry Shepherd, Mike Kumpel, and George Hopkins. The company grew into a well-respected organization that offered an invaluable service to residents and businesses owners. By 1922, the Firemen's Band was formed and provided entertainment in parades, even winning a national title for best appearance during a Labor Day competition in Washington, DC, in 1931. (Courtesy of the author.)

After the Volunteer Hose Company of Middletown was chartered in 1887, the first purchases made by the company were a hook-and-ladder truck and a steam whistle. For years, the company had a system of alerting firefighters to a fire or other emergency, with six blasts of the siren indicating a town fire and four blasts indicating a fire in the country. The company also sounded its siren every Sunday at noon for the townspeople. The current siren has long stood behind the company's former South Broad Street location, and its distinctive, loud sound is an endearing and minor disruption to those who live or work close to it. Motorized equipment was purchased with funds raised from the company's annual Fireman's Carnival, which was first held in 1922. This 1930 petition (below) from concerned citizens requests that the town allow the fire company to hold its carnival in town limits to pay down the debt on a "new motorized truck." (Both, courtesy of Middletown Historical Society.)

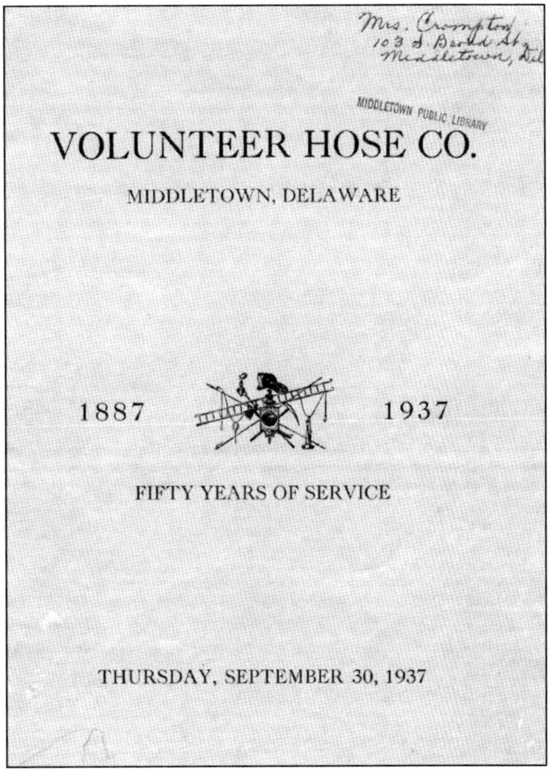

VOLUNTEER HOSE CO.

MIDDLETOWN, DELAWARE

1887 1937

FIFTY YEARS OF SERVICE

THURSDAY, SEPTEMBER 30, 1937

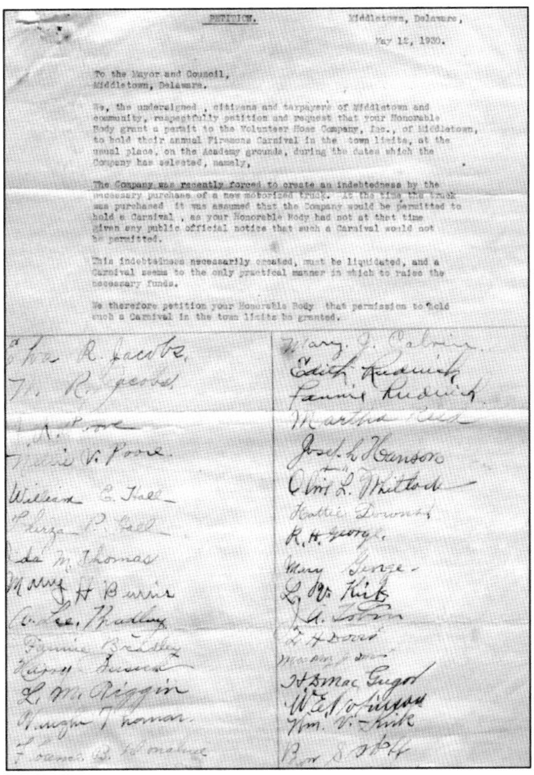

PETITION. Middletown, Delaware,

May 12, 1930.

To the Mayor and Council,
Middletown, Delaware.

We, the undersigned , citizens and taxpayers of Middletown and community, respectfully petition and request that your Honorable Body grant a permit to the Volunteer Hose Company, Inc., of Middletown, to hold their annual Firemens Carnival in the town limits, at the usual place, on the Academy grounds, during the dates which the Company has selected, namely,

The Company was recently forced to create an indebtedness by the necessary purchase of a new motorized truck. At the time the truck was purchased it was assumed that the Company would be permitted to hold a Carnival , as your Honorable Body had not at that time given any public official notice that such a Carnival would not be permitted.

This indebtedness necessarily created, must be liquidated, and a Carnival seems to the only practical manner in which to raise the necessary funds.

We therefore petition your Honorable Body that permission to hold such a Carnival in the town limits be granted.

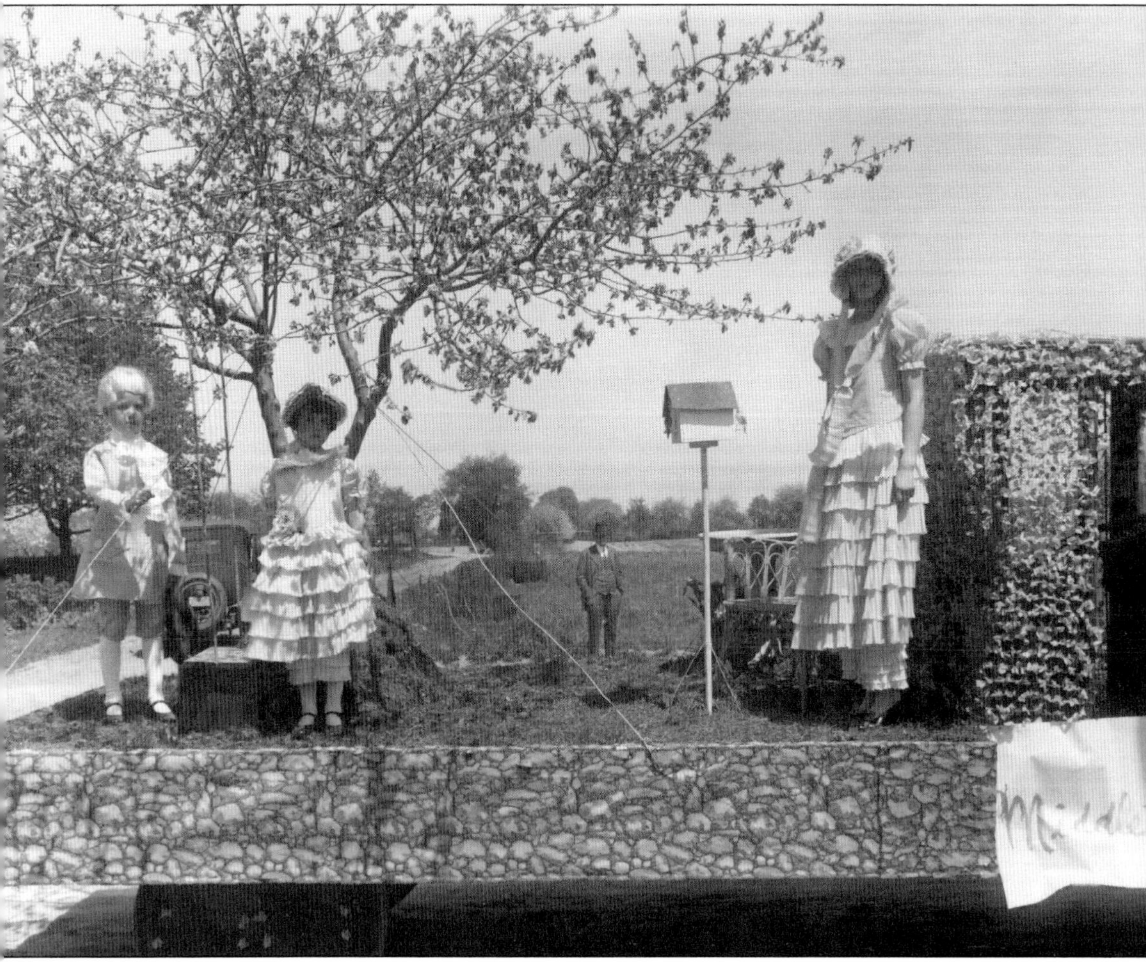

The Middletown New Century Club displayed this "garden scene float" during the May 1928 Apple Blossom Festival parade in Dover. The club was founded in 1897 and had a clubhouse built at 438 North Broad Street in 1916. Members of the club used their special skills to raise money for the clubhouse and were also paid from those funds. A *Middletown Transcript* article published on October 28, 1916, tells that the building's cornerstone—with the inscription, "New Century Club, 1916,"—was laid the previous Tuesday with ceremonies by the Masonic Order. An opening was carved into the side of the building for the cornerstone, which was placed alongside a metal box that contained a Bible; a US flag; photographs of Pres. Woodrow Wilson; names of federal, state, and town government and other officials; copies of the *Middletown Transcript*, *New Era*, and daily newspapers; the Masonic code of Delaware; a sketch of the Union Lodge No. 5; and many more gifts. The building cost about $6,500 and offered rental space for dances and other "entertainments." (Courtesy of Delaware Public Archives.)

SOUP

General Rules

Beef ranks first for soup making. Wipe meat with damp cloth, separate from bone, cut in inch cubes. Put in cold water and let stand 1 hour, then let come to a boil, if it boils at all it must be gently. The proportion of water to meat depends on the strength of the soup desired. All meat, or meat and bone may be used. The best is made from meat and bone, the more bone used, the stiffer will be the stock. Put on fire and bring to a boiling point. As scum rises it should be removed. Cook slowly 4 or 5 hours. To give the desirable golden color, brown 1-3 of the meat in hot frying pan in marrow from a marrow bone. In place of this sugar may be added or 1½ teaspoons kitchen boquet. Brown stock is made from beef 2-3 lean meat and remainder bone or fat highly seasoned. White stock is made from chicken or veal with delicate seasoning.

Brown Soup Stock

6 lbs. shin of beef — 3 qts. cold water
½ teaspoon peppercorns — 6 cloves
1 bay leaf — 3 sprigs thyme
1 tablespoon salt — 2 sprigs parsley

½ cup each cut in dice, carrot, turnip, onion and celery. Follow directions given under general rules.

White Soup Stock No. I

4 lbs. knuckle veal — 2 qts. cold water
1 tablespoon salt — ½ teaspoon peppercorns
2 stalks celery — 1 onion

Remove meat from bone and cut in small pieces. Add water and seasoning. Heat gradually to boiling point. Skim often, simmer 4 or 5 hours and strain.

White Soup Stock No. II

The water in which fowl or chicken is cooked makes White Stock.

Potato Soup

Peel and cut in dice 6 potatoes, ½ onion grated. Cut fine the rough pieces of 1 stalk of celery. Nearly cover with water, add salt to taste. Boil until tender. Add 1 pt. milk, 1 cup cream. Let come to a boil. Then drop in piece of butter size of walnut cut in bits and rolled in flour. Let cook a minute and serve.

—*Mrs. Clarence E. Pool.*

5

The Middletown New Century Club published a 1919 book, entitled *Reliable Recipes*, full of recipes from the kitchens of its members. In addition to soups, the book also includes recipes for fish and oysters, croquettes, fancy cakes, and candy. The dedication page reads: "The fate of nations depends on how they are fed." The club offered much to the community through volunteerism. A 1919 article in the *Middletown Transcript* states that the club would hold a meeting "in conjunction with some of the leading men of the town with the purpose of organizing a Law and Order Society in the hope of improving the general order of the town, especially on Saturday nights." More lighthearted offerings included meetings that featured the state chairman of arts and crafts and sponsorship of the local Parent-Teacher Association (founded in 1940) and a local Girl Scout troop in 1945. (Courtesy of Middletown Historical Society.)

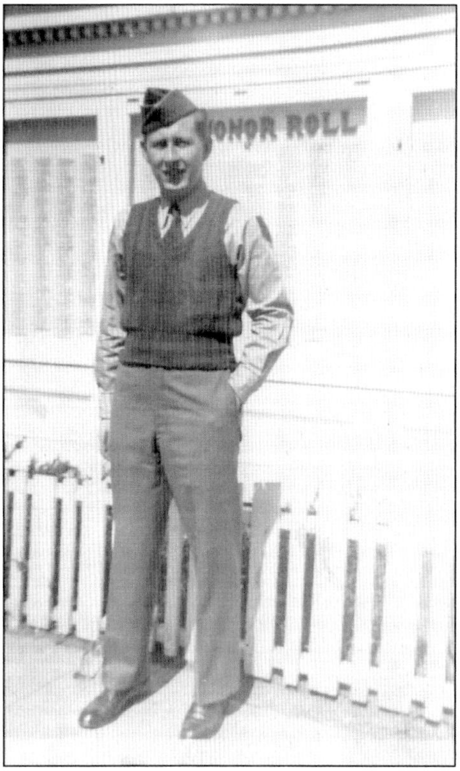

The unidentified soldier at left stands in front of the Middletown World War II Honor Roll, which was installed on May 31, 1944, in honor of local soldiers who fought in the war. The honor roll was located next to the (now former) Delaware Trust Bank building at the northwest corner of Main and Broad Streets, but was removed in June 1972 to make way for the bank's drive-through lane. Below, Middletown soldier W.W. Fellows is shown in his official military photograph that was sent to his mother, Ada Fellows. (Left, courtesy of *Middletown Transcript*; below, courtesy of Delaware Public Archives.)

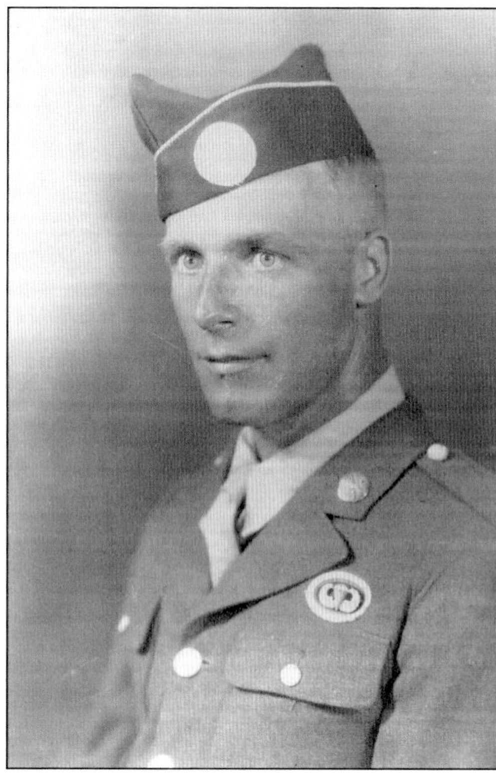

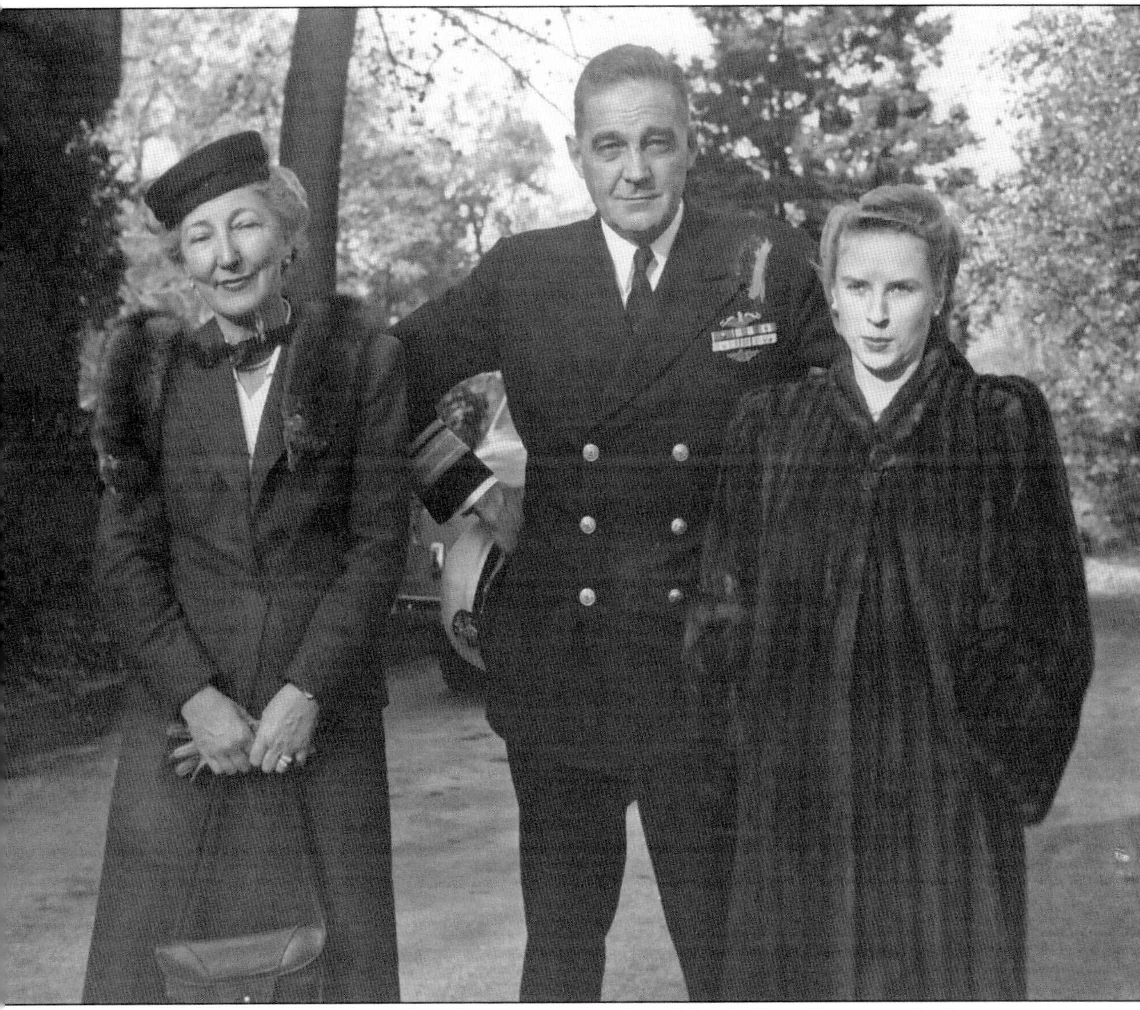

Rear Adm. John H. Brown Jr. and Nellie Janvier lived on North Cass Street with their two children, John H. Brown III and Mariana Brown. Admiral Brown, pictured here with Nellie and Mariana, was born in Canton, Pennsylvania, and entered the Naval Academy in 1910, where he excelled at football and also competed in rowing and track. After graduating in 1914, he went through submarine training and became commanding officer of the USS *C-2* in World War I. In the early 1930s, Admiral Brown became an instructor at the Naval Academy Department of Physical Training and managed athletics. He then became commander of the USS *Richmond*, which was stationed near Peru during Japan's attack on Pearl Harbor. Admiral Brown served as commander of Submarine Squadron Four from July 1942 to November 1943, when he became commander of Training Command, Submarine Force, Pacific Fleet. He also served as Deputy Commander, Submarines, Pacific Fleet. Admiral Brown was awarded the Distinguished Service Medal and the Legion of Merit with a gold star for his service during World War II. (Courtesy of Delaware Public Archives.)

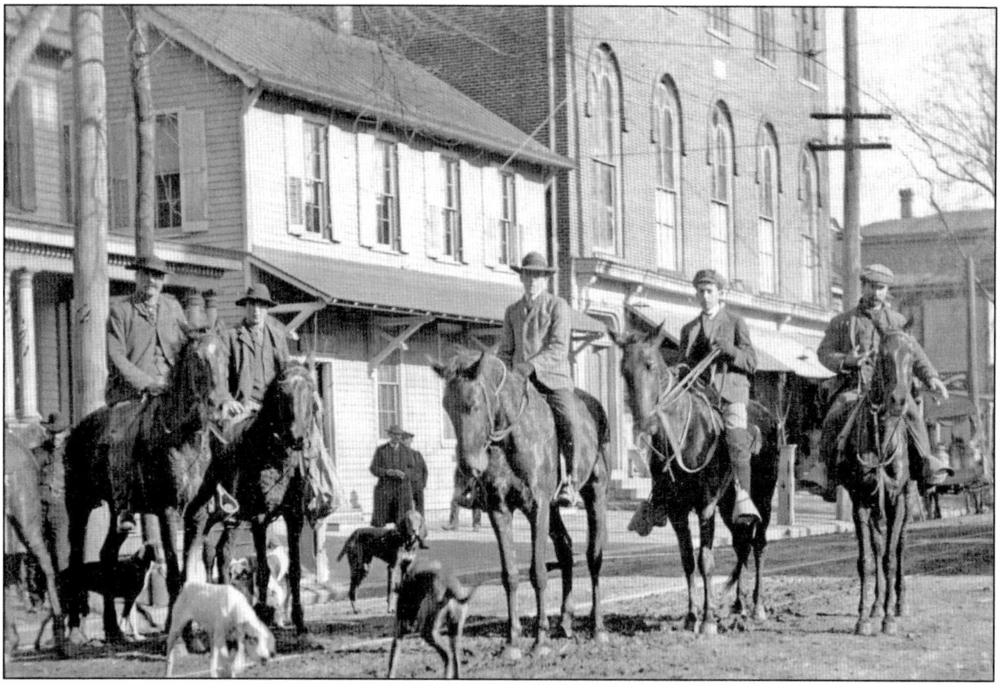

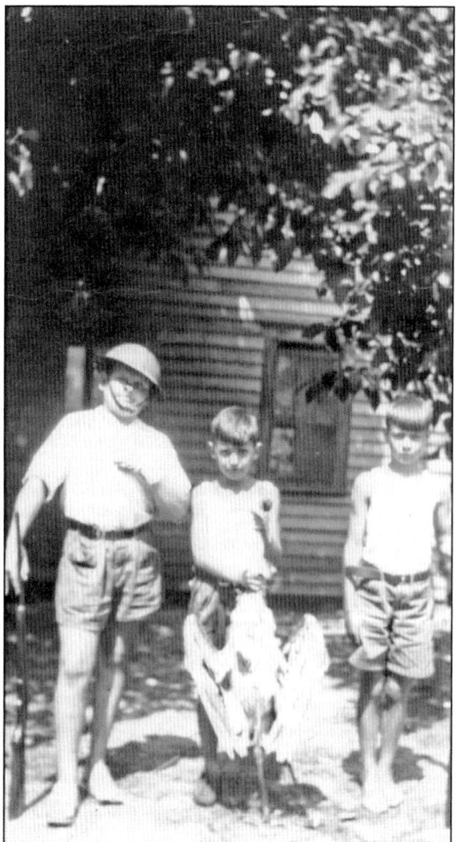

Maryland Fox Hunters gather in front of the Middletown Town Hall in this undated photograph. Fox hunts were announced in the *Middletown Transcript* newspaper. An article from December 28, 1886, mentions a hunt such as this. (Courtesy of Middletown Historical Society.)

Johnny Niles (left), Jack Ray (center), and Jimmy Barnhill pose for this 1932 photograph while attending Appoquinimink Boys' Camp at Silver Lake. The camp was founded the previous year with the backing of the Protestant Episcopal Church, Diocese of Delaware. The plan was to allow each church in the district to occupy the camp each week, but that proved to be impossible, and campers from multiple churches in the diocese came together for one-week stays. Each week, an average of 20 campers built skills in athletics, woodcraft, and Red Cross work. The Rev. H. Lee Marston led the camp throughout the year and held a special service at Old St. Anne's Church every Sunday. The camp was open from June through August and cost $10 per week to attend. A *Middletown Transcript* article states that its "interesting program" and nominal fee led to the camp reaching full capacity each week. (Courtesy of Middletown Historical Society.)

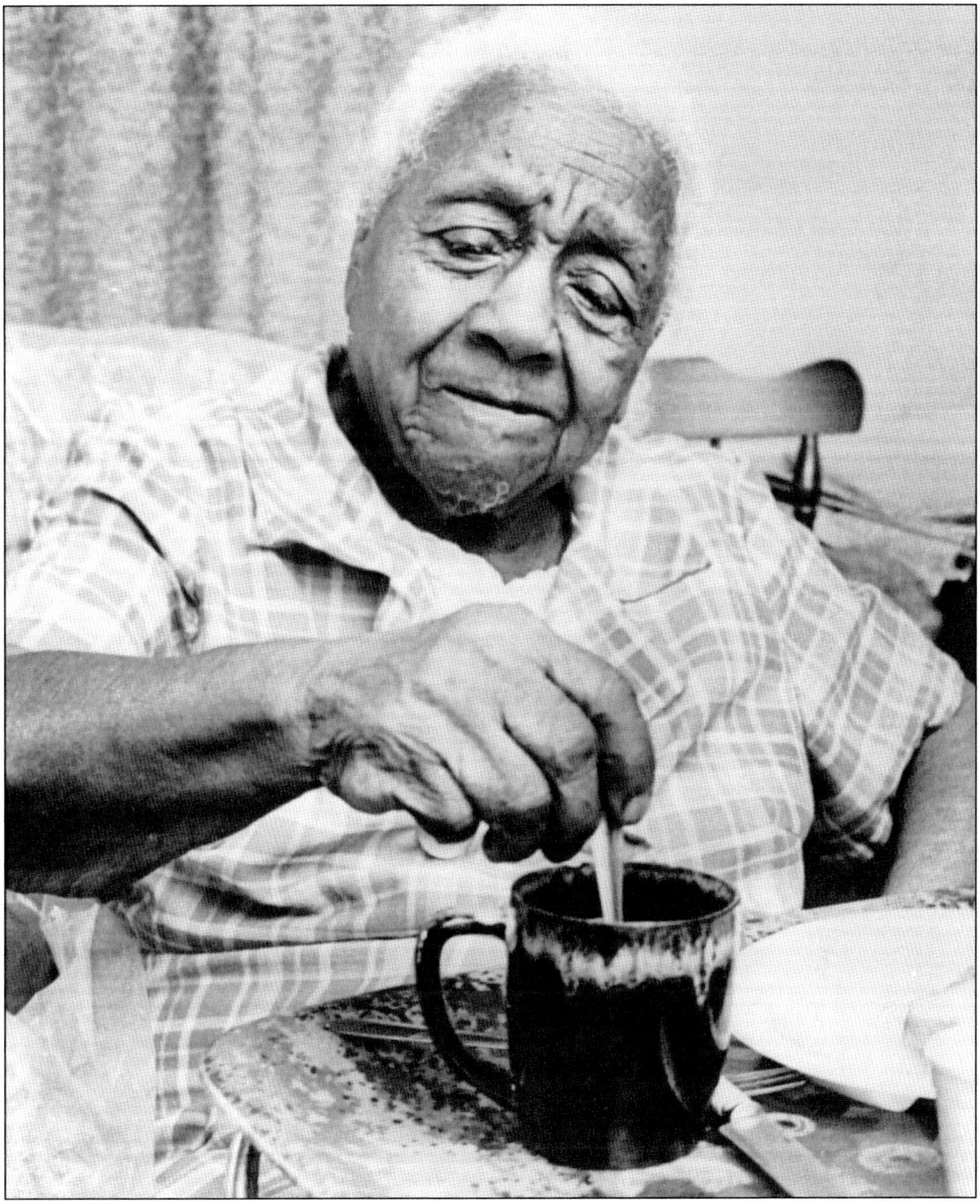

Clara Todd, who moved from Blanca (near Smyrna and Cheswold) to Middletown, is shown here at age 90. She and her husband, Oscar, had 17 children together: Francis, Emma, Viola, Sylvia, Cassie, Estella, Clara, Maryanna, Norman, Elwood, Elmer, Charles, Harry, Leroy, Courtney, Edward, and Solomon. Clara and Oscar resided at 308 New Street for decades. While Oscar worked on area farms, Clara washed clothing and cooked for local residents. She was a talented baker who made pies and other baked goods to sell for the benefit of Dale United Methodist Church. The Todds and their neighbors were very friendly and helpful, and kept an eye on each other's children. Clara and Oscar taught their children and grandchildren to put their faith first, to love others, and to work hard for what they want in life. They were very family-oriented, and their many descendants continue to hold a family reunion every two years, with an informal gathering during off years. (Courtesy of Betty Todd.)

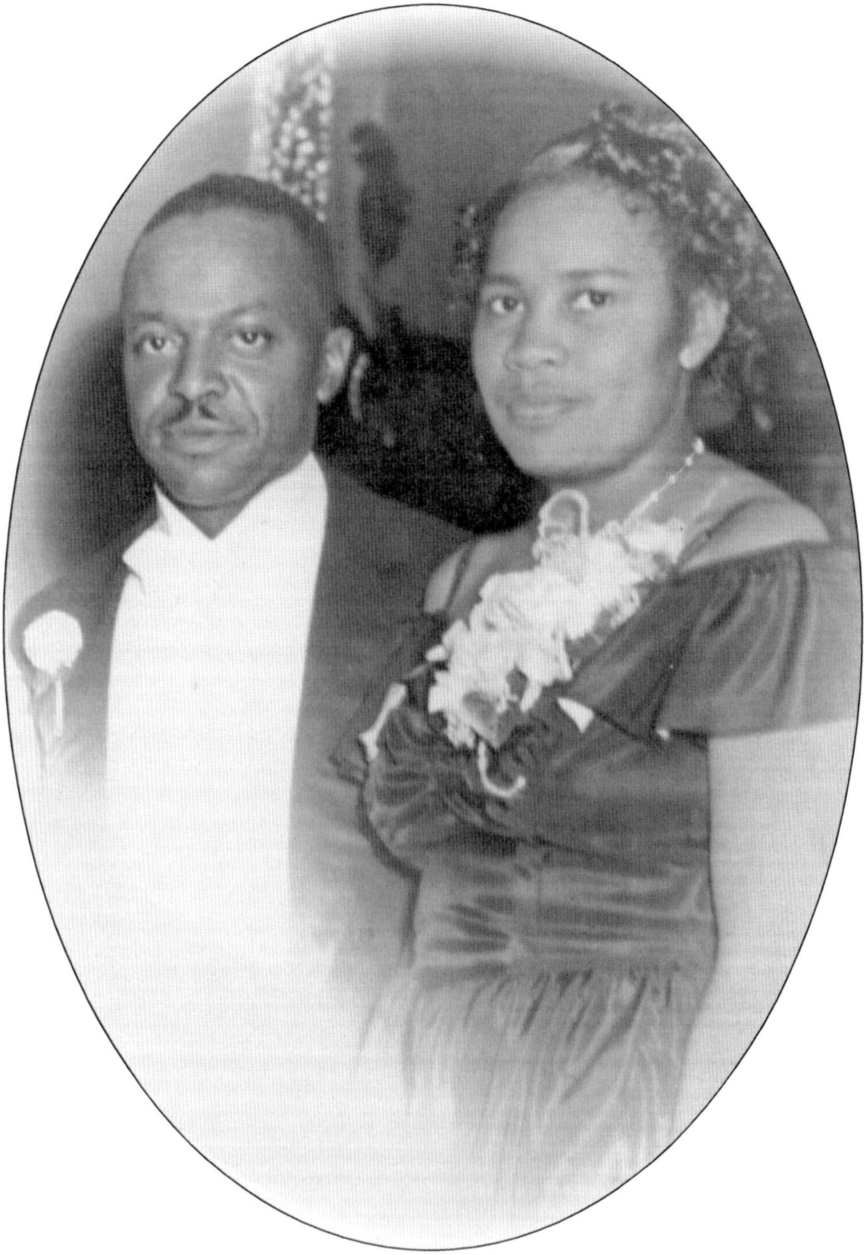

Ethel and John F. Lloyd of Mount Pleasant are pictured at the Cotton Club, a nightclub and beer garden on East Lake Street in the mid-20th century. Russell and Leah Draper owned the club and operated it out of their house with the help of Leah's brother, Otis Jefferson. It was a popular spot for black people, many of whom came from Townsend, Warwick (Maryland), and as far away as Wilmington to socialize and listen and dance to music on Friday and Saturday nights. Live music was provided by an all-female group, the Sweethearts of Rhythm, and a variety of four- and five-piece bands, who played many genres of music and featured saxophones, pianos, and horns to entertain the packed venue. A bar was located at the front of the building, with a dance floor, a stage, and open space toward the back. During the week, patrons could purchase beer and bottles of liquor from the club. (Courtesy of Betty Todd.)

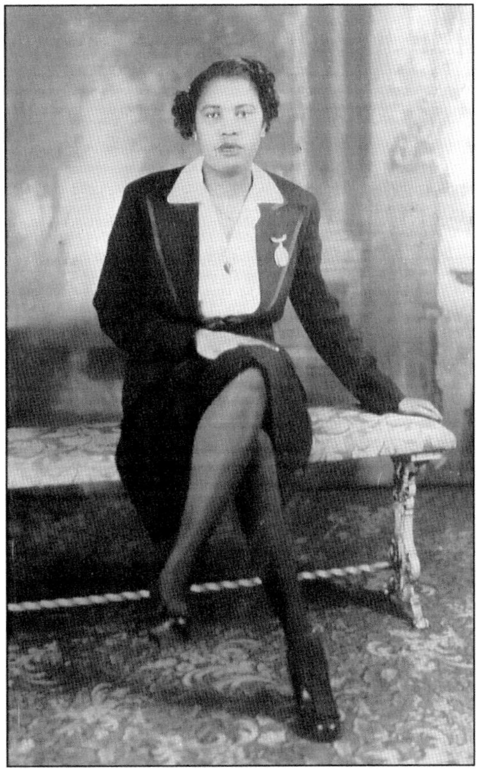

The daughters of Frank and Grace Blackson, Ethel May (Blackson) Lloyd (right) and Frances (Blackson) Hopkins (below), were raised in a house on Route 896 in Mount Pleasant, just north of Middletown. They both attended the Mount Pleasant School 119c. Both sisters worked at a powder plant in Elkton, Maryland, where they helped make explosives for use in World War II. Frances then worked for the University of Delaware, from which she retired. One of Ethel's three children was Betty Todd, a longtime resident of East Lake Street. Her two other children were Frank A. Scott and Martina (Lloyd) Ortiz. The family later lived in downtown Middletown. (Both, courtesy of Betty Todd.)

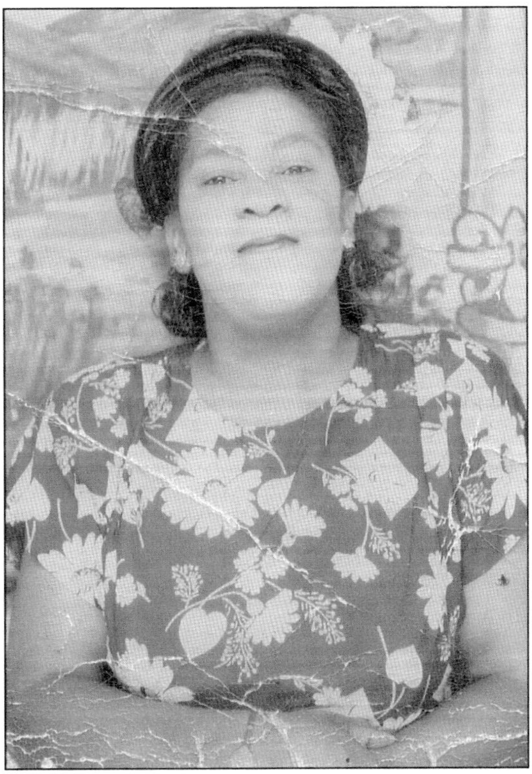

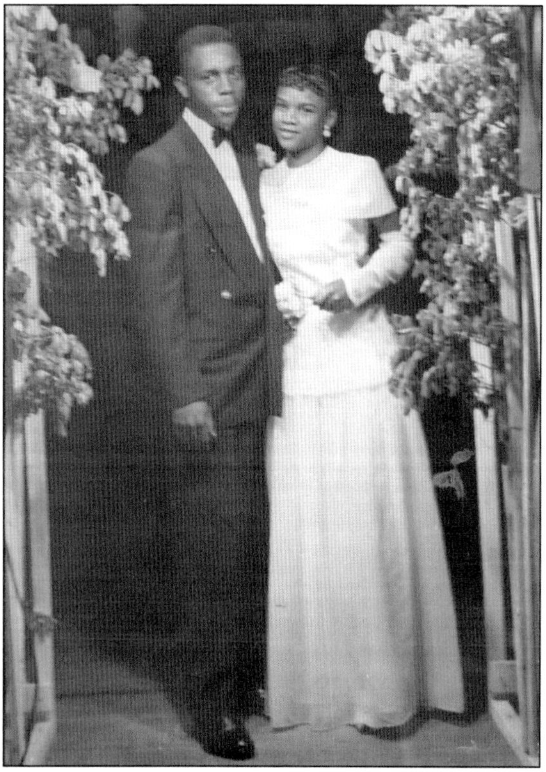

Longtime Middletown residents Betty (Blackson) and Norman H. Todd met in school and starting dating in 1948. The 1950 prom photograph at left shows the beginning of their lives together. Betty was a 1950 graduate of the Middletown School 120c, and Norman served in the Army from 1950 to 1952. They lived on Jefferson Street until Norman built their home on the corner of East Lake and New Streets, where they raised six children together—three boys and three girls. They are pictured in the 1960s photograph below at a dance held by the Noble Gentlemen social club at the National Guard armory on North Cass Street. Other longtime residents who lived in the East Lake Street area included the Saunders, Walker, Frisbee, Henry, Draper, Williams, Wiggins, Jefferson, Perkins, Hanks, Morris, Miles, Moody, Rhodes, Marvel, Waters, Empsons, Satterfield, Gomez, and Brinkley families. (Both, courtesy of Betty Todd.)

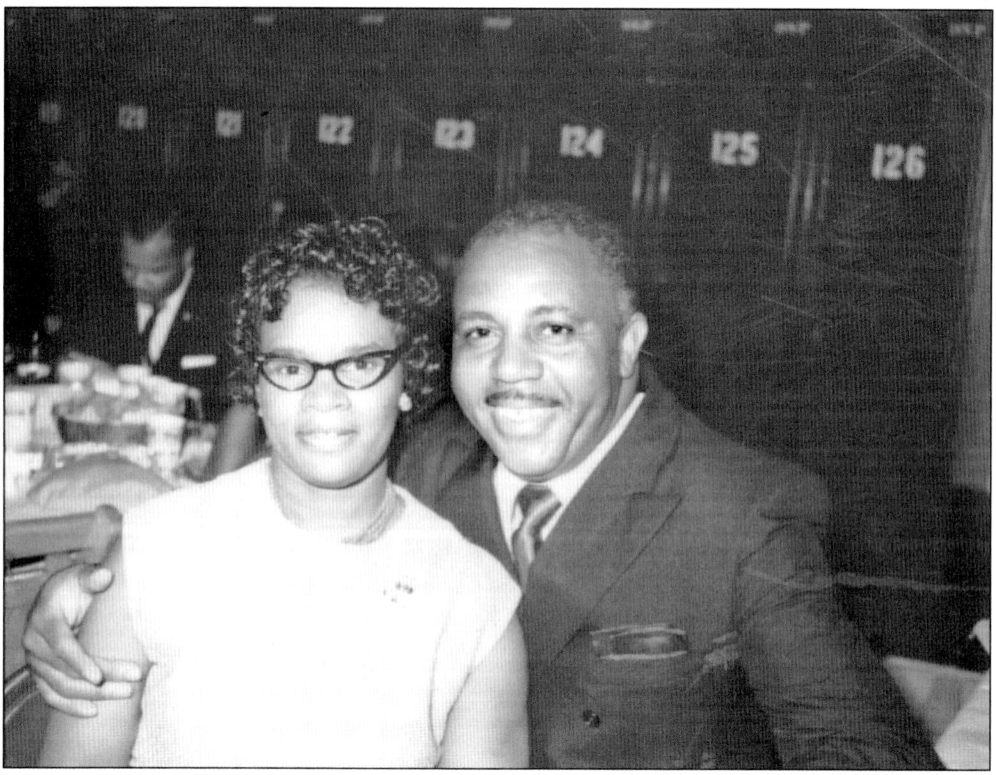

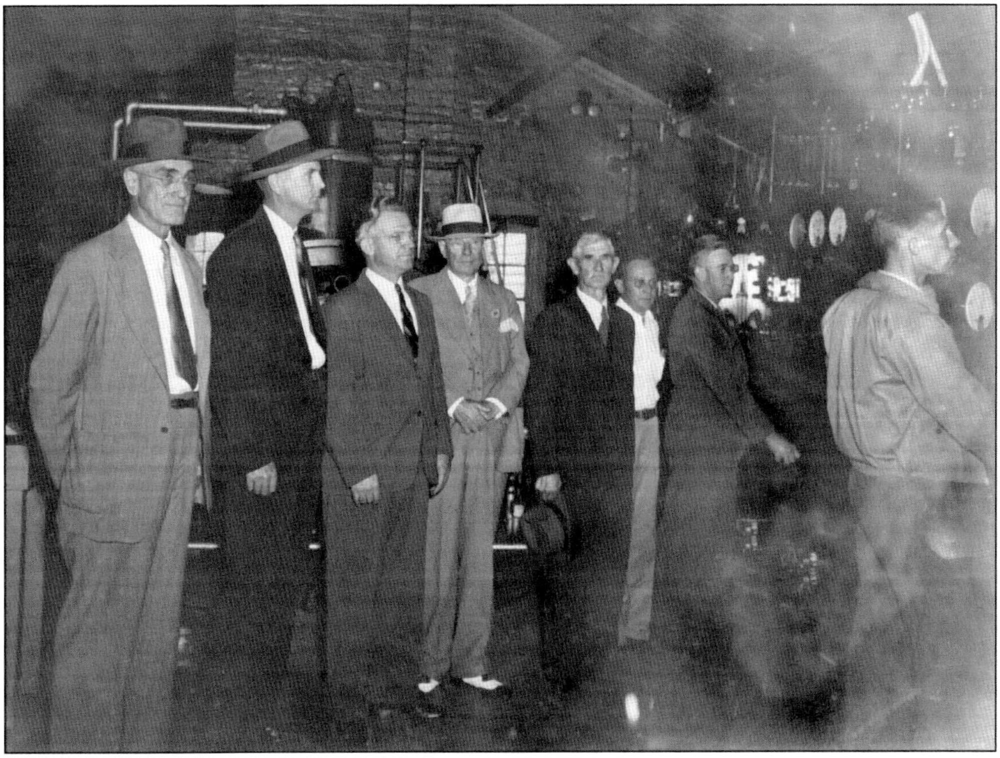

This September 4, 1946, image shows C.E. Taylor, J.D. Waddell, C.D. Appleby, M.G. Kennedy, William Price, Wallace Hufnal, acting mayor Herbert Phillips, and L. Clark Ennis in an unspecified location. (Courtesy of Middletown Historical Society.)

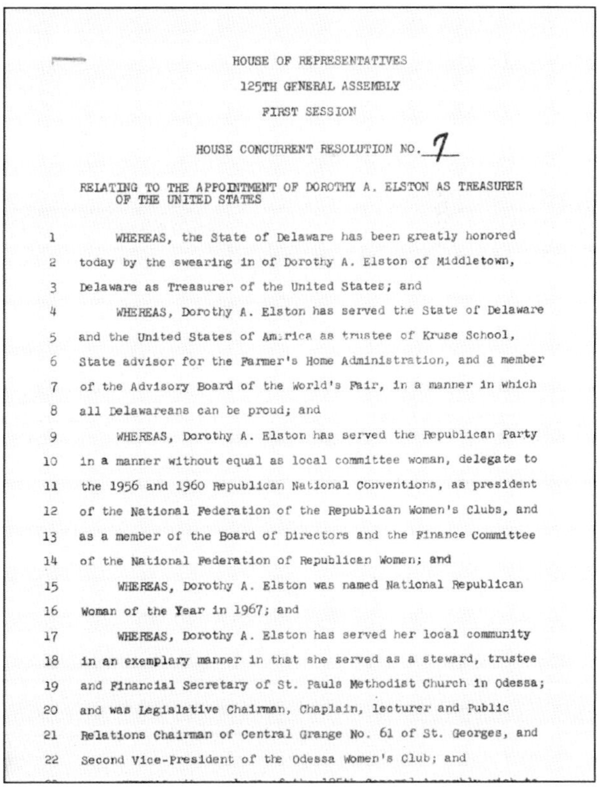

HOUSE OF REPRESENTATIVES

125TH GENERAL ASSEMBLY

FIRST SESSION

HOUSE CONCURRENT RESOLUTION NO. 7

RELATING TO THE APPOINTMENT OF DOROTHY A. ELSTON AS TREASURER OF THE UNITED STATES

WHEREAS, the State of Delaware has been greatly honored today by the swearing in of Dorothy A. Elston of Middletown, Delaware as Treasurer of the United States; and

WHEREAS, Dorothy A. Elston has served the State of Delaware and the United States of America as trustee of Kruse School, State advisor for the Farmer's Home Administration, and a member of the Advisory Board of the World's Fair, in a manner in which all Delawareans can be proud; and

WHEREAS, Dorothy A. Elston has served the Republican Party in a manner without equal as local committee woman, delegate to the 1956 and 1960 Republican National Conventions, as president of the National Federation of the Republican Women's Clubs, and as a member of the Board of Directors and the Finance Committee of the National Federation of Republican Women; and

WHEREAS, Dorothy A. Elston was named National Republican Woman of the Year in 1967; and

WHEREAS, Dorothy A. Elston has served her local community in an exemplary manner in that she served as a steward, trustee and Financial Secretary of St. Pauls Methodist Church in Odessa; and was Legislative Chairman, Chaplain, lecturer and Public Relations Chairman of Central Grange No. 61 of St. Georges, and Second Vice-President of the Odessa Women's Club; and

Middletown resident Dorothy A. Elston was appointed treasurer of the United States in 1969 and was sworn into office by the 125th Delaware General Assembly with this House Concurrent Resolution No. 7. Elston served as a delegate to the Republican National Convention in 1956 and as an alternate in 1960, was president of the National Federation of Republican Women from 1962 to 1967, and was named Republican Woman of the Year in 1967. (Courtesy of Middletown Historical Society.)

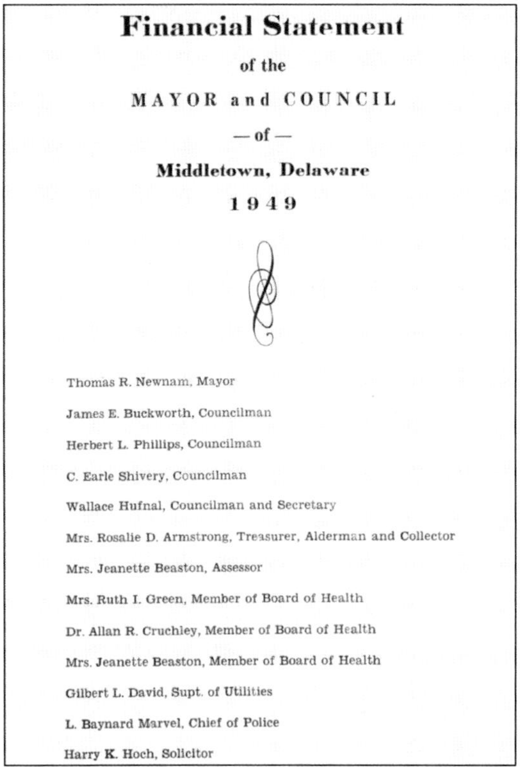

Financial Statement

of the

MAYOR and COUNCIL

— of —

Middletown, Delaware

1949

Thomas R. Newnam, Mayor

James E. Buckworth, Councilman

Herbert L. Phillips, Councilman

C. Earle Shivery, Councilman

Wallace Hufnal, Councilman and Secretary

Mrs. Rosalie D. Armstrong, Treasurer, Alderman and Collector

Mrs. Jeanette Beaston, Assessor

Mrs. Ruth I. Green, Member of Board of Health

Dr. Allan R. Cruchley, Member of Board of Health

Mrs. Jeanette Beaston, Member of Board of Health

Gilbert L. David, Supt. of Utilities

L. Baynard Marvel, Chief of Police

Harry K. Hoch, Solicitor

This financial statement of the 1949 mayor and council includes the financial expenditures of the town for that year, as well as prominent people who served the town. Names include Mayor Thomas R. Newnam; councilmen James E. Buckworth, C. Earle Shivery, and Wallace Hufnal; Rosalie D. Armstrong, treasurer, alderman, and collector; Jeanette Beaston, assessor; Gilbert L. David, superintendent of utilities; L. Baynard Marvel, police chief; and Harry K. Hoch, solicitor. The 1955 photograph below shows Mayor John N. Sparks (in bow tie), who was instrumental in starting the Middletown Historical Society, to which he donated a large collection of pictures and information. (Both, courtesy of Middletown Historical Society.)

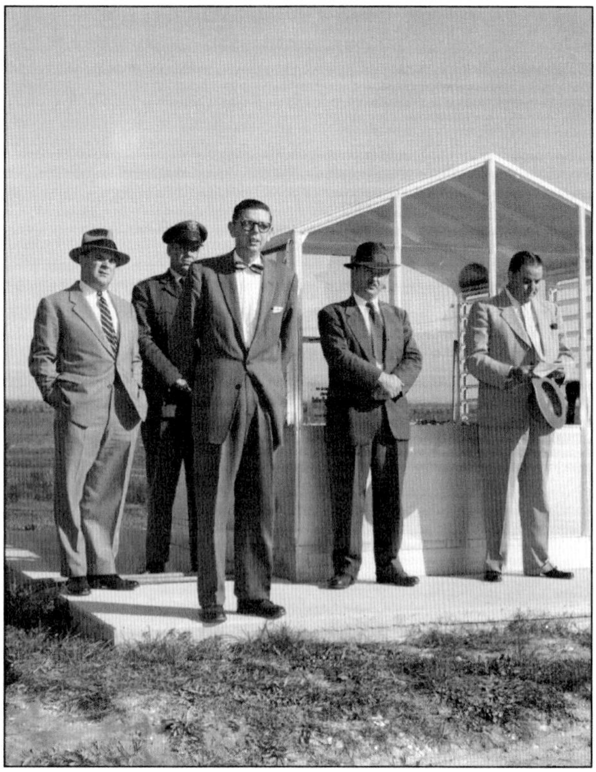

Six

EDUCATION

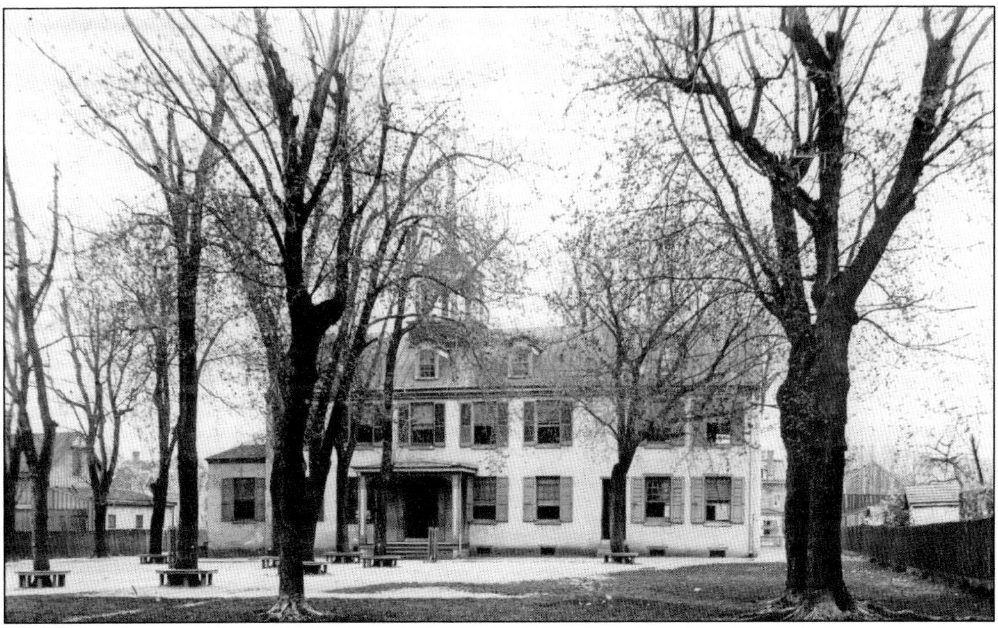

The Middletown Academy, the oldest educational institution on record in the area, opened in 1827 as a private school on North Broad Street and offered English and classical education, with two sessions held each year. The cost for education in the "English branches of education" was $8 per session, and mathematics and languages cost $10 per session. Rev. Joseph Wilson was first to supervise at the school, with Isabella Anderson serving as head of the female students. In the 1840s, some residents expressed displeasure at the management of the school, but education was not affected. The academy became public in 1876 when School Districts 60 and 94 merged and rented the building for $5 per term, which was later reduced to $1 per term. Once the public school building opened on South Broad Street in 1929, the academy was no longer needed. (Courtesy of Scott Lawrence.)

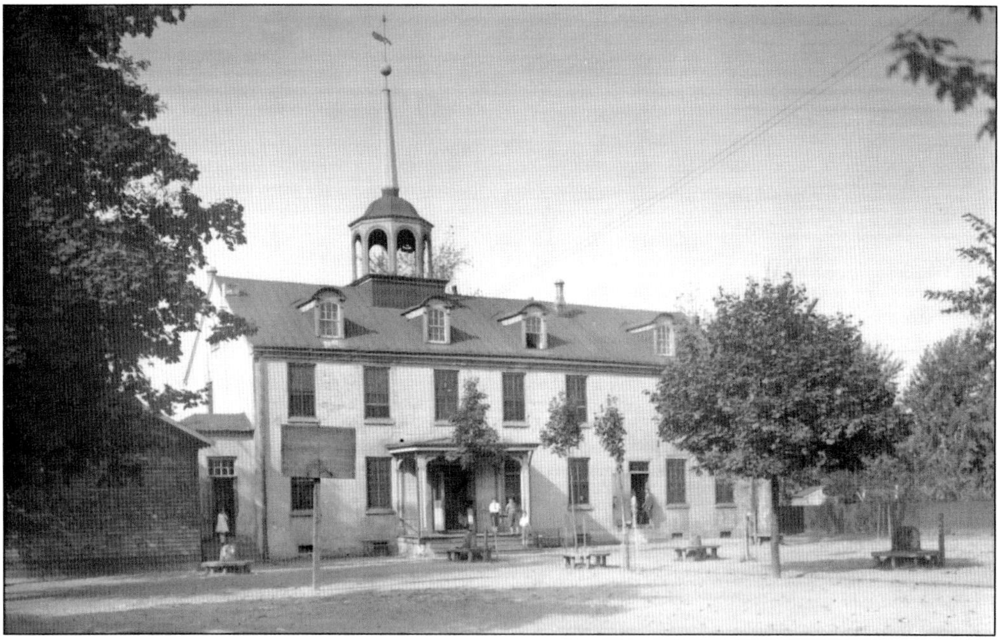

The appearance of Middletown Academy, known as "Old Academy," has changed throughout the years. The school added a dining room and kitchen in 1865, plus another $4,700 section in the late 1800s, when it became a public school. The academy suffered a fire in January 1903 and had to close its doors for several months. In 1945, the government sold the building to the St. George's Hundred Historical Society, which was organized to save it. Its central structure remains relatively the same, and in 1960, it was deeded by the historical society to the town for community use. It has housed the town hall, the Middletown police, a public library, and, at the date of publication, is shared by the Middletown Historical Society and the Middletown Area Chamber of Commerce. (Above, courtesy of Delaware Public Archives; below, courtesy of Middletown Historical Society.)

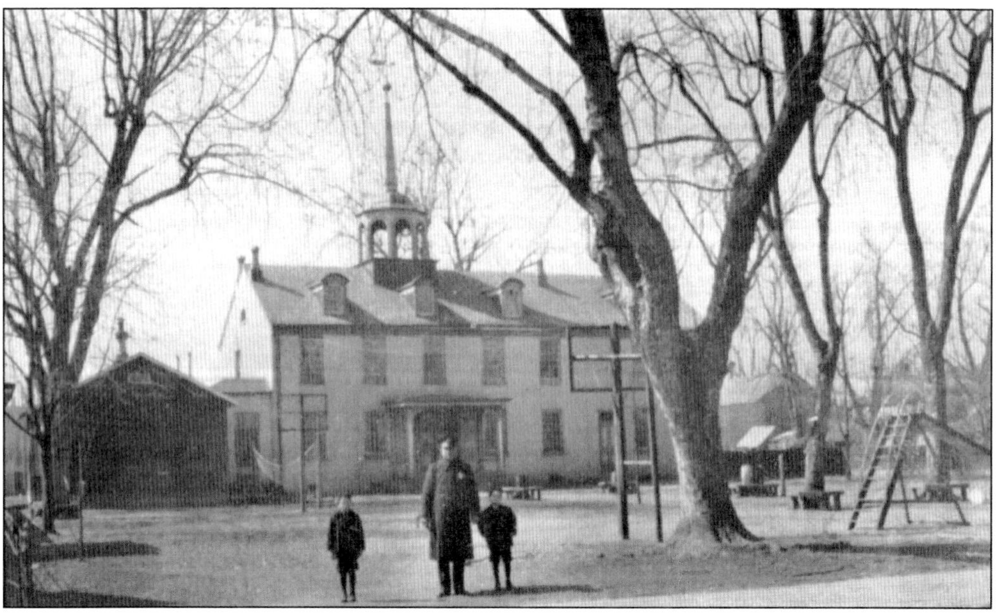

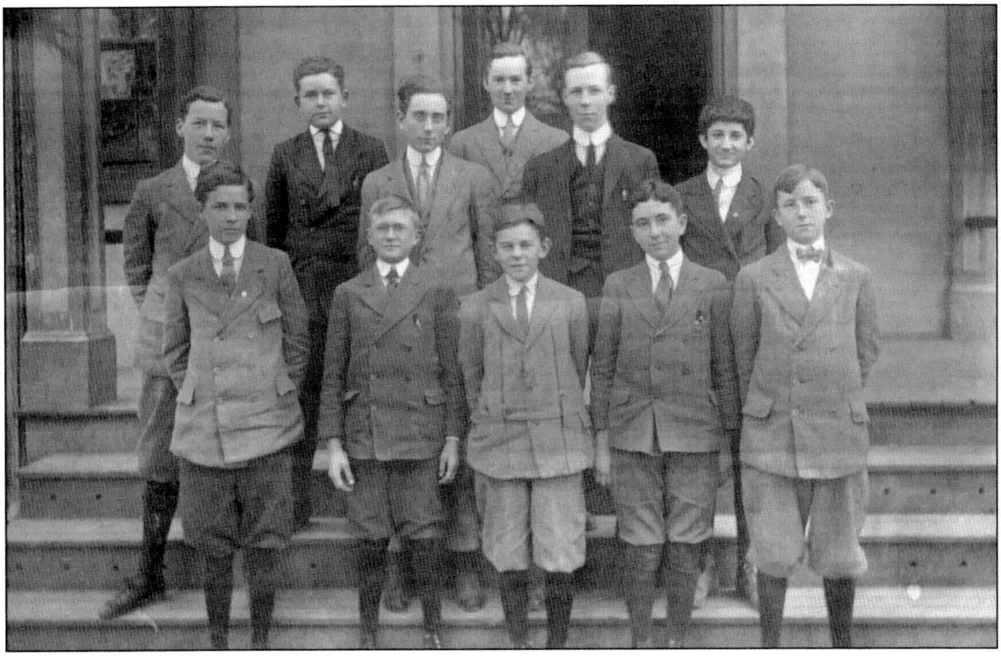

The private Middletown Academy offered students a "good English and classical education." The school year included two sessions with a short break in between. In 1840, principal William Harris reported that 33 pupils attended school in the building, and tuition was $430. Discipline was to be "administered with firmness, yet with parental kindness," and students were encouraged to "behave toward one another in a mild, obliging manner, carefully avoiding all angry disputes and quarrels" when out of school. They were not allowed to visit taverns, balls, dances, or other similar events, nor were they permitted to partake in card games or other "harmful and destructive games." The men of the class of 1911 are pictured above, and the class of 1914 is below. (Both, courtesy of Middletown Historical Society.)

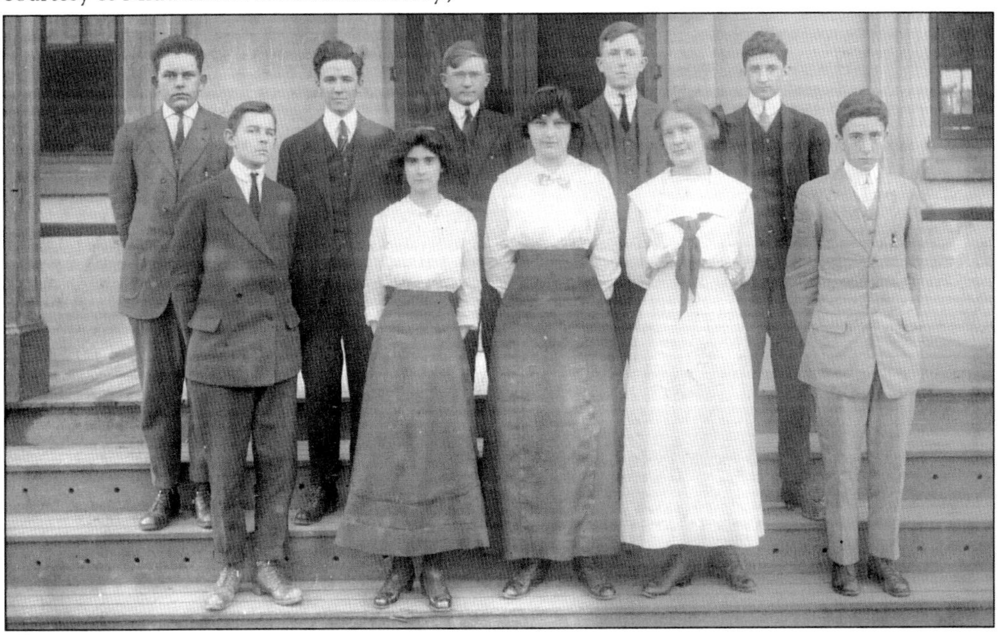

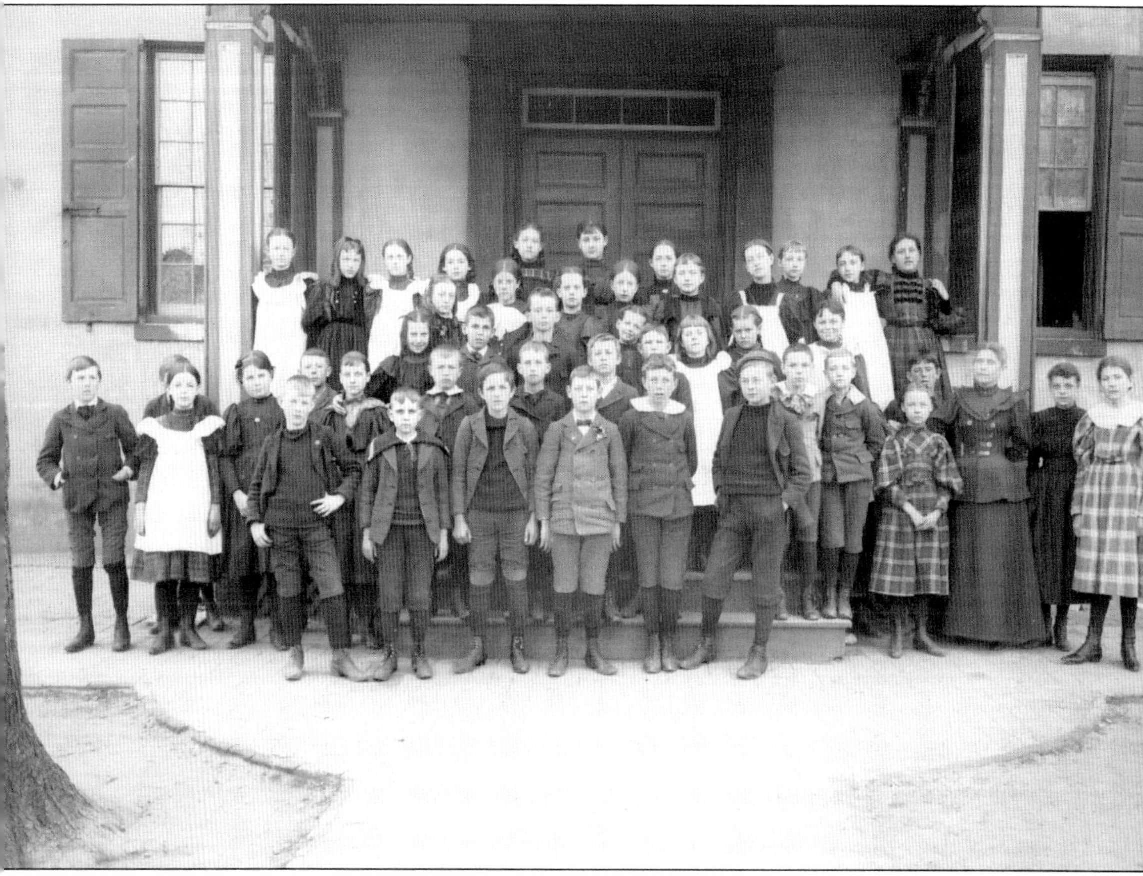

This Middletown Academy class photograph shows how the school grew to educate many more than 33 students by the late 1800s. In this 1897 image, the fifth-and-sixth-grade class is shown in front of the historic building with teacher Mary Price. (Courtesy of Middletown Historical Society.)

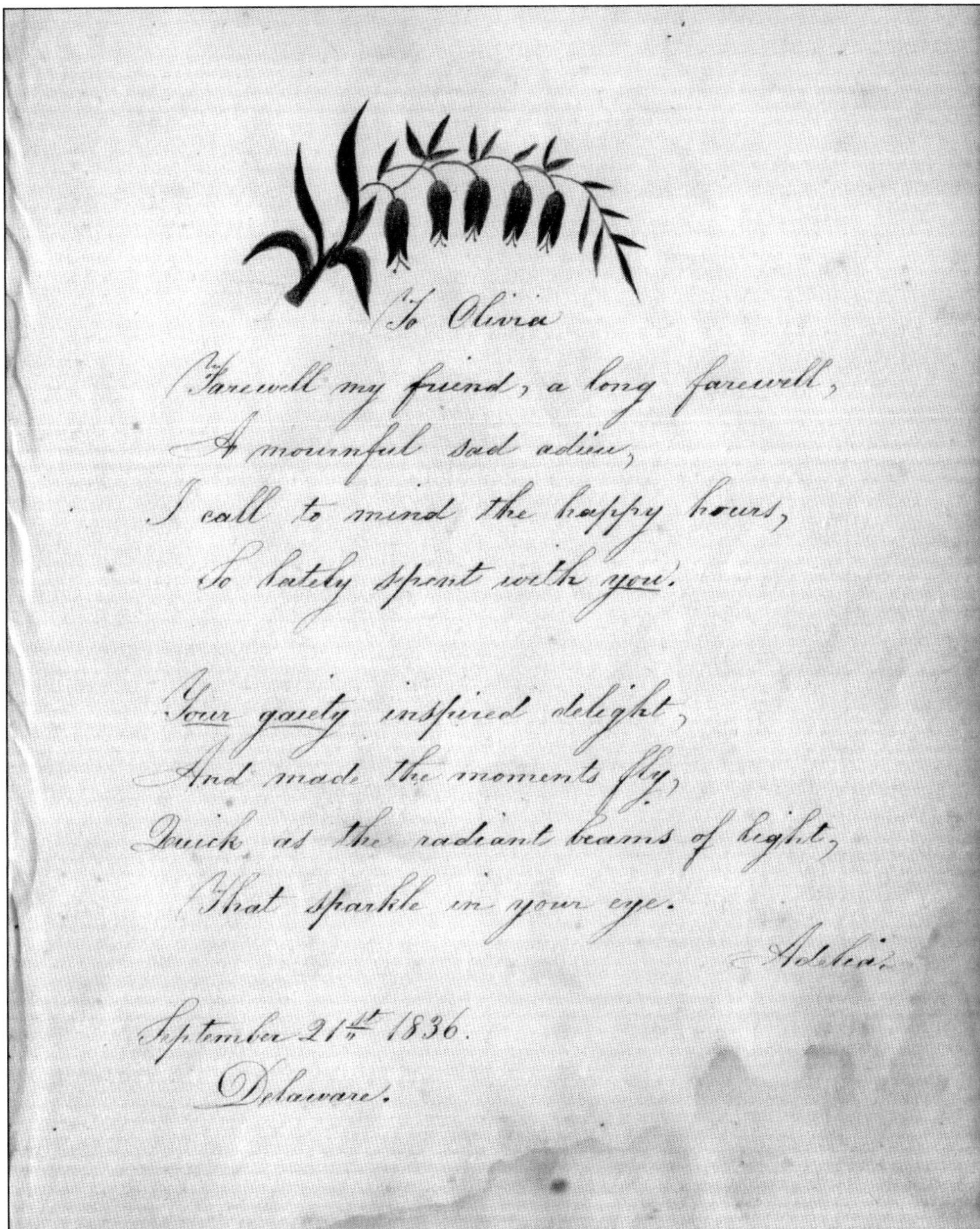

To Olivia

Farewell my friend, a long farewell,
A mournful sad adieu,
I call to mind the happy hours,
So lately spent with you.

Your gaiety inspired delight,
And made the moments fly,
Quick as the radiant beams of light,
That sparkle in your eye.

Adelia.

September 21st 1836.
Delaware.

This poem was written on September 21, 1836, in Olivia Rebecca Cochran's friendship book. Cochran, who lived just west of Middletown, used the book to collect autographs, artwork, and poems from Delaware friends and classmates from Christiana, Newark, and Cantwell's Bridge, as well as from friends and classmates at a boarding school in Pennsylvania. The poem "To Olivia" reads: "Farewell my friend, a long farewell, / A mournful sad adieu, / I call to mind the happy hours, / So lately spent with you. / Your gaiety inspired delight, / And made the moments fly, / Quick as the radiant beams of light, / That sparkle in your eye." The green leaves and red flowers at the top were delicately painted. (Courtesy of David and Alison Matsen.)

Middletown's 'Old Academy'

THE OLD ACADEMY

By Al Berkman

Old Derelict, with sagging sills and dome—
The welcome worn from off thy rotting door,
You seem so bare, so friendless and alone,
The dust lies thick upon your splintered floor.
Although the Hand of Time has passed your way
And stilled the merry voices you once knew
Some wandering sons and daughters far away,
Remember still—and cherish thoughts of you.

Those empty rooms. They were not always so.
Their memories—how they clutch my very heart.
With life and laughter once they seemed to glow
And of our lives became an active part.
From primary thru graduation day
By woes made dark, by happiness made bright,
Their teachings more than once have paved the way,
And proved a watchword thru the lonely night.

The bell up in the belfry rings no more—
A relic—yes—but what a priceless gem.
Ah! would its tongue could clamor as of yore
To call the ones now grown to women and to men.
Hundreds once made haste its dictates to obey
Some with a laughing heart, while others yet felt blue
And now, the whispering breezes seem to say,
"School's out for you old bell—school's out for you."

Deep scarred and old and touched by frosts of Fall—
A grey old monk, philosopher and sage!
A prideless place, yet very proud withal,
A beauty's pride that scorns the touch of Age.
Despite thy scars, despite thy sagging sill,
You sense good cheer from mossy step to dome,
No breath of Time nor Winter frosts can chill
The love we bear to thee, no matter where we roam!

Lines written December 1931, upon seeing the old forsaken schoolhouse crumbling in decay.

Al Berkman crafted this poem in 1931 about the Old Academy building, which sat vacant at the time. In 1945, he wrote a letter to Clarence P. Weber requesting that certain lines be omitted and the final eight be replaced with, "Though old and scarred and crumbling in decay / A wise old Sage, with wisdom of the years. / Forsaken once—You'll know a brighter day, / And soon will take your place with other seers. / Though once, we passed you by in proud disdain: / We hallow now your sagging walls and dome. / Through winter's coldest frost, there will remain / The love we have for you, no matter where we roam." Berkman was not alone in his nostalgia for the treasured school; in 1918, former academy instructor Ida Howell, who continued to teach local students after the academy closed in 1929, also penned a poem with lines such as, "The laughing boys and girls of yore / Whose voices come to us no more" and "The breezes sigh—our hearts do, too, To break with the old is hard to do." (Courtesy of Middletown Historical Society.)

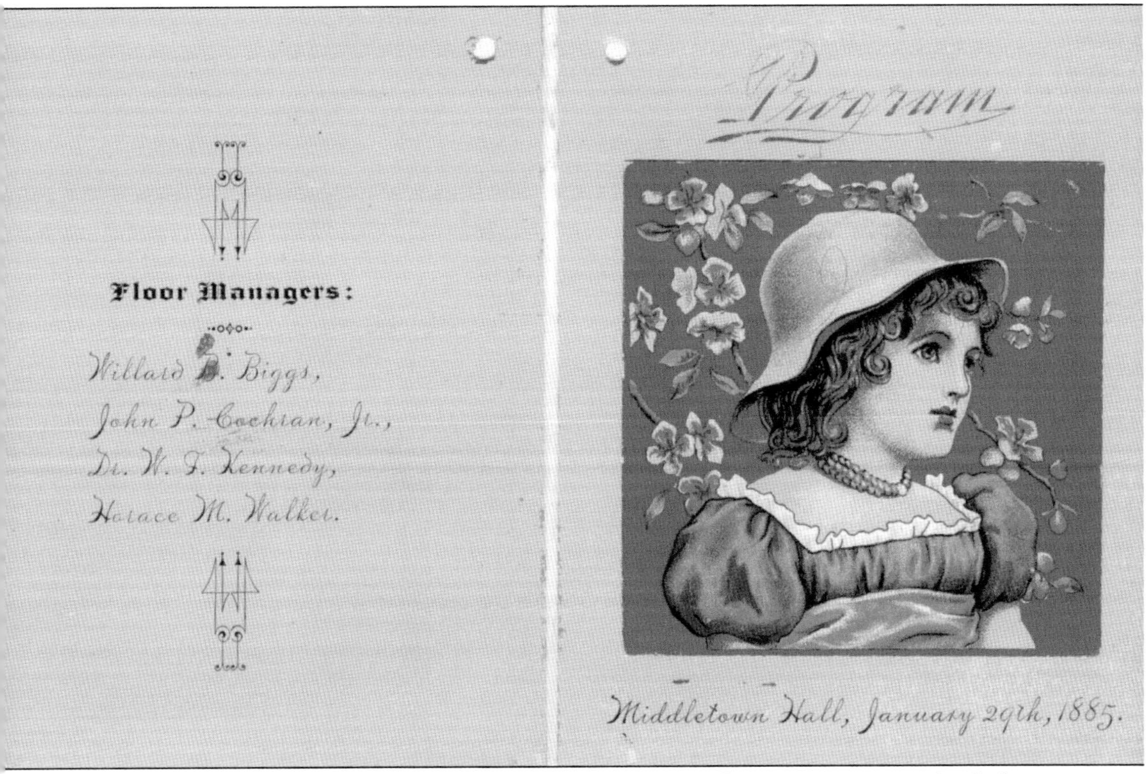

This 1885 dance card, printed by Middletown-based Freeman and Reeve, is an example of what was given to each young lady who attended such dances. The cards listed the schedule of dances, also called "engagements," for the evening. A young man would "reserve" a dance with a lady by signing his name next to one of the engagements on her dance card. Reserving one lady for more than four dances was frowned upon. The style of dance, the name of the song, and the composer were included, along with many opportunities for young ladies to dance with young gentlemen. This particular card shows that the dance was held at the Middletown Hall with an evening of 20 separate engagements and a range of dance styles, including a waltz-glide to "Queen's Lace Handkerchief" by Johann Strauss II and a schottische to "Hurry Little Children, Sunday Morn" by David Braham. (Courtesy of Middletown Historical Society.)

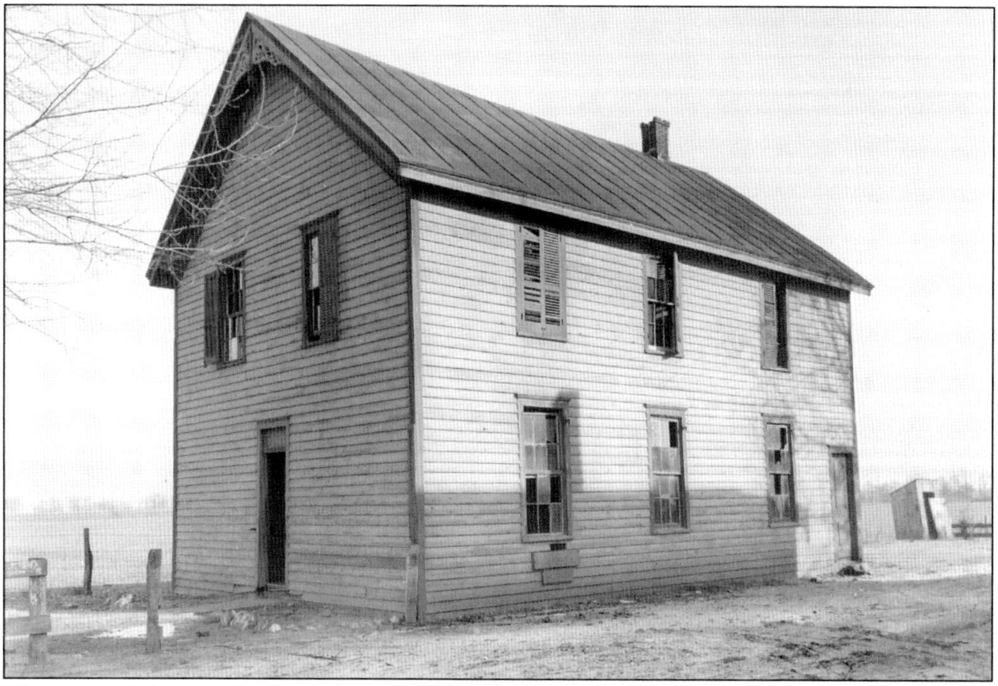

The original Summit Bridge School 116c for black children (above) was abandoned after the construction of a new two-room building (below) that was erected in 1922 and cost $10,730.40. Construction began on May 25, 1922, and the structure was completed on October 17, 1922. The school served students from grades 1 through 6 in the Summit area (north of Middletown) until it was closed after the 1942–1943 school year. Students then went to the Louis L. Redding Comprehensive School 120 in Middletown. Trustees and teachers during the Summit Bridge School's final year were chairman Andrew Davis, clerk Thomas Gould, Herbert Chandler, Vince Lilly, and Carrie Raisin. Other southern New Castle County schools for black children included St. George's 117c, Mount Pleasant 119c, Middletown 120c, Odessa 121c, Port Penn 122c, Congotown 123c, Lee's Chapel 124c, Townsend 125c, Ebenezer 126c, Taylors Bridge 127c, and Green Spring 128c. (Both, courtesy of Delaware Public Archives.)

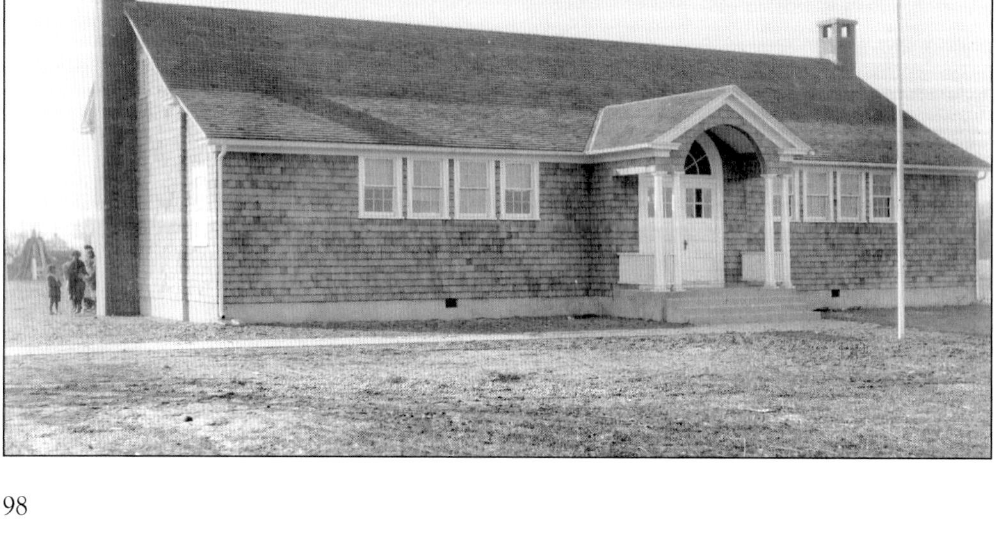

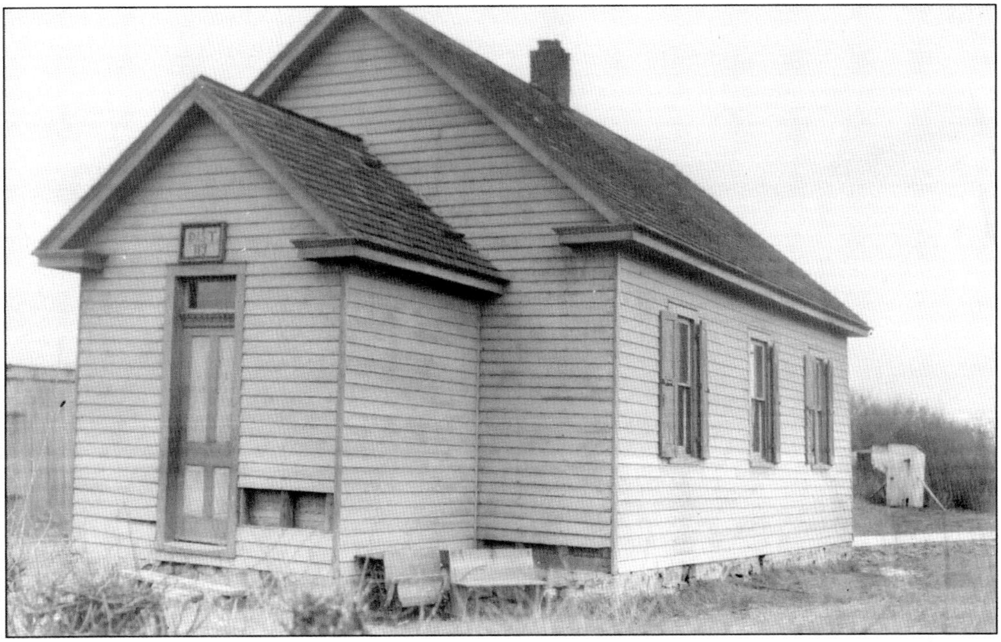

The original Mount Pleasant School 119c for black children (above) was abandoned to make way for a new one-room building (below), which was constructed from September 19, 1922, to January 30, 1923. It served students in grades 1 through 6 who lived a few miles north of Middletown town limits. The cost to build the school was $7,808.74. Anna Russum prepared students in grades 1 through 6 for education at the Middletown School 120c in downtown Middletown. Russum wore many hats during the school day. According to former students Martha Harvey and Elizabeth Ross, she made the fire; cooked breakfast and fed her students; served as gym teacher, choir conductor, and drama teacher; and also held spelling bees. An educational directory from 1914 shows teachers at schools for black children earned an annual salary of between $30 and $35. (Both, courtesy of Delaware Public Archives.)

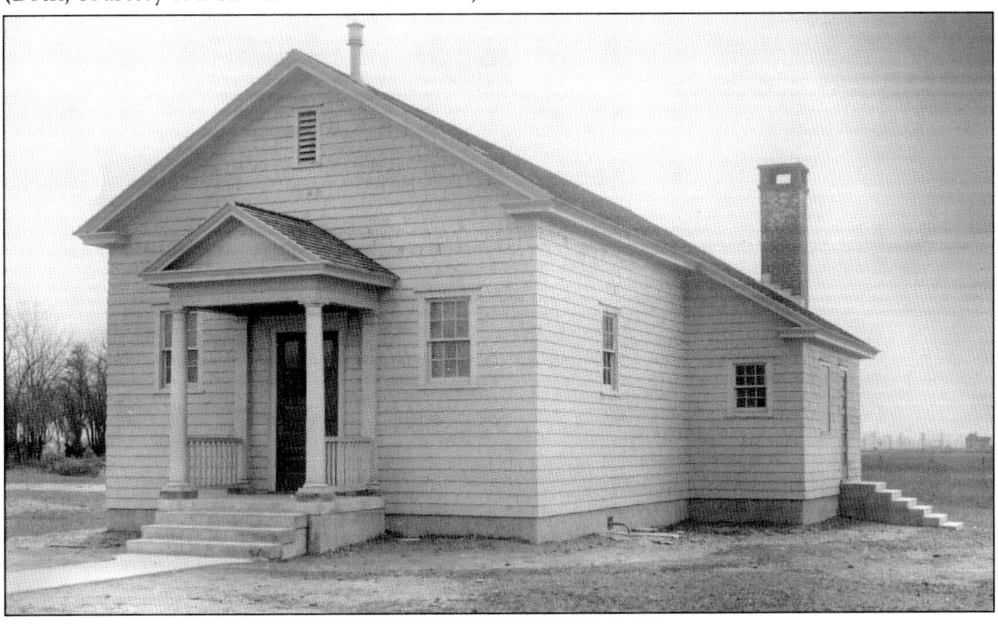

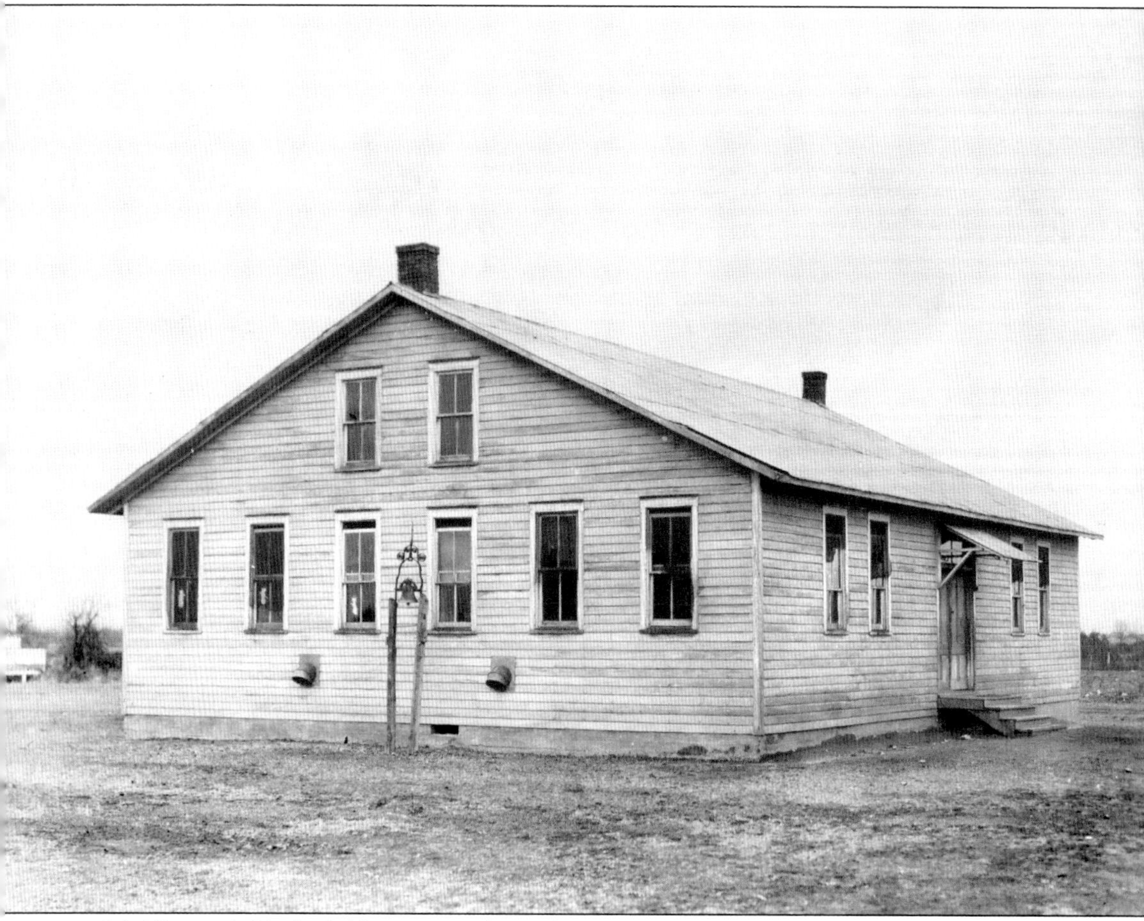

Middletown's black children were educated at several locations in the area, including on East Lockwood Street. After grade 9, they had to travel to Dover or Wilmington if they wished to graduate from high school. This unidentified school was abandoned, and in 1922, the Middletown School 120c building was constructed on New Street. The school was adjacent to the location of the Louis L. Redding Comprehensive School for black students in grades 1 through 12, which was built in 1953. (Courtesy of Delaware Public Archives.)

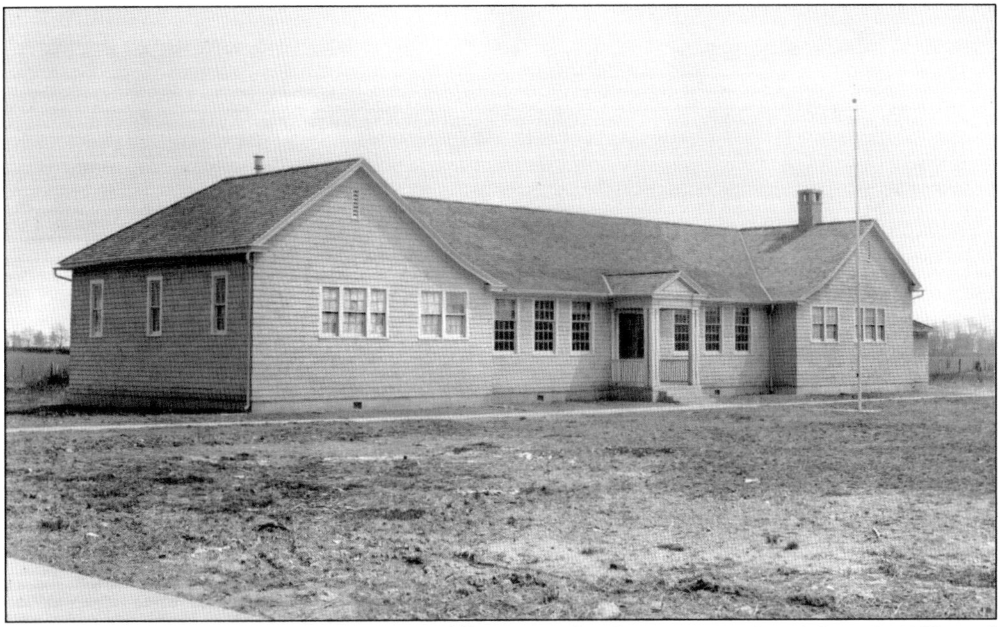

Construction of the new, three-room Middletown School 120c started on May 19, 1922, and was finished on January 30, 1923, at a total cost of $21,258.44. Students who lived in downtown Middletown attended the school from grades 1 through 9 and were joined by students from schools such as the Mount Pleasant School 119c during grades 7 through 9. The building was located adjacent to the present-day location of Louis L. Redding Middle School, named after the famous Wilmington attorney who took part in the landmark *Brown v. Board of Education* court case. (Both, courtesy of Delaware Public Archives.)

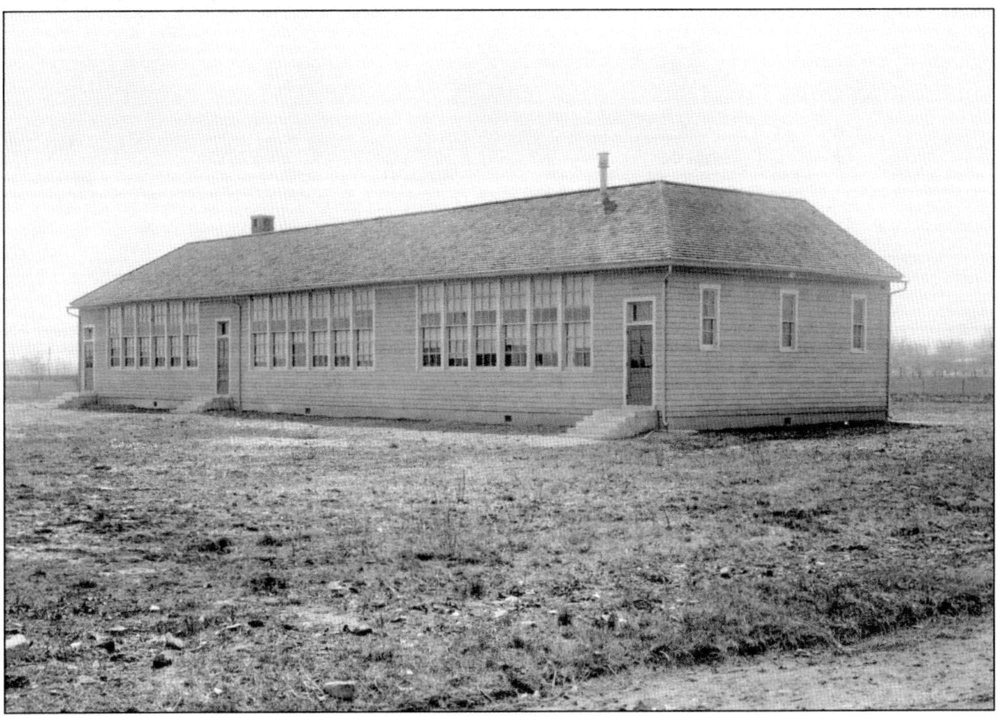

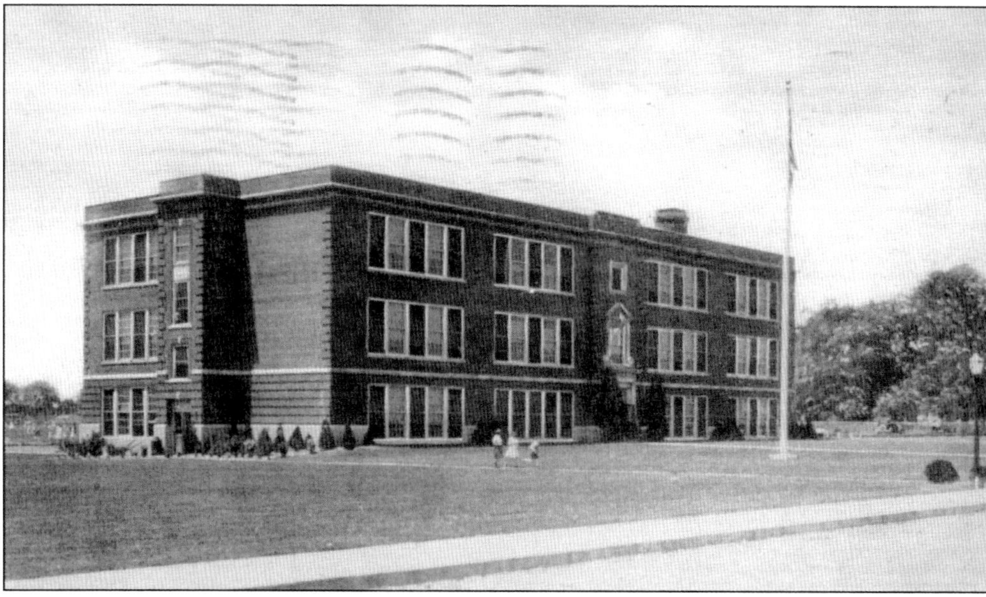

The two-story Middletown public school on South Broad Street opened its doors in September 1929 for students in grades 1 through 12. The initial 21-room building, which included an auditorium, cost an estimated $185,000. A cafeteria was added around 1940, ground was broken for a gymnasium addition in 1961, and multiple other additions and renovations to the school have taken place over the years. It is now Everett Meredith Middle School, but it is commonly referred to as "the old high school" due to its long history as Middletown High School. The campus is home to the Cavalier football stadium, where fans pack the stands for every home game. (Above, courtesy of Middletown Historical Society; below, courtesy of Delaware Public Archives.)

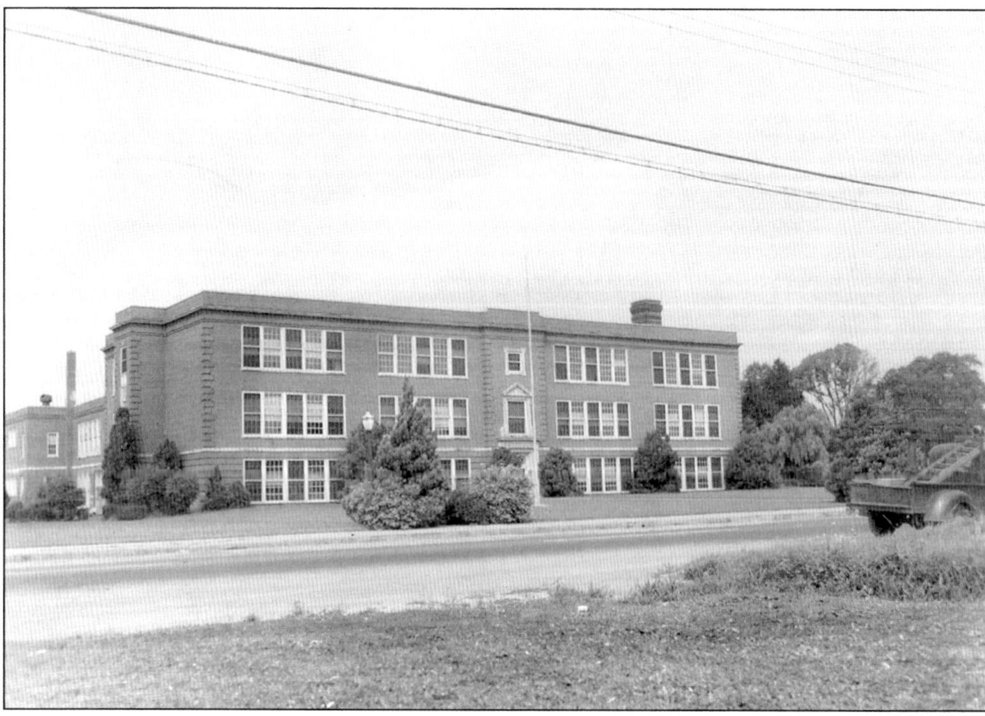

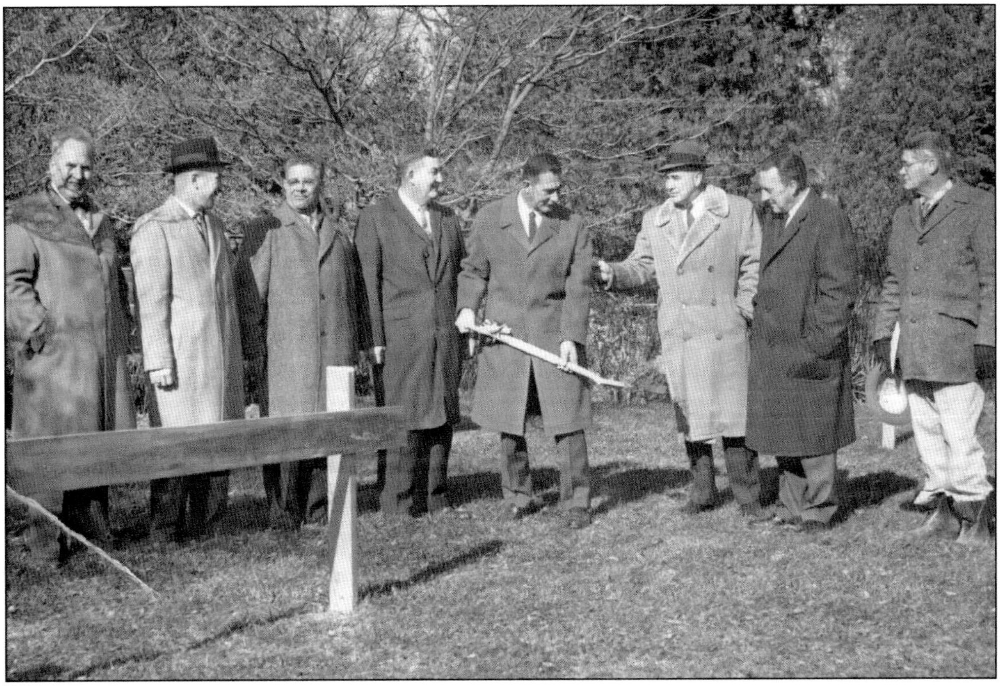

The image above shows the ground-breaking ceremony for the 1961 gymnasium addition at the Middletown public school on South Broad Street. Pictured are, from left to right, George McDermott, architect of the gym; Groome Mears Jr.; Dr. Alan R. Crutchley; James A. Johnston, district superintendent; John W. Fennimore, board president; John Healy, contractor; George Pope, architect; and Walter Howard, construction inspector. Below, students stand outside the addition. (Above, courtesy of *Middletown Transcript*; below, courtesy of Delaware Public Archives.)

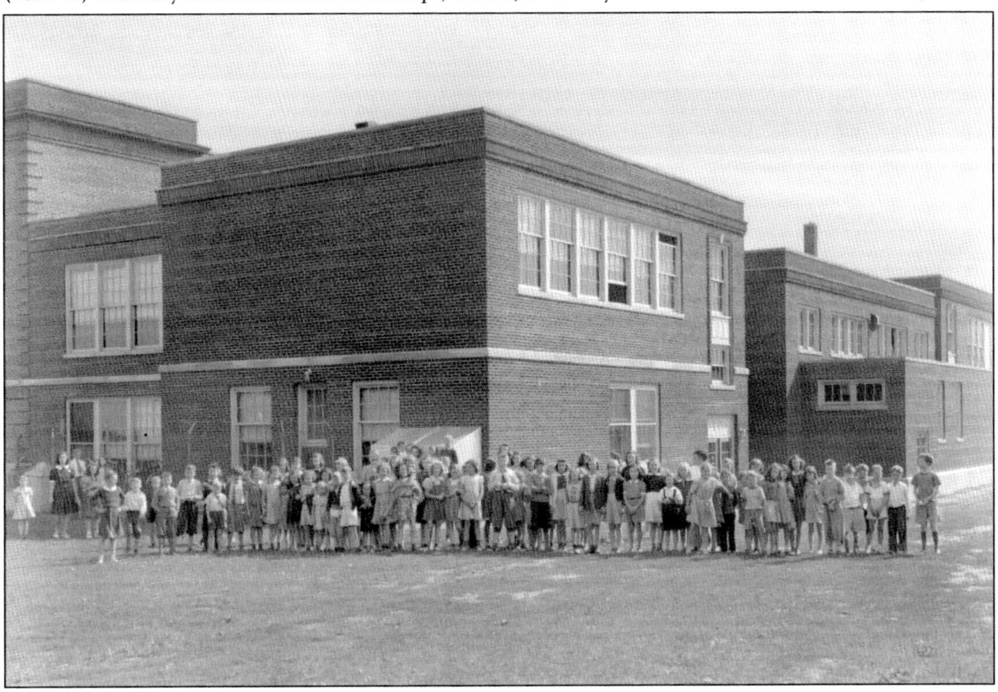

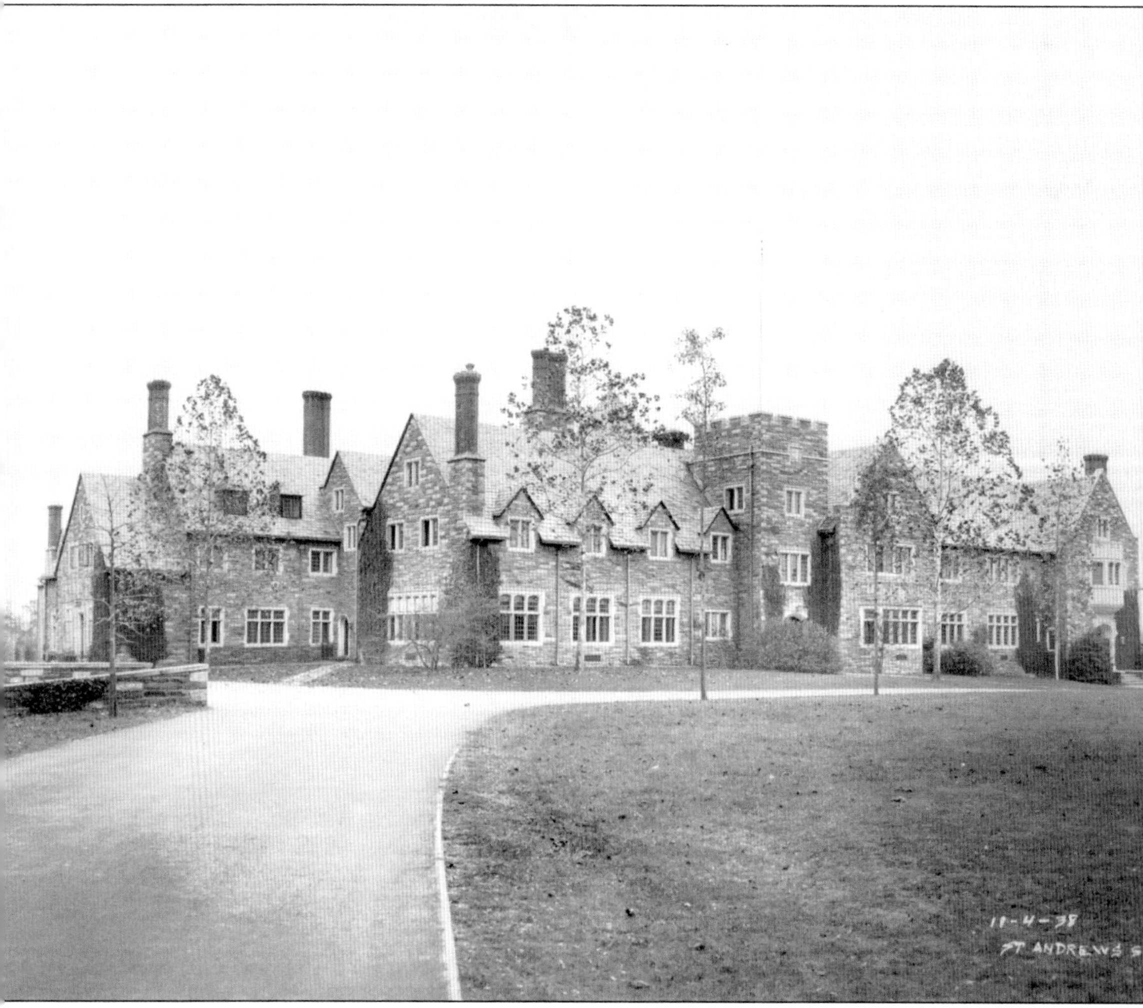

St. Andrew's School, a private boarding school, was founded in 1929 by A. Felix duPont, who stated, "The purpose of St. Andrew's School is to provide secondary education of a definitely Christian character at a minimum cost consistent with modern equipment and highest standards." Under the administration of the Episcopal Church School Foundation, the school was initially for grades 8 through 12 and allowed only boys, 11 of whom comprised its first graduating class in 1934. Grades are taught in accordance with the British education system, in which 9th grade is known as third form, 10th grade is fourth form, 11th grade is fifth form, and 12th grade is sixth form. In 1961, St. Andrew's School had more than 150 students; it now serves more than 300 students under the direction of 72 faculty members. Students at St. Andrew's School learn and live among their instructors in a highly engaged academic and natural environment. (Courtesy of Delaware Public Archives.)

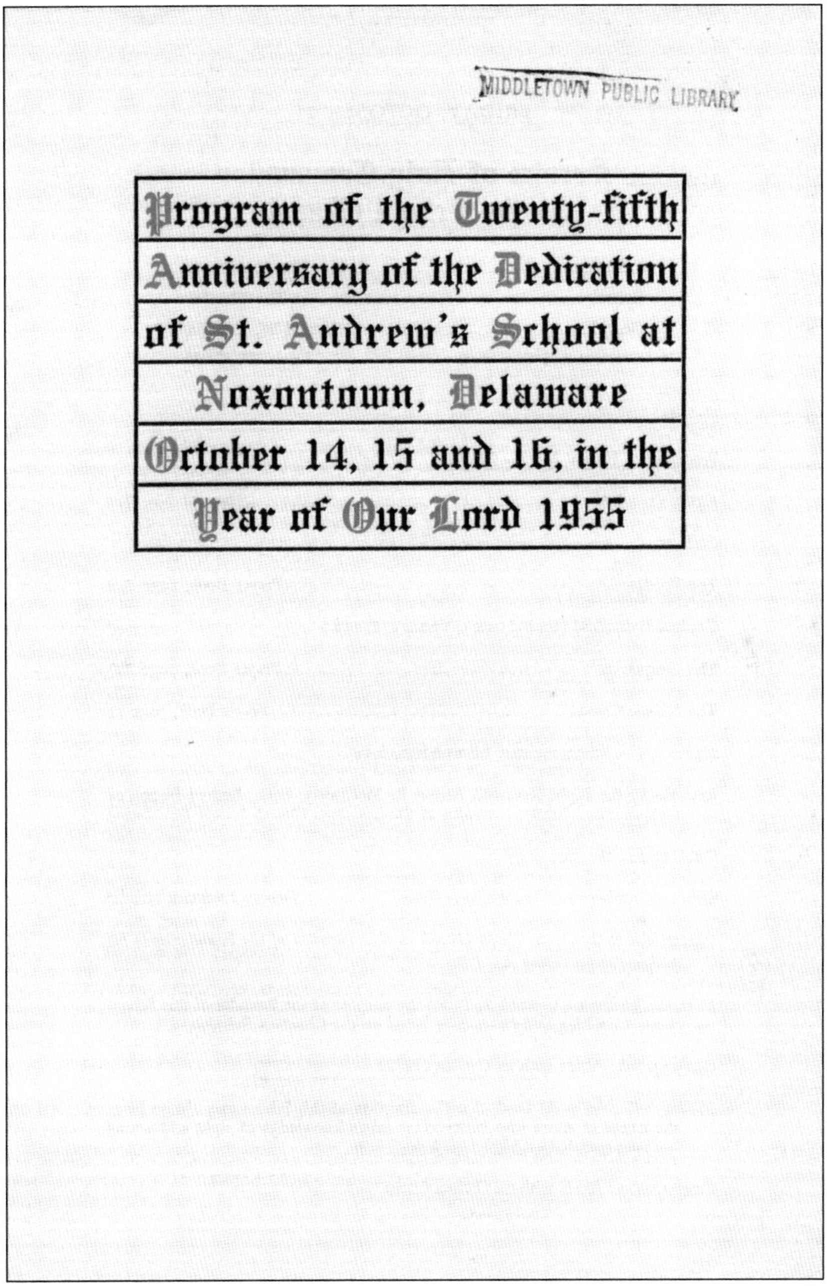

Program of the Twenty-fifth Anniversary of the Dedication of St. Andrew's School at Noxontown, Delaware October 14, 15 and 16, in the Year of Our Lord 1955

St. Andrew's School celebrated its 25th anniversary in 1955. It now operates as a coeducational high school that houses its students, many of whom come to the school from other countries, in English-style buildings around the immediate campus. The initial campus encompassed 100 acres along Noxontown Pond and became a gem known for its pristine buildings and surrounding grounds. The campus now spans 2,200 acres and includes woodlands, wetlands, farmland, a pond, 14 tennis courts, an organic garden, an indoor pool, and gorgeous stone buildings such as the Founders Hall, Amos Hall, and the O'Brien Arts Center. In the late 1980s, *Dead Poets Society*, starring Robin Williams, was filmed at St. Andrew's School and across town at the Everett Theatre. (Courtesy of Middletown Historical Society.)

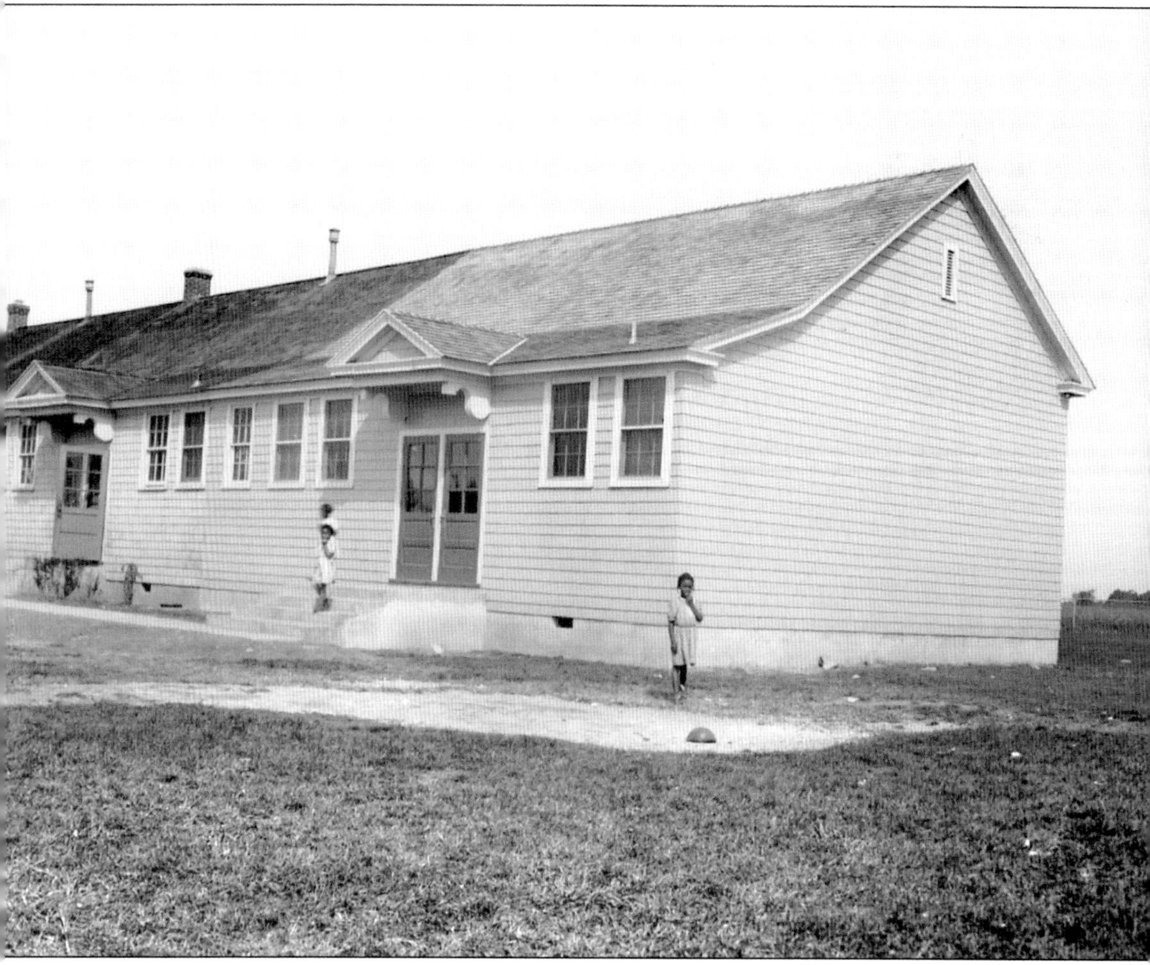

These students are shown outside the agriculture studies addition to Middletown School 120c for black children. The addition provided agricultural education to male students, who learned to tend to and care for farm animals and how to work the land as a farmer. The school was led for many years by principal Dr. Alfred G. Waters, a "forward-thinking professor" who based his curriculum on the system developed by German educator Friedrich Froebel. Dr. Waters offered students the right to play with play materials, or "gifts," and activities, or "occupations." He encouraged his students, who faced many obstacles, to learn to reach their goals. Although the landmark *Brown v. Board of Education* decision to desegregate public schools throughout the United States was reached in 1954, Middletown's schools remained segregated until the mid-1960s. The *Brown* case was argued before the Supreme Court by the first black attorney in Delaware, Louis L. Redding. (Courtesy of Delaware Public Archives.)

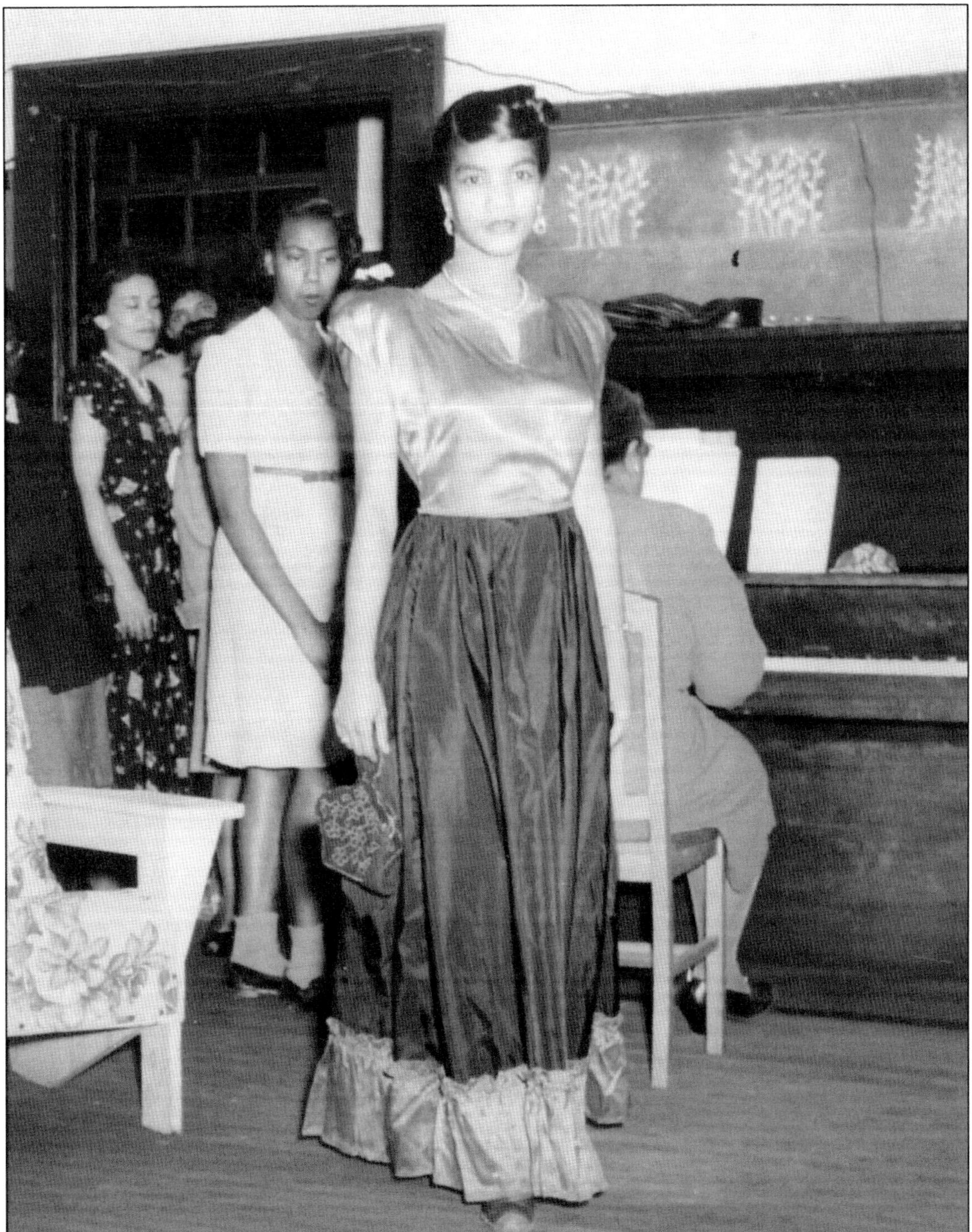

The Middletown School 120c for black students offered home economics classes as one way to expand education under the direction of principal Dr. Alfred G. Waters. Students showed off the skills they learned in class at events such as this fashion show, which was held on April 18, 1948. Courtney Stevenson and Minnie Wynder taught home economics by instructing young women on many important skills for the time. The curriculum taught students to make their own clothes, cook, bake, do laundry, iron laundry, and answer the telephone. Students also displayed their canning, needlework, and clothes-making skills to the community at events like community fairs. Female students could also take part in a drama group that packed the auditorium during performances. (Courtesy of Delaware Public Archives.)

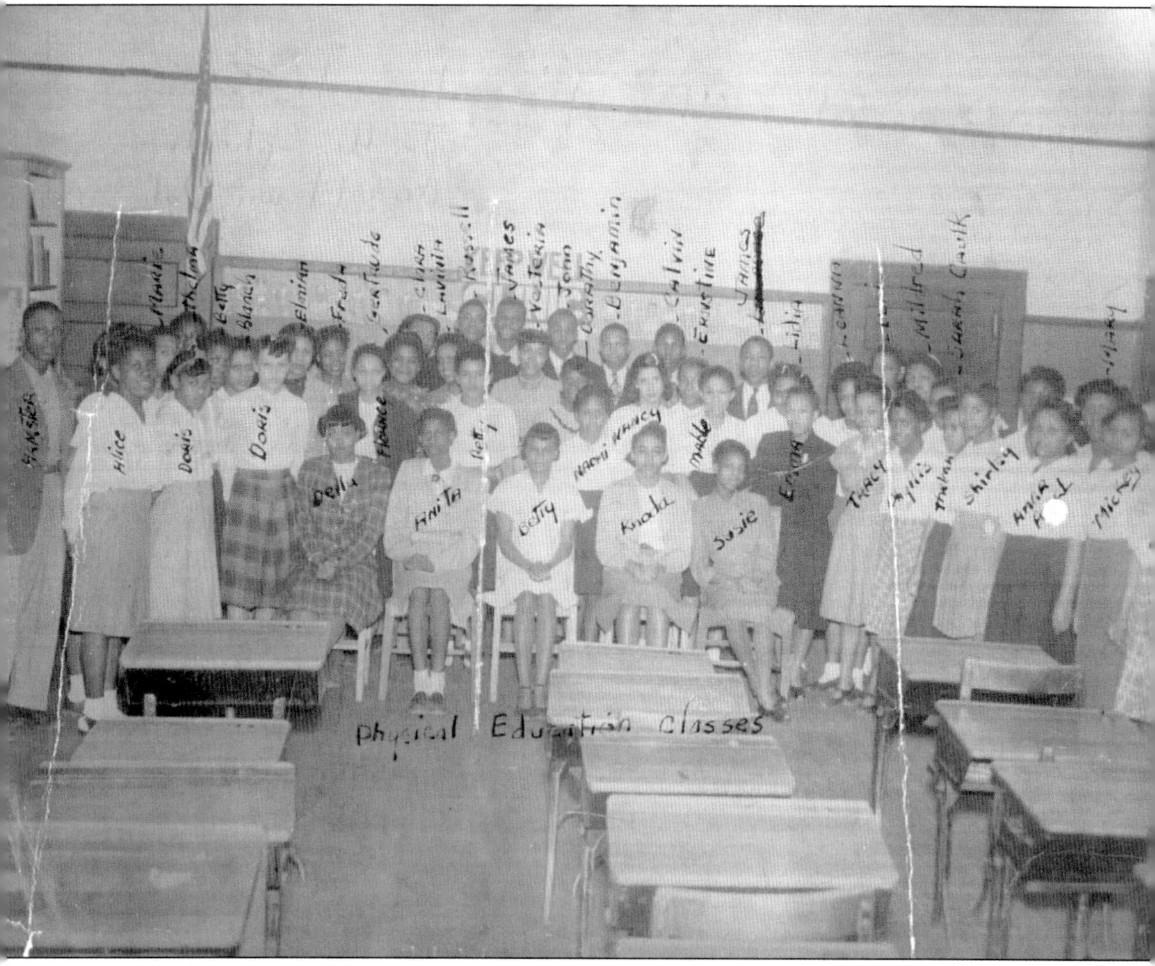

This photograph shows a physical education class at Middletown School 120c in the late 1940s. Longtime East Lake Street resident Betty Todd is pictured at center, along with female classmates such as Della, Anita, Victoria, Rhoda, Susie, Emma, Tracy, Phyllis, and Clara, and male classmates such as Russell, James, John, Benjamin, and Calvin. Female students learned to compete athletically in these classes, as they were offered basketball, field hockey, and track alongside their male peers. Redding alumna Dorothy Taylor said the girls set a record or two with their athletic talents. The school's male athletes stood out under the direction of basketball coach Oliver Thompson, a talented leader who ran a tight ship of a team and commanded respect that paid off on the court. People came from miles around to watch the Redding Eagles play basketball and football. (Courtesy of Betty Todd.)

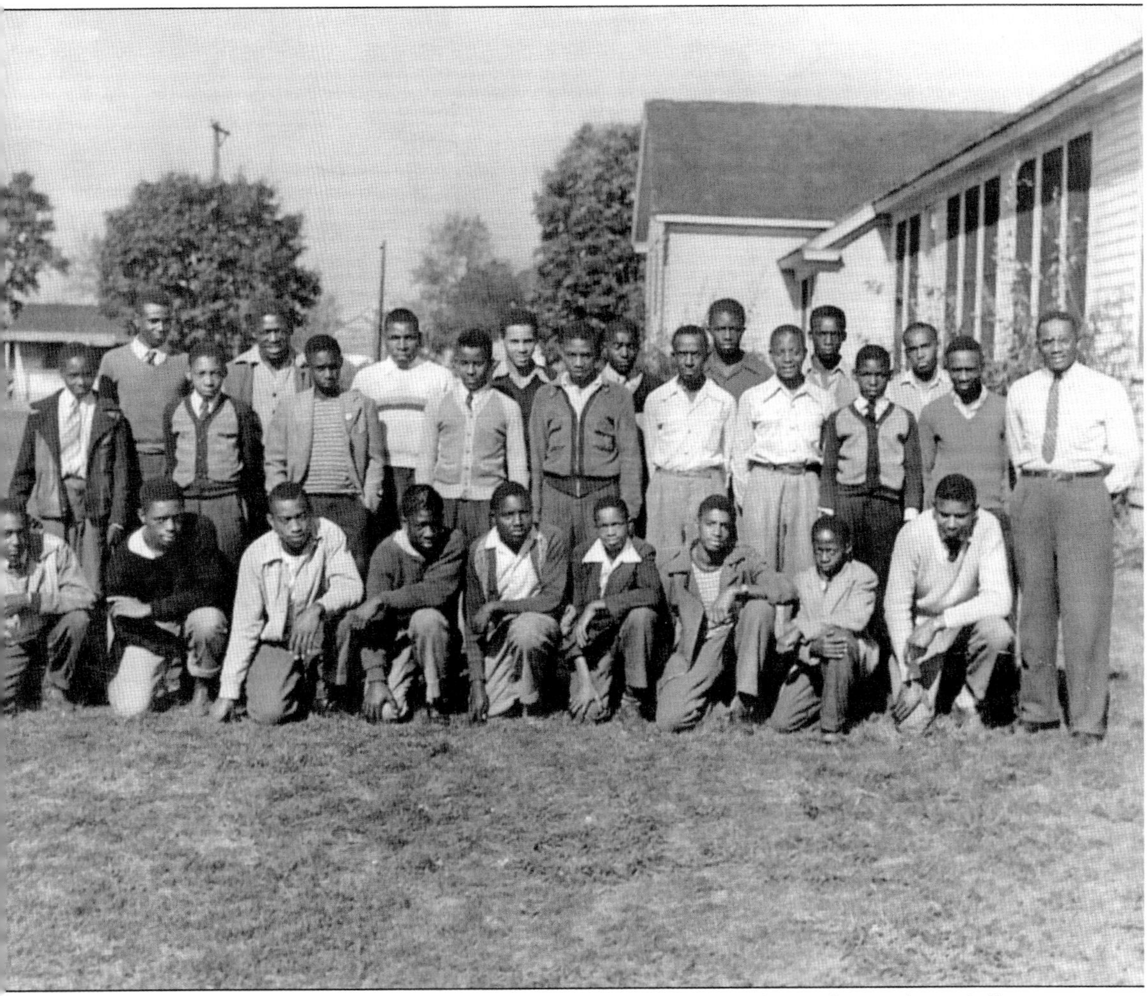

While home economics was offered to female students, male students learned agriculture skills at Middletown School 120c (next to where the Louis L. Redding Comprehensive School was built). Principal Dr. Alfred G. Waters incorporated a sense of community in the school by offering several alternative subjects to students. Athletics, music, and agriculture were taught in addition to reading, writing, and arithmetic. Once the Louis L. Redding Comprehensive School was built adjacent to Middletown School 120c, student dances were held on Saturday nights and featured future musical stars such as James Brown, Ike and Tina Turner, Otis Redding, and Sam Cooke. Students needed permission from their parents to attend the dances, and parent chaperones were brought in when musical acts performed. The school's enrollment also increased when the comprehensive school was built, as it offered high school education to black students in southern New Castle County. By 1961, Redding had an enrollment of 650 students. (Courtesy of Betty Todd.)

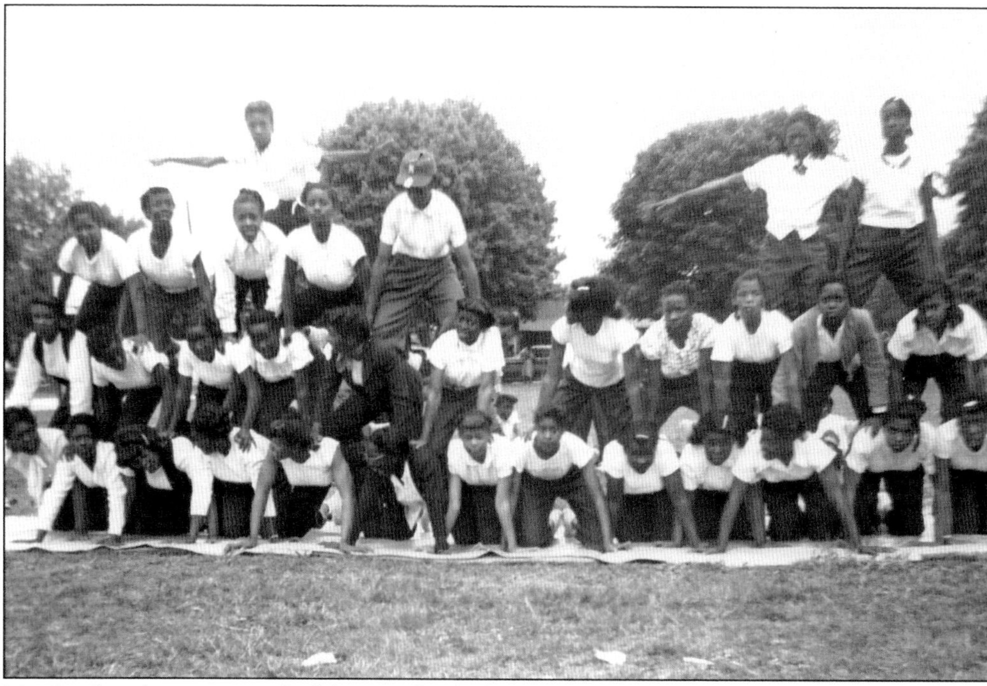

May has long been a time of celebration for the black community in the East Lake Street vicinity. The May 1951 photograph above shows students in pyramid form during a performance in a "circus" at the Middletown School 120c during its annual play day for children and families. Many came out to watch stunts like this. Teachers showed girls how to wrap the maypole, a dance they performed in white dresses. Parents brought food to share with those in attendance, while male students played baseball. The annual event was held into the late 1950s, but was then discontinued. (Both, courtesy of Delaware Public Archives.)

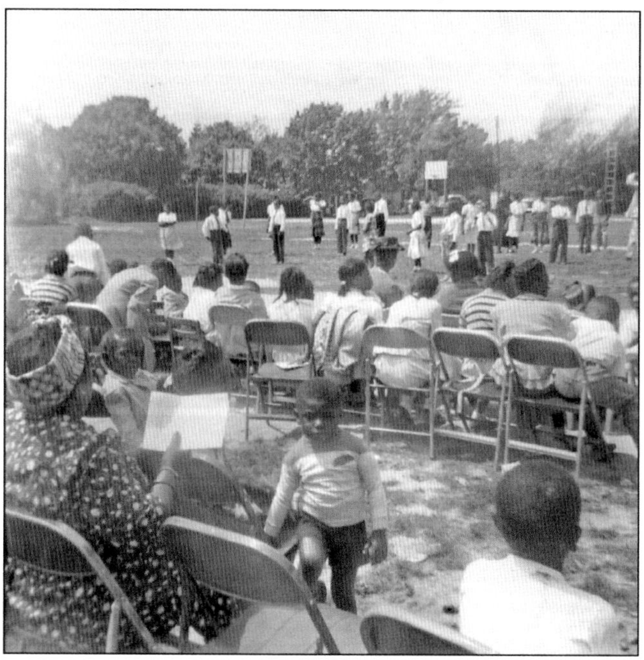

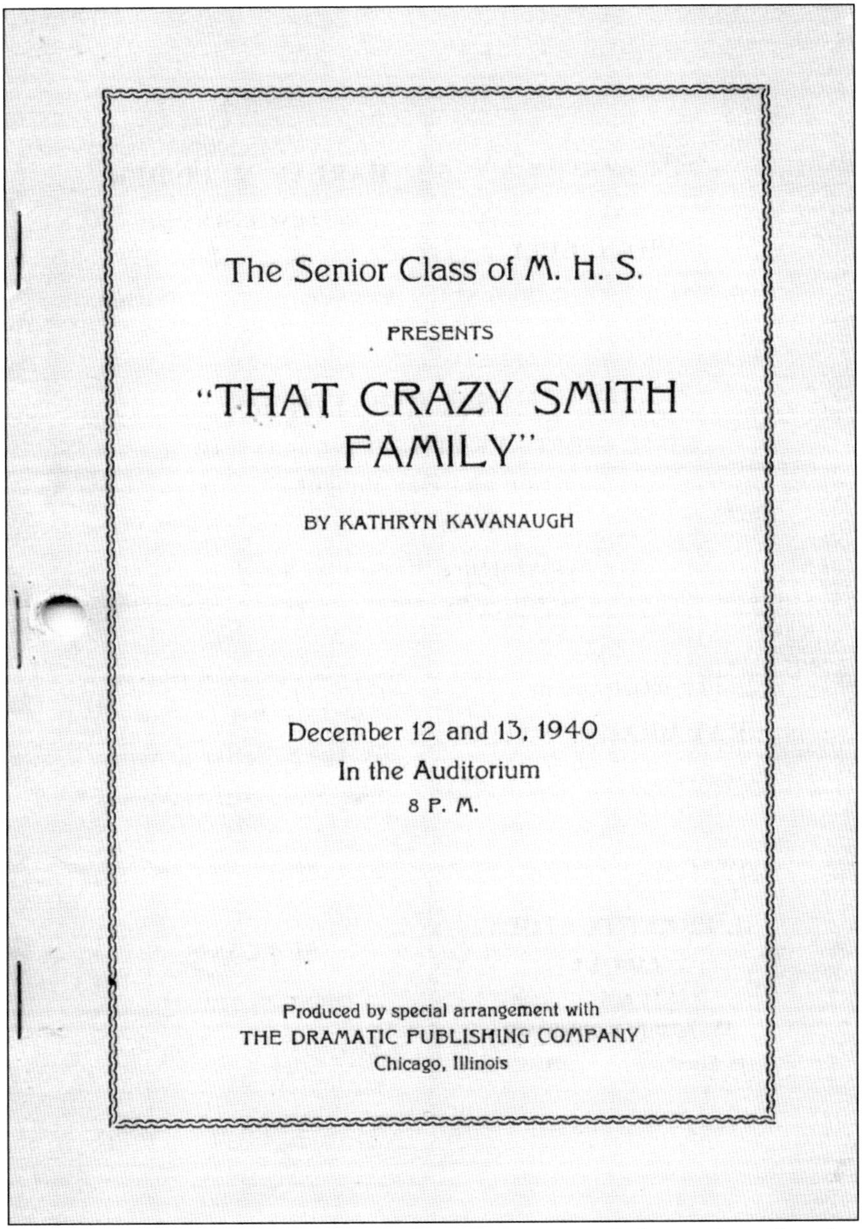

The Senior Class of M. H. S.

PRESENTS

"THAT CRAZY SMITH FAMILY"

BY KATHRYN KAVANAUGH

December 12 and 13, 1940

In the Auditorium

8 P. M.

Produced by special arrangement with

THE DRAMATIC PUBLISHING COMPANY

Chicago, Illinois

Middletown High School has become known for its spring musicals, but students there have long had a passion for putting on plays. The class of 1941 produced *The Crazy Smith Family* with a cast including Marion Daniels, Marvel Argoe, Richard Jones, Beatrice Atkinson, Arthur Shivery, Mary Guessford, Alma Lou Dunkelberger, Rose Jenn Guessford, George Schreppler, William Phillips, James Smith, and Catherine Burke. Volunteer directors Roy Smith and Ted McClain were instrumental in keeping plays alive at MHS for some time. In 1978, Mike Atkins and Jane Ironside put on a Christmas play for the school. Later that year, the one-act play *Wurzel Flummery and My Client Curley* was performed for the community, leading to other one-act shows. One year, *Guys and Dolls* was performed by students at the Everett Theatre, and the stage crew had to transport the sets it constructed across town. Crew members sometimes had to get creative to place props such as a carriage or a car on stage. (Courtesy of Middletown Historical Society.)

MIDDLETOWN SCHOOL DISTRICT SIXTY
504 South Broad Street
Middletown, Delaware 19709

March 20, 1969

Mr. John N. Sparks
Middletown, Delaware

Dear Mr. Sparks,

The School Board of the reorganized School District #12, which includes Middletown-Townsend and Odessa, is requesting that you serve on the citizens school Board Advisory Committee. The first meeting of the Board with the Advisory Committee will be held in the High School Cafeteria on Tuesday evening, April 1, 1969 at 8:00 P.M. Refreshments will be served beginning at 7:45 P.M. The public will be invited to attend this meeting but you are especially invited as one of our leading citizens.

The Board would like to get your thinking on several important problems with which it is faced. One problem of immediate concern is the naming of the reorganized School District, the board must clear the selected name with the State Archivist and give the name to the State Board by Tuesday, April 7th. Please come to the meeting on the 1st with some good suggestions for a name.

The school board is counting on you, remember the children.

Sincerely,

James A. Johnson, Jr.

James A. Johnson, Jr.
Clerk of the Board.

JAJ:mem

Middletown, Odessa, and Townsend schools operated under separate administrations until they were united to form one district in 1969. To lead the consolidation, a Citizens Advisory Committee was founded and tasked with the search for a proper name. The input of Middletown mayor Jack Sparks was solicited via this letter. Sparks suggested the name should reflect the area's early history, and Appoquinimink was chosen in homage to the river from which the area's first trade and settlements were established. Townsend resident Helen Kimmey, who served on the Townsend School Board and was appointed by a judge as the first woman on the Appoquinimink School District Board of Education, still serves the district as a volunteer at the time of this publication. The Appoquinimink School District has since grown immensely with the addition of countless students and many new schools due to a large increase in population below the Chesapeake & Delaware Canal. (Courtesy of Middletown Historical Society.)

Seven

ATHLETICS

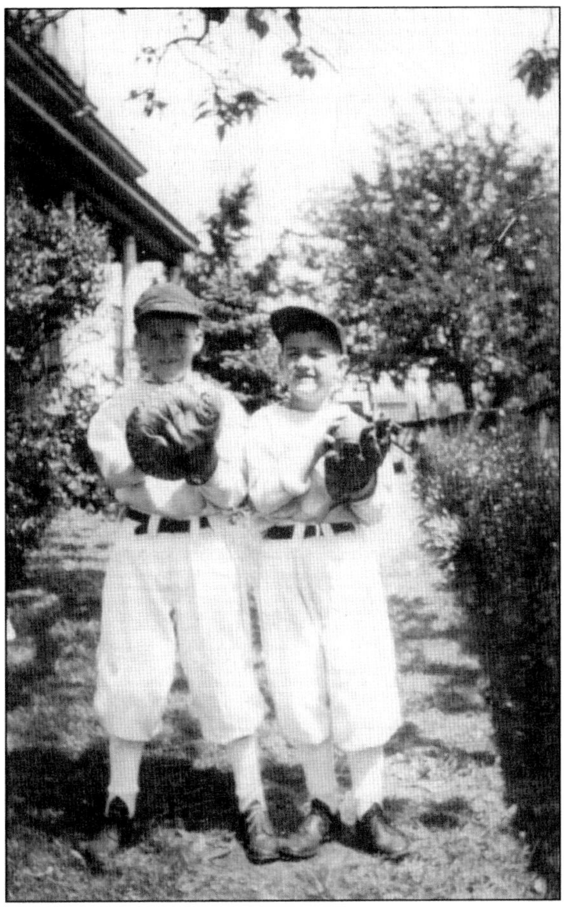

Jack (left) and Richard Green are shown here in their youth baseball uniforms. The brothers grew up on the Green farm on East Main Street and did not have to come home from school to milk cows so long as they played a sport. Their father, John C. "Jack" Green, offered his cow pasture on the south side of East Main Street to all children to play baseball together. There were no umpires and no adults, unless the boys' father came out to toss an easy pitch to some of the youngest players to ensure that they did not strike out. Two of the children went on to play minor league baseball. Jack later played baseball and football for Middletown High School, from which he graduated in 1955. Richard, a 1956 graduate, played baseball, basketball, and football, and later served as the school's athletic director. (Courtesy of Richard and Marlene Green.)

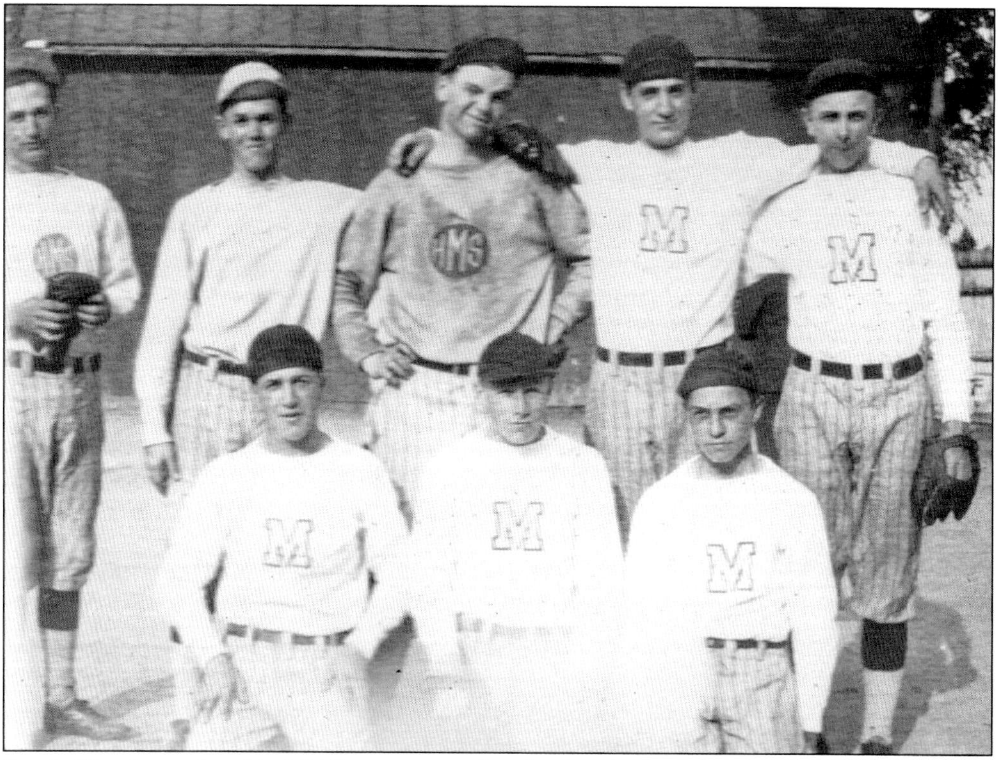

Baseball has been played in Middletown since shortly after the game was invented. A professional team once played on a diamond behind Bethesda United Methodist Church. The game was later played on lots on the east end of town until a more permanent field was constructed, with grandstands, in town. The first game at that location was played in 1914. In 1929, the Middletown High School team beat Laurel to take the state title. Pictured above are, from left to right, (first row) Clarence Reihms, Roy Rawley, and Leon Roemer; (second row) Pete Reynolds, John C. "Jack" Green, Henry Brady, Jack Swain, and Robert Armstrong, Pictured below are, from left to right, Dick Reihms, who played shortstop, and outfielders Jack Green, Bob Armstrong, and Leon Roemer. (Both, courtesy of Richard and Marlene Green.)

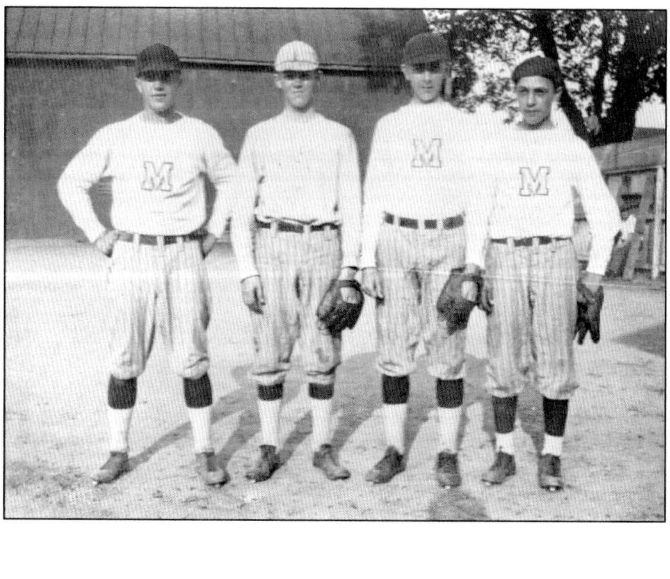

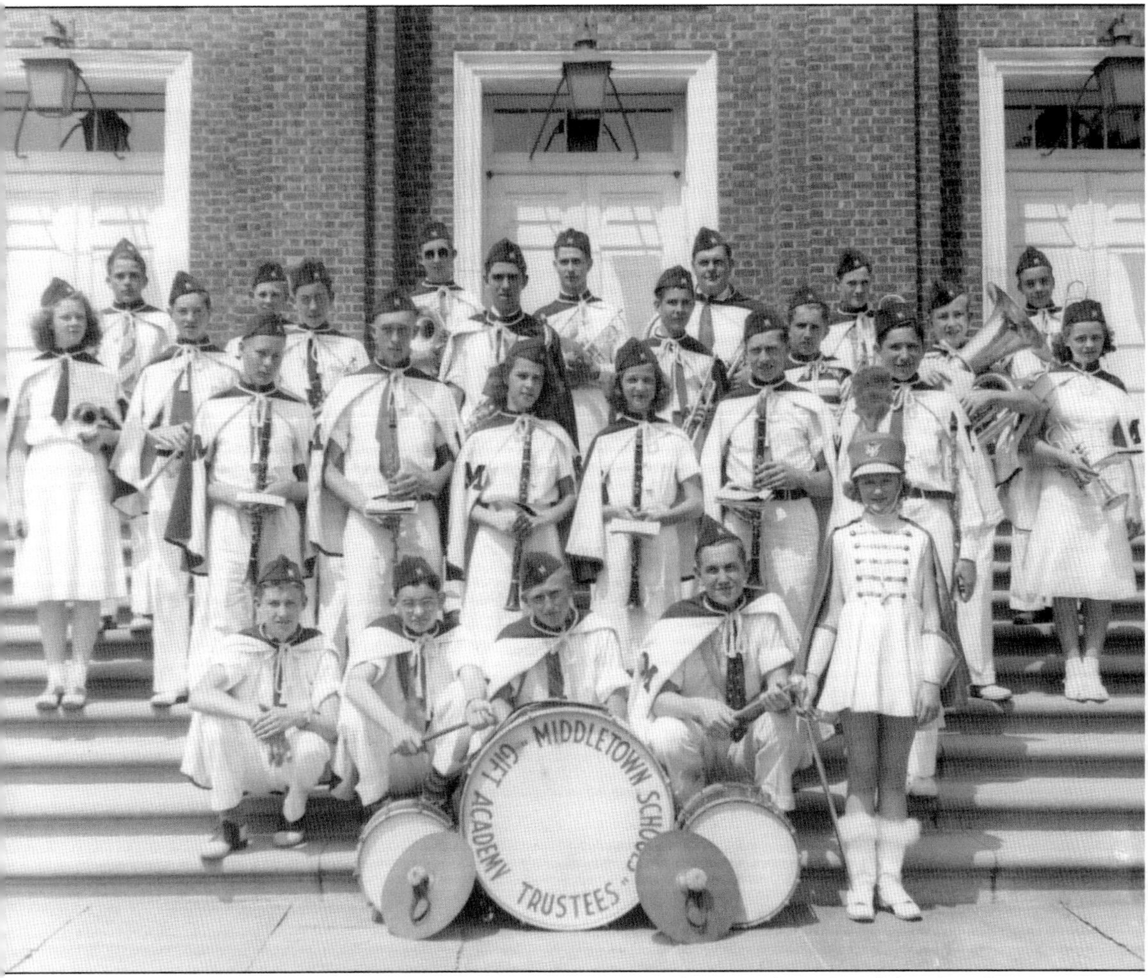

The Middletown High School Band, now known as the Cavalier Marching Band, has long been the sound of the school at varsity football games. The 1938 band pictured includes, from left to right, (first row) Warren Buckingham, Jimmy Hart, Peter Savin, Woodall Cochran, and Jean Jones; (second row) Early Robinson, Joe Jarrell, Lucille Dunkelberger, Nan Dunkelberger, Bill Phillips, and Harry Smith; (third row) Ann Stafford, Herman Price, Thomas Donovan, Linwood Robinson, Eugene Ennis, Jimmy Wise, Groome Mears, and Anna Crossland; (fourth row) Arthur Shivery, James Jarrell, Willard Robinson, Horace Ginn, C. Merrill Wagner, Harry Sadoff, and Howard Boyd. (Courtesy of Delaware Public Archives.)

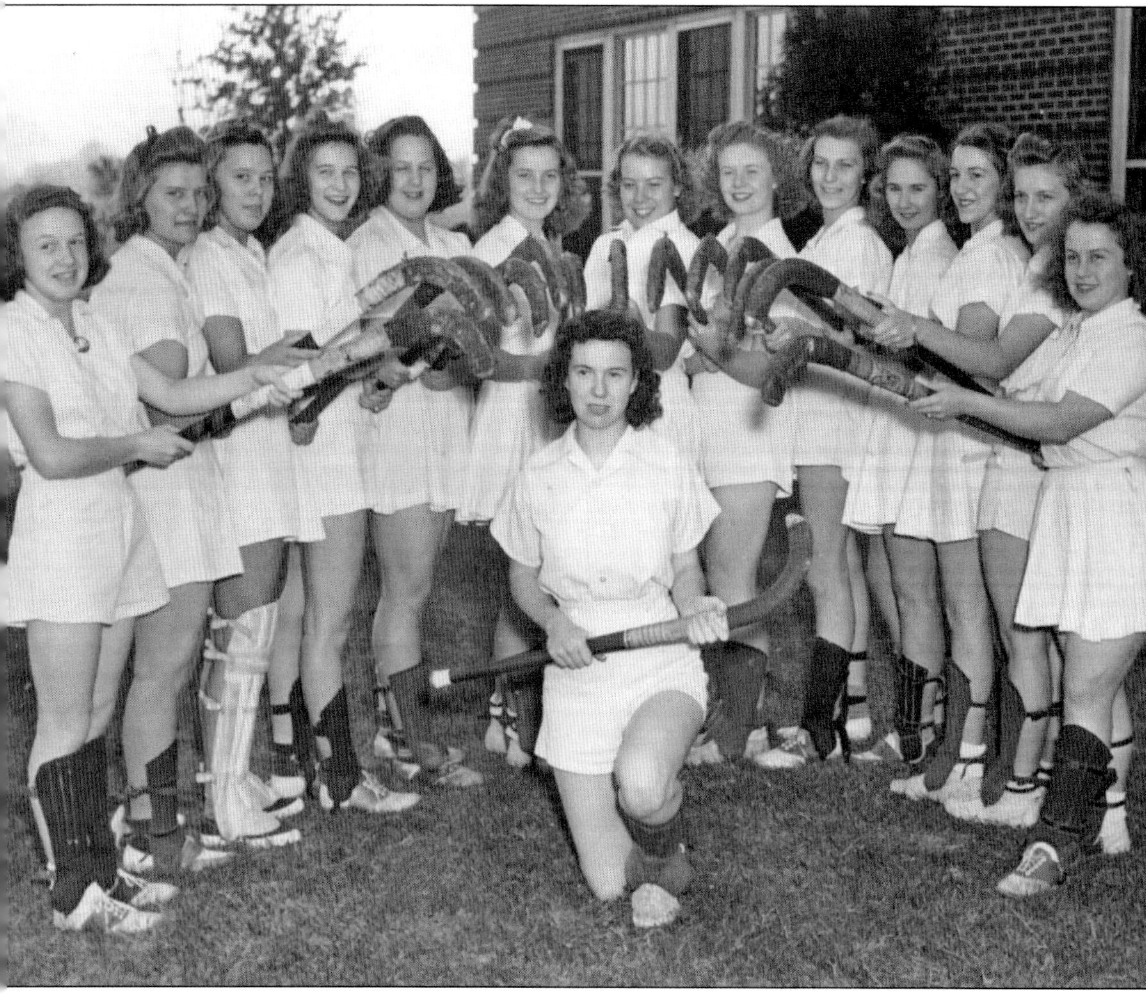

The 1941 Middletown High School girls' field hockey Team went undefeated. A brief article printed in the *Middletown Transcript* on behalf of the school states that the team's season "started out with a bang!" after the girls scored 10 goals and allowed Harrington none. Fans were credited as encouraging the team to play a vigorous game. Pictured here are, from left to right, Louise Hill, Jane Farrow, Gladys Boyd, Nan Dunkelberger, Bertha Ogden, Mary Krejci, Ruby Dawson, Ann Stafford, Nanny Lou Fouracre, Louetta Jacobs, Joan Keith, Maryellen Phillips, and Jean McElwee, with captain Eleanor George in the center. Middletown is described in the article as winning under the direction of coach Kenneth Steers. (Courtesy of Delaware Public Archives.)

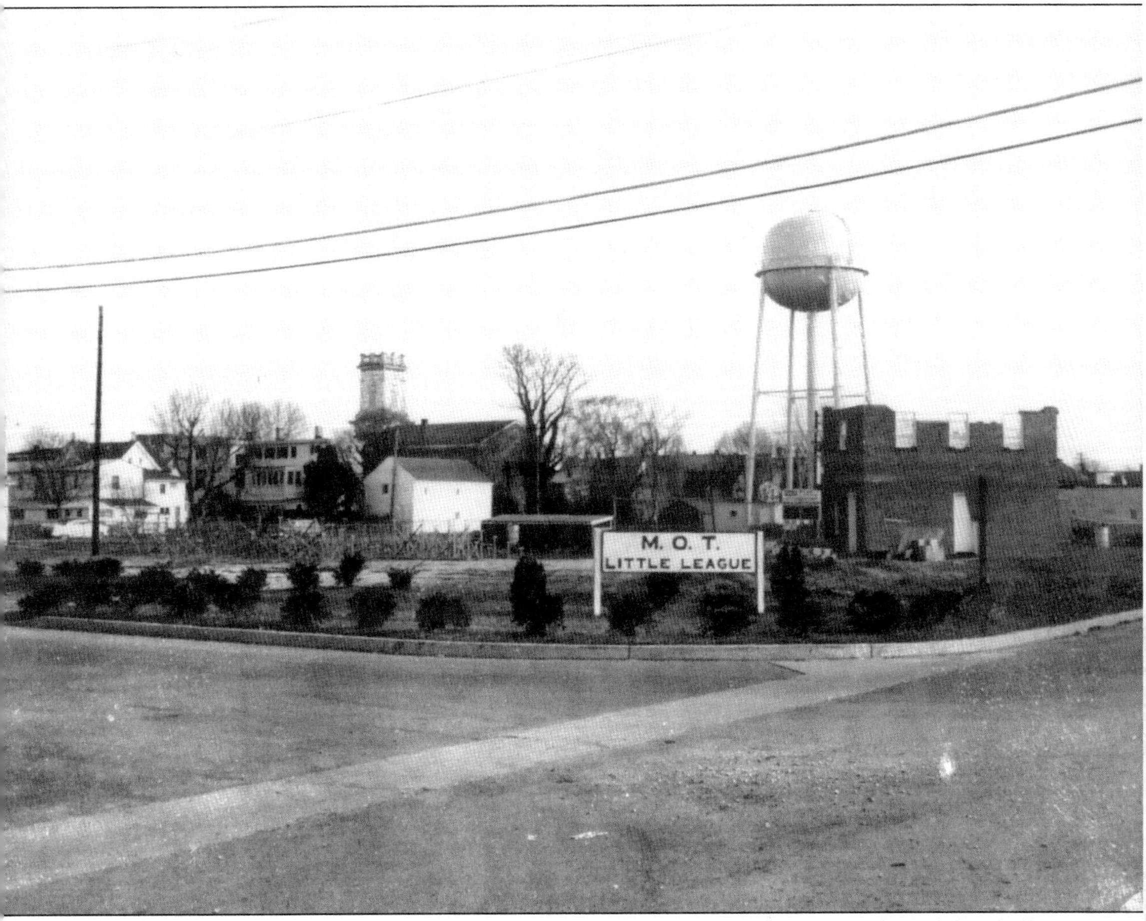

In 1956, Forest Men's Fellowship of Forest Presbyterian Church formed an integrated youth baseball league for Middletown, Odessa, and Townsend players as a community project. The M.O.T. Little League found its home on a town lot at West Green and Scott Streets. The Lions Club sponsored the field and erected a backstop and fences. Robert McDowell was chairman of the project and served as secretary of the league alongside president Jack Sparks, vice president Jesse Watson, and treasurer Sherman Tribbitt. The M.O.T. Little League Ladies' Auxiliary, composed of league mothers, supervised Tag Day and the sale of refreshments. League boundaries at the time stretched north to Newark, south to Smyrna, east to the Delaware Bay, and west to the Maryland state line. Teams included the Corvettes, the Whirlwinds, the Rangers, the Wheels, the Texateers, and the Jaycees. (Courtesy of Middletown Historical Society.)

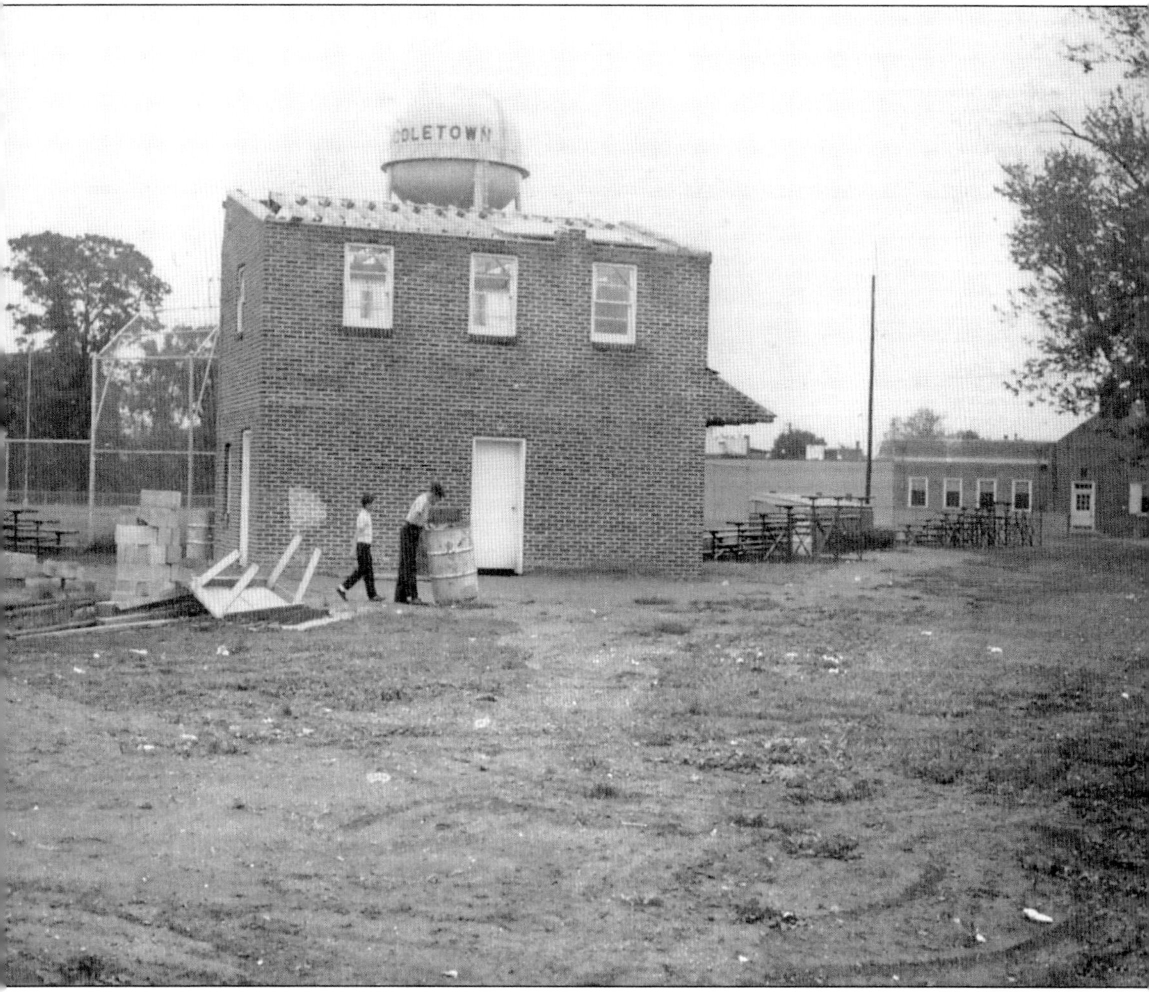

M.O.T. Little League launched a renovation program in 1960 with a new lease from the Middletown Town Council that allowed for an enlargement of the field. Renovations also included a newly landscaped field, block dugouts, a Cyclone fence and backstop, a broadcasting building and concession stand, an electric scoreboard, and a recreation area. Additionally, two buildings were donated by the Volunteer Hose Company of Middletown. Lighting was added later. The M.O.T. Little League Field, which became known as Duke Field, opened on May 20, 1961, and remained a popular hangout for countless players and residents. The Little League season opened annually with a parade of its teams up South Broad Street, onto West Main Street, and onto South Scott Street, where ceremonies were held on the field. Duke Field was replaced by a new fire company building, Middletown Memorial Hall, in the early 2000s. (Courtesy of *Middletown Transcript*.)

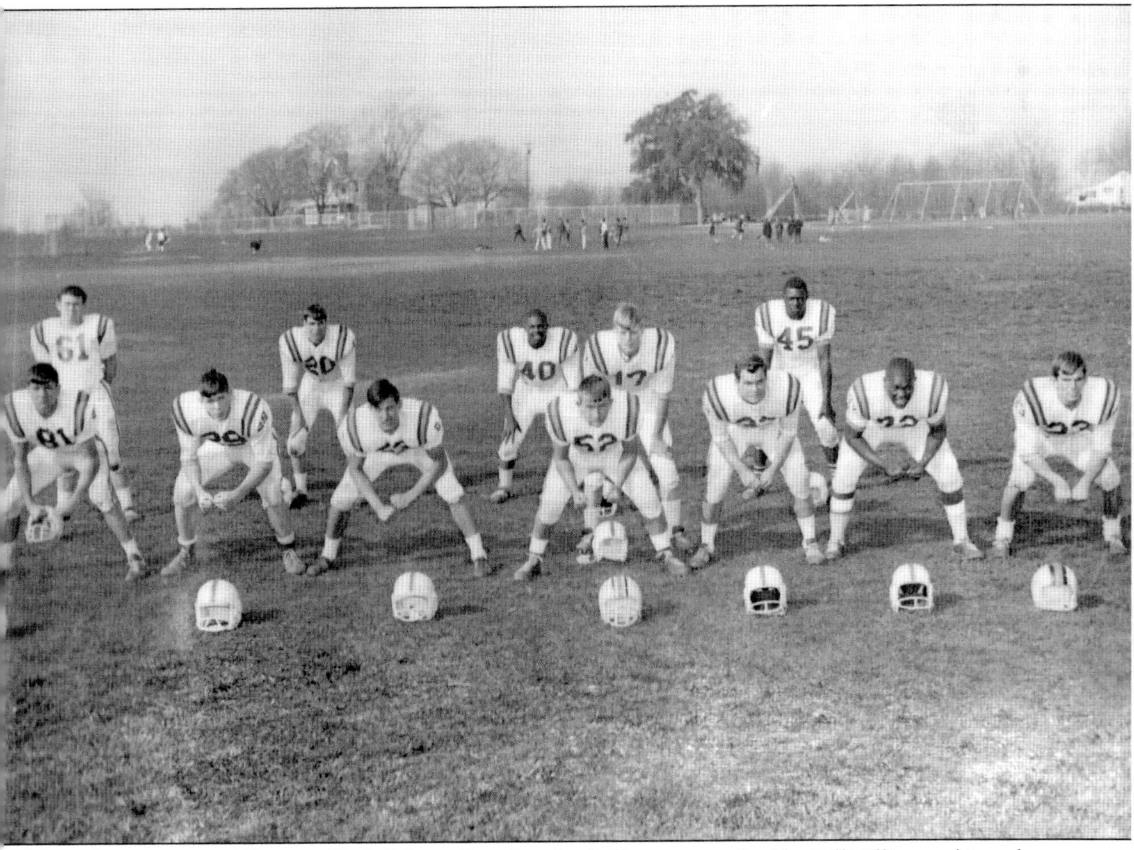

The 1962–1966 Middletown High School Cavalier football teams coached by Bill Billings achieved legendary status for their five-year, 45-game winning streak. The 1966 team capped its season with a 14-13 win over Salesianum in a much-anticipated game that drew at least 6,500 fans. Billings expressed worry about the end-of-season opponent; at the start of the season, he stated it "might be the worst mistake I ever made in scheduling that team," well before his team proved it to be the best decision he ever made. This photograph shows the 1966 offense in formation. Pictured here are, from left to right, (first row) John Henderson, end; Lester Holland, tackle; George Atkinson, tackle; Jim Reynolds, center; Bob Shetzler, guard; Rock Saunders, tackle; and Frankie Cale, halfback; (second row) Kenny Walker, guard; John Branner, halfback; Wayne Brown, fullback; Sonny Merkel, quarterback; and Quentin Stokes, halfback. (Courtesy of Jimmy Reynolds Jr.)

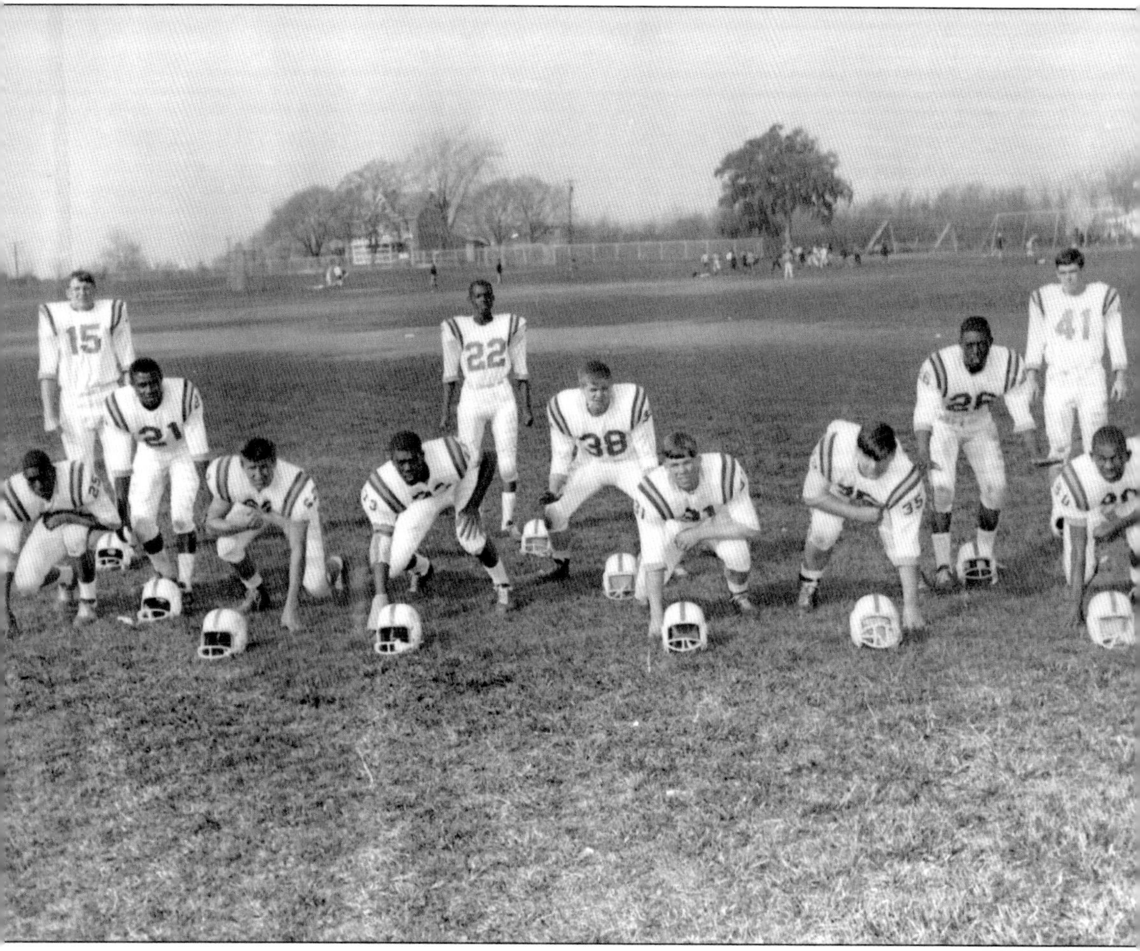

The 1966 roster also included Scott Reihm, quarterback; Greg Simendinger, quarterback; John Combs, end; Marvin Younger, end; Allen Stokes, guard; Ed Harvey; Geoff Perry, end; Andrew Cale, halfback; Robert Skinner, halfback; Bob Chambers, guard; Reggie Henderson, end; Joe Chas, tackle; Glen Fennemore, end; Ricky Laws, center; Robert Hall, end; Ray Filasky, fullback; Herky Billings, halfback; Quinton Stokes, halfback; John Filasky, center; Robert Grau, guard; Pete Whitlock; Albert Scott; Eddie Heverin, tackle; Dewittfield Henry, end; David Webster, end; Bill Hutchison, end; Lewis Saunders; and Ronald Gitaitis. Clifford Towe and Dennis Loftus assisted coach Bill Billings that year. With only four players from the 1965 season returning to play in 1966, Billings was quoted in a newspaper article about the team's outlook that year as saying, "The rest are fairly new and don't have much game experience," and that the team was "counting heavily on newcomers." (Courtesy of Jimmy Reynolds Jr.)

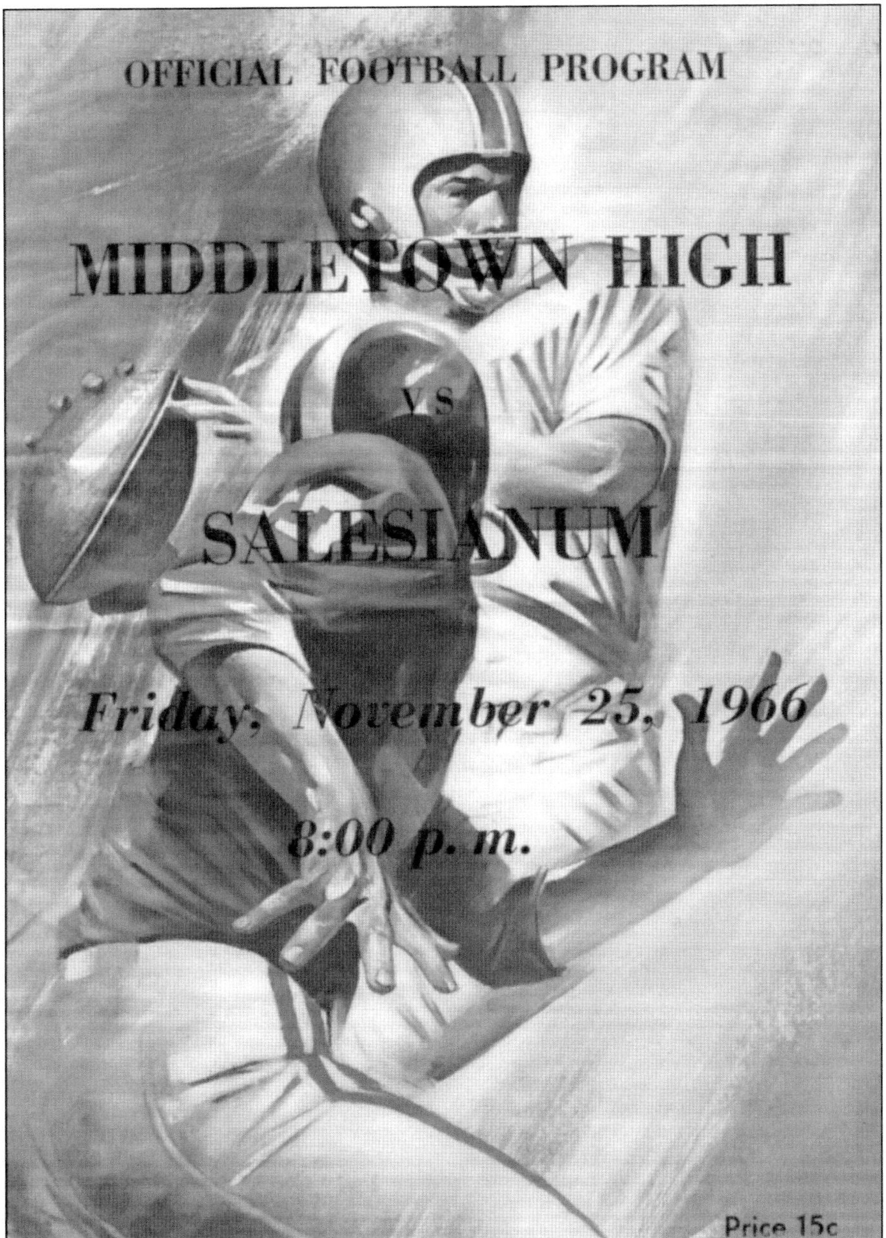

The November 25, 1966, matchup between the Middletown High School Cavaliers and Salesianum Sallies high school football teams was the equivalent of a state championship, which were not yet held in Delaware at the time. The season kicked off with headlines of "Middletown picked—to lose 1st game," incorrectly predicting the outcome against Caesar Rodney, and "Middletown hangs 38-0 shocker on Dover" to describe the 1966 season opener against Dover High School. The game against Dover was predicted to be the "game of the year," but that title was claimed when the upstate, private-schooled Sallies met the farm-raised, public-schooled Cavaliers steps away from a banner that hung over Broad Street and read "Beat Sallies." Headlines such as "It's David vs. Goliath" and "Big Sals out to snap 44-game Middletown grid streak tonight" show Middletown was the clear underdog going into its 45th win. (Courtesy of Jimmy Reynolds Jr.)

Cavaliers do it!

How Middletown won 45 straight

1962 (Won 9, Lost 0)

19	Caesar Rodney	6
27	Smyrna	7
34	Dover Air	0
33	Shanahan	26
30	Lewes	0
28	North Caroline	14
47	Georgetown	8
20	Milford	19
28	Dover	7

1964 (Won 9, Lost 0)

40	Caesar Rodney	0
*52	Smyrna	6
33	Dover	6
61	Lewes	6
34	Laurel	6
32	Georgetown	0
37	Milford	0
73	North Caroline	12
48	Elkton	7

* Used ineligible player.

1963 (Won 9, Lost 0)

35	Caesar Rodney	0
20	Smyrna	13
47	Dover Air	0
28	Lewes	0
40	Laurel	6
53	Georgetown	6
20	Milford	6
40	North Caroline	6
42	Dover	6

1965 (Won 9, Lost 0)

26	Caesar Rodney	0
20	Smyrna	0
26	Elkton	0
20	Dover	6
33	Lewes	13
46	Laurel	6
40	Georgetown	13
41	Milford	0
41	Seaford	13

1966 (Won 9, Lost 0)

34	Caesar Rodney	0
44	Smyrna	6
38	Dover	0
68	Lewis	0
53	Laurel	0
52	Georgetown	13
53	Milford	6
35	Seaford	7
14	Salesianum	13

The day after Middletown High School beat Salesianum, November 26 headlines read, "Little Middletown pulls off grid upset" and "Game of Decade Surprises All But Loyal Local Fans." Several Middletown players were strategically placed out of their regular positions, which was practiced during an off-week at the beginning of the season. The Cavalier defense delivered multiple hard hits that were unexpected by the hard-to-defeat Sallies, who earned their two touchdowns of the night on Cavalier fumbles. Middletown was losing until the fourth quarter, when a 69-yard drive resulted in a touchdown with less than five minutes left in the fourth quarter. Sallies coach Wayne Allen stated, "They kept coming up with those weirdo plays to keep their drives alive." Middletown became known for its football and eventually created a youth league that cultivates great players. (Courtesy of Jimmy Reynolds Jr.)

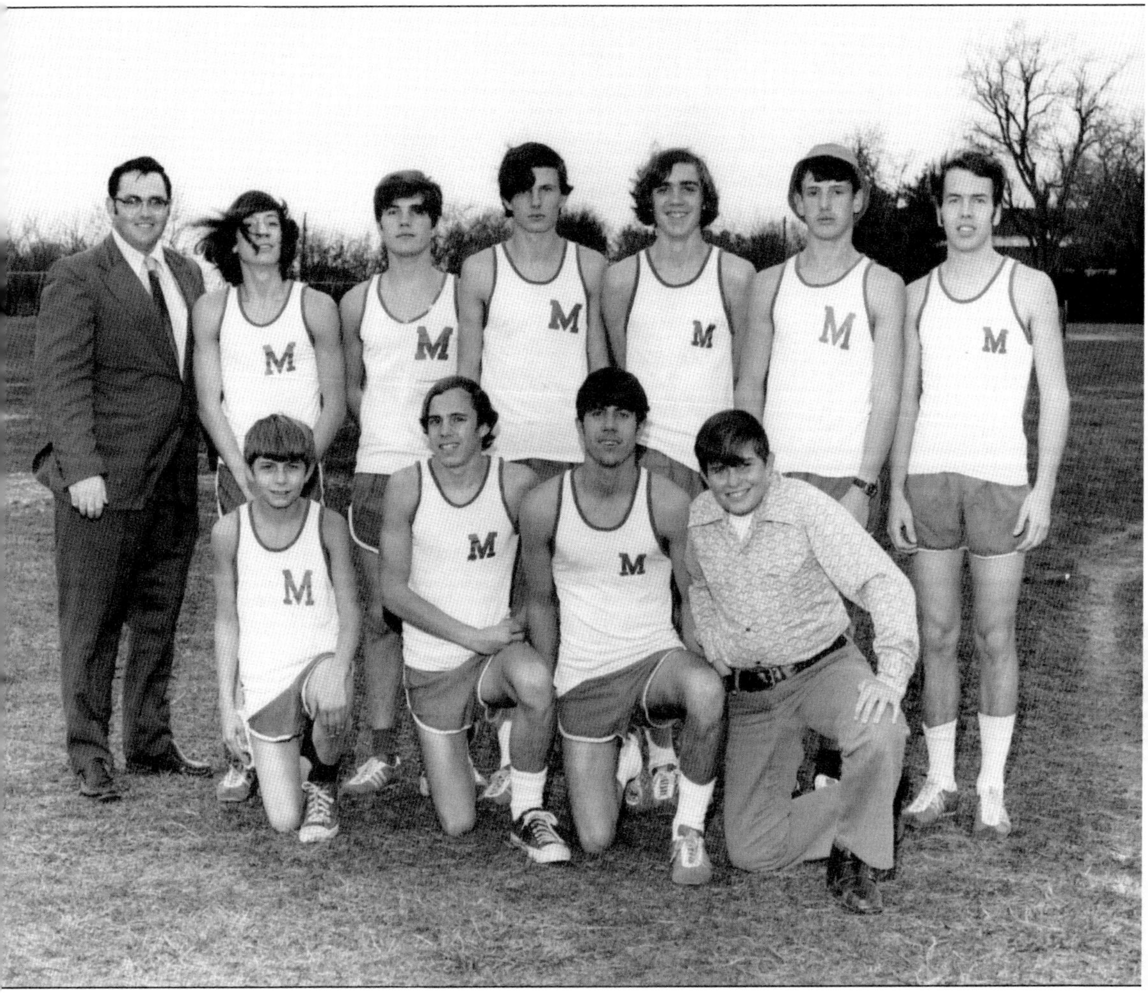

Middletown High School was the first to offer high school cross-country running when Kenneth Steers founded the team in the late 1930s. The first teams competed against college freshmen until other high schools started their own teams. A September 22, 1938, *Middletown Transcript* article states that boys' sports were quickly developing, with the first cross-country practice drawing 14 runners. Five meets were scheduled that season, with one home meet, two in Pennsylvania, and two in New Jersey. Team members included W. Buckworth, F. Cleaver, C. Ennis, I. Ginn, J. Guessford, J. Jarrell, R. Jones, J. Lawrence, L. McCabe, W. Phillips, V. Reed, L. Robinson, F. Rudnick, A. Sheats, J. Smith, A. Staut, J. Voshell, L. Walker, R. Wilson, M. Yearsley, A. Nabb, H. Smith and W. Fennimore. Steers also coached girls' basketball and field hockey, track and field, and boys' basketball, baseball, and football. This 1960s-era team photograph was not taken during Steers's tenure at MHS, but it shows the result of his efforts. No one is identified in this image. (Courtesy of Richard and Marlene Green.)

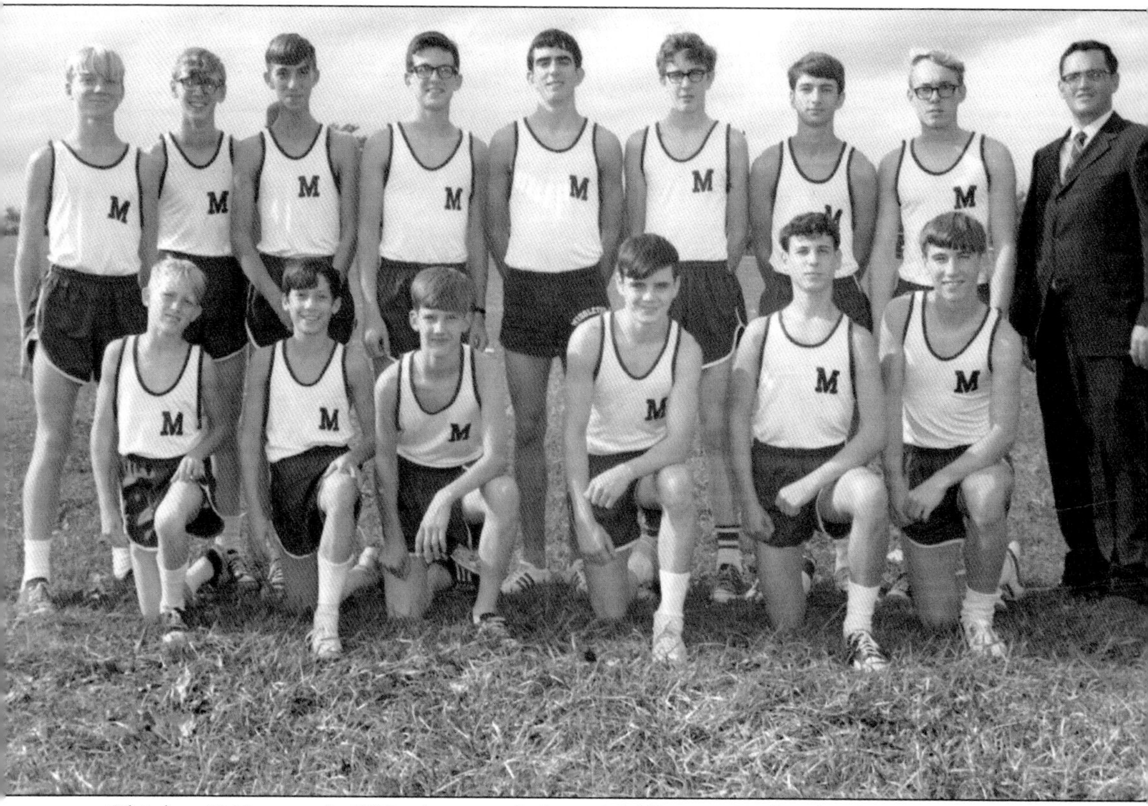

This late-1960s or early-1970s photograph shows Middletown High School cross-country runners, from left to right, (first row) Steve Wyatt, Craig Wynne, Tom Owens, Elmo Lancaster, Bob Cox, and John Meredith; (second row) Dave Wilson, Dave Rawley, Glenn Frazer, Lee Reynolds, Kevin Douglas, Bob Weaver, Bob Damon, and Andy Howell. Early notable runners at MHS included Bill Buckworth, the first state high school cross-country champion, who also took the one-mile track title, and Merritt Yearsley, who held state track titles for cross-country and the 100-yard and 200-yard dashes. Yearsley was also one of the first cross-country captains—if not the first—and one of the first to earn a varsity letter in the sport along with Ralph Wilson, William Buckworth, and Alfred Sheats in 1938. The team initially ran a 2.3-mile course, but cross-country eventually increased to the standard 3.1 miles, or 5 kilometers. (Courtesy of Richard and Marlene Green.)

Eight

Modern Times

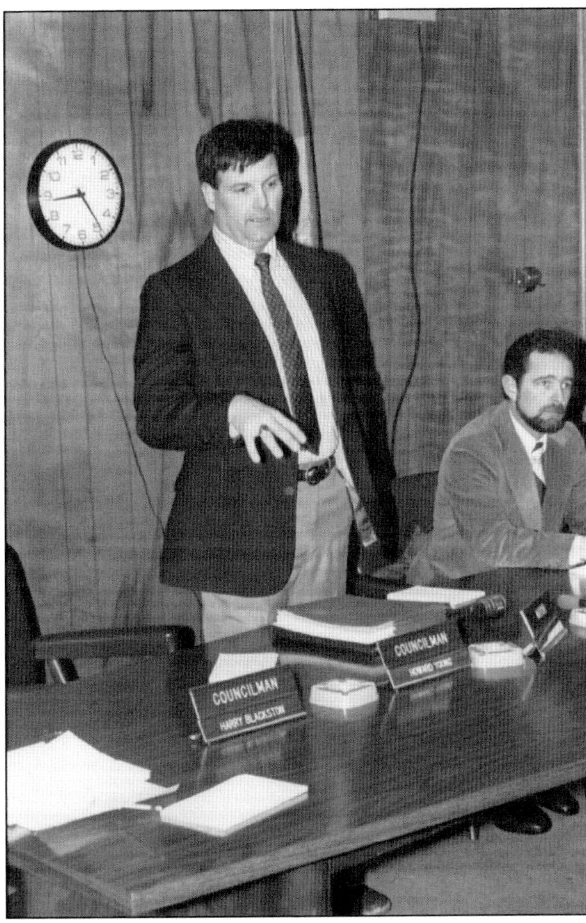

Mayor Kenny Branner Jr. has served as Middletown's mayor since 1989 and will leave a legacy of bringing much growth to the town. He and his council took a proactive approach to impending construction by extending town limits to allow for more town control over building and putting the necessary infrastructure in place for commercial growth. New neighborhoods and stores replaced farm crops, forever changing Middletown's landscape. The population as of 2012 was close to 19,000 people. (Courtesy of *Middletown Transcript*.)

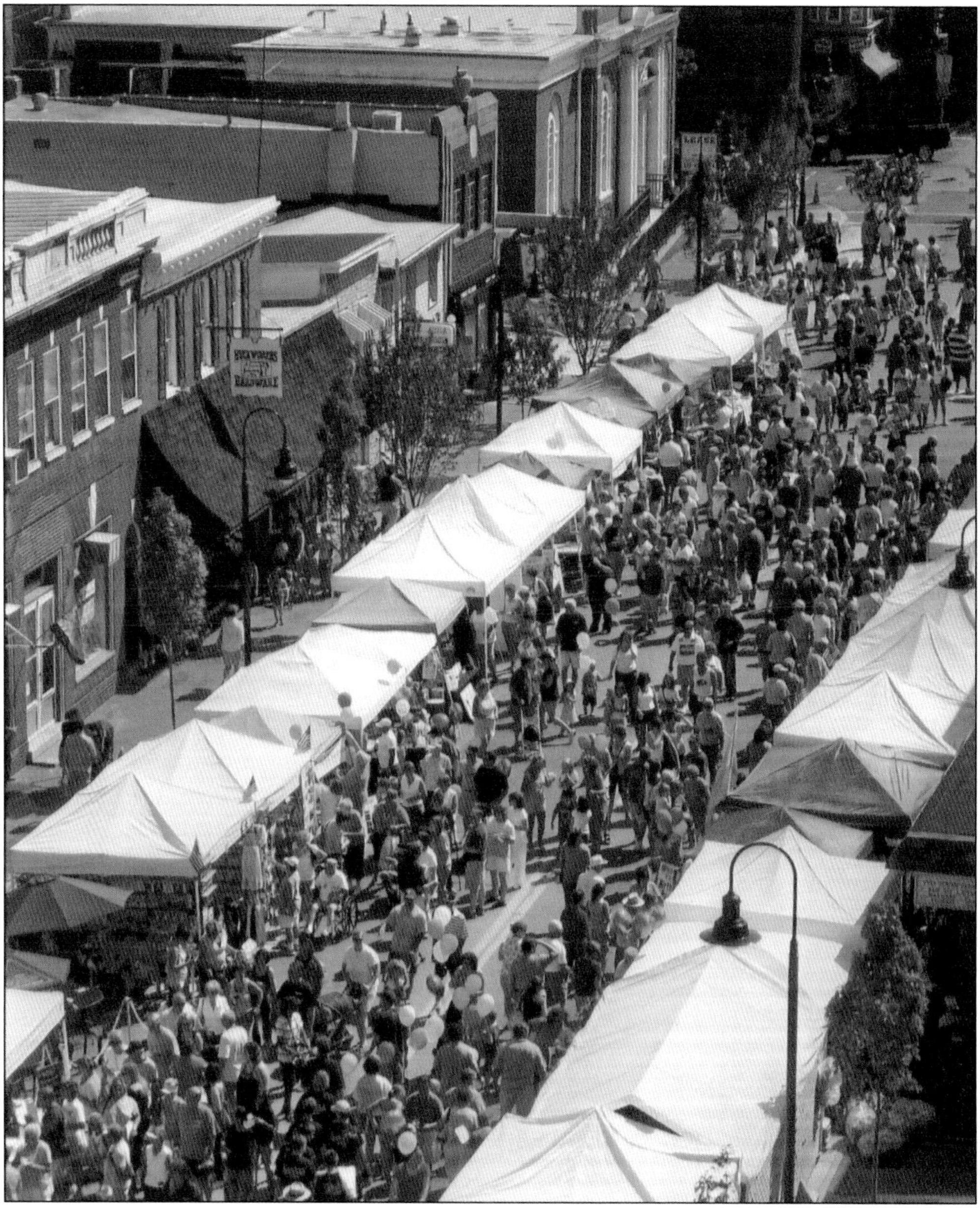

Middletown pays homage to its history during its Victorian Stroll Parade, held in early winter, and the Middletown Historical Society's Olde-Tyme Peach Festival, pictured here. During the Peach Festival, several of the town's original streets are closed to regular traffic on the third Saturday of every August as tens of thousands of residents and visitors swarm the festival to enjoy its historical exhibits, peach pie contest, family activities, and an array of vendors that sell crafts, art, food, and more. (Courtesy of Middletown Historical Society.)

Bibliography

Clark, Elaine. *Middletown Memories, 2nd Peach Festival booklet*. Middletown, DE.

Committee for the Slide Presentation "Middletown: Yesterday & Today." *Middletown Yesterday*. Odessa, DE: Corbit-Calloway Memorial Library.

Conrad, Henry C. *History of the State of Delaware*. Lancaster, PA: Wickersham Co., 1908.

Cox, Harold E. *Diamond State Trolleys: Electric Railways of Delaware*. Forty Fort, PA: self-published, 1991.

Department of Public Instruction, State of Delaware. *Educational Directories*. 1914–1943.

DuPont, A. Felix. www.standrews-de.org/aboutus/mission/index.aspxe. Middletown, DE: St. Andrew's School, 2013.

Gelber, Ben. *The Pennsylvania Weather Book*. Piscataway, NJ: Rutgers University Press, 2002.

Kee, Ed. *Delaware Farming*. Charleston, SC: Arcadia Publishing, 2007.

Lewis, Dorsey. *Dorsey Waitman Lewis Papers*. University of Delaware Special Collections Department, 1878–1958.

Lewis, Dorsey. *RG 9200LO3*. Delaware Public Archives Small Manuscript Collection.

Montefiore, Gene T. *Middletown Centennial*. Wilmington, DE: Wm. N. Cann, Inc., 1961.

Middletown: Esteemed Despite Loss of Diamond Shape. Wilmington, DE: Evening Journal, April 29, 1961.

Middletown Transcript, 1886–2013.

Norton, Joan M. Middletown Historic District, National Register of Historic Places Inventory—Nomination Form. United States Department of the Interior, National Park Service, 1978.

Raimo, John and Robert Sobel. *Biographical Directory of the Governors of the United States, 1789–1978, Vol. 1*. Westport, CT: Meckler Books, 1978.

RG 1325.008, Newspaper Clippings, General, World War II. Delaware Public Archives.

Rear Admiral John Herbert Brown, Jr., U.S. Navy. Delaware Public Archives.

Scharf, J. Thomas. *History of Delaware, Vol. II*. Philadelphia: L.J. Richards & Co., 1888.

Wilmington News Journal, August–November 1966.

Zebley, Frank R. *The Churches of Delaware*. Wilmington, DE, 1947.

Consistent with our mission to preserve history on a local level, this book was printed in South Carolina on American-made paper and manufactured entirely in the United States. Products carrying the accredited Forest Stewardship Council (FSC) label are printed on 100 percent FSC-certified paper.

MADE IN THE USA